Golf REACHES THE Seven Hills

Golf REACHES THE Seven Hills

GERRY A. LANHAM

ORANGE *frazer* PRESS
Wilmington, Ohio

ISBN 978-1949248-555 Hardcover
ISBN 978-1949248-487 Softcover
Copyright ©2021 Gerry A. Lanham
All Rights Reserved

Published for the copyright holder by:
Orange Frazer Press
37½ West Main St.
P.O. Box 214
Wilmington, OH 45177

For price and shipping information, call: 937.382.3196
Or visit: www.orangefrazer.com

Book and cover design by:
Orange Frazer Press with Catie South

Library of Congress Control Number: 20219152111

First Printing

For Nick, Elise, Sofia, Joey, Alex,
Nathan, Julia, Carmen,
and the people who created them

Table of Contents

Foreword

Since 1890, golf has been deeply woven into the fabric of Cincinnati's sports culture but little is known of its colorful and famous golfers, golf courses, and related events. Gerry Lanham put together a collage of accomplishments and facts while sprinkling human interest stories that all contributed to the rich history of Queen City golf. These important and interesting historical fragments get lost over time, unless someone like Gerry commits painstakingly and selflessly to research, collate and print them. This requires an enormous amount of time to pour over old newspapers and books, while conducting personal interviews with people involved at the time. He has devoted countless days and months that he could have spent on a golf course, chronicling these facts for our pleasure and education.

I have been intimately involved in Ohio golf, and specifically the Greater Cincinnati—Northern Kentucky area, for over sixty years and on almost every page of this book I found new, entertaining and interesting tidbits that shaped golf in the area. Gerry's writing style flows so smoothly it was a challenge for me not to binge read the entire book, but there is so much information I wanted to go slowly and savor his research. He was able to cover the whole spectrum of the golf industry from course architects and builders, famous men and women Amateurs, and equipment, to local Professionals and even noteworthy caddies. Gerry documents the growth of private clubs and public courses, as well as ghost courses that no longer exist. There is scarcely a golf topic that is not covered.

I believe myself to be a golf historian and a voracious golf book collector, so I consider Gerry's volume to be a major contribution to both of those worlds. If someone like him doesn't unselfishly sacrifice the time, effort and creativity to capture the area's golf history, it has less and less chance of being discovered and preserved in one place. This book is a "must read" for anyone who is passionate about golf and how it impacted the Tri-State area. It is my distinct pleasure to offer this foreword and encourage you, dear reader, to make this one of your favorite and most used golf books.

Dr. Michael J. Hurdzan, ASGCA Fellow,
Hurdzan Golf Design

Introduction

Golf became a national game in Scotland around 1860 and eventually grew throughout Great Britain. In the 1880s the game began to spread all over the world and was particularly popular in the United States. This book presents a history of golf as it made its way from the East Coast to the Midwest and Cincinnati in the 1890s. This includes all directions from Fountain Square and into the region we call Greater Cincinnati. The game had an impact on our city's lifestyle and culture, and the area's special flavor in turn affected the game's growth.

As we began our research, we traced the game's movements as the surrounding hills were conquered by the transportation system. But it was also the growth of a sport that has been a large part of my life. We wanted to educate all golfers, young and old, on where and when the seeds of the game were planted and especially those who promoted its growth. Internet, library, museum and newspaper searches unearthed a lot of the information available. But one of the difficulties was navigating the dead ends caused by the lost records of many of the courses and clubs themselves. Records, correspon-

dence, trophies and photos were lost during clubhouse fires, moves and redecorating.

In the beginning, golf was in the hands of a few Scottish Professionals who migrated here to educate and promote the game. People such as Robert White, Phil Honeyman and Archie Simpson were considered not only Golf Professionals (called Experts in the day) but architects, superintendents, club makers, teachers and players. Soon to follow came nationally revered designers like Tom Bendelow, Donald Ross and Bill Diddel. They would build the new places to play and add their prestige to the growth that continued at the beginning of the Twentieth Century. Later, other designers like Palmer, Nicklaus and Norman would add to that legacy as the Century ended.

The growth was fueled even further by the local and national media and sports journalists such as Ralph Love and others who wrote for the *Post-Times Star* and *Enquirer*. In addition, sporting goods companies such as Spalding and MacGregor developed mass manufacturing and marketing of equipment to bring the game closer and more affordable to the average American.

Time-Worn Score Card Recalls Old-Time Golf

BY WALLY FORSTE

Cliff Bell, the locker room man at Losantiville Country Club, found an old score card at the club the other day. It was yellow with age and had no writing on it. And since Cliff has been around Losantiville only 22 years, it didn't mean much to him.

But to old-time Losantivillers, members and caddies and employes, the card was of high interest.

And likewise to some "old boys" around Pleasant Ridge who used to sneak in an evening round unbeknownst to the late Jim Muirden, greenskeeper, and Caddy Master George Benvie when they were perhaps off to the gathering of some Scottish clan.

The clansmen gathered often in those days, the smokey grog costing only about 12 bits per quart.

Course Opened In '06

The score card was of interest to oldtimers because it was the card of the old Losantiville 18, laid out in 1906 and "modernized" into the present layout more than 25 years ago.

The days of the old Losantiville were elegant ones and the game was played along the old traditional lines in a gentlemanly sort of way.

Golf has changed a lot since and perhaps not for the better. The old card listed the names of all the holes. They don't name holes any more, at least around here.

Devil's Own Still Here

The only hole in town with a name nowadays is Hyde Park's "Devil's Own."

The old Losantiville card, names and yardages:

No.	Name	Yds.	No.	Name	Yds.
1	Fairview	270	10	Gateway	390
2	Toboggan	450	11	The Bog	375
3	The Knoll	296	12	Saucer	472
4	Sunset	350	13	Little Lake	137
5	Punch Bowl	470	14	Milky Way	362
6	The Ridge	352	15	Barn Yard	323
7	Middle March	200	16	Church Hill	366
8	Bunker Hill	400	17	Orchard	389
9	Beeches	390	18	Home	350

Par for the old course was 37-36—73.

Most of the names fitted the holes perfectly, others didn't. No. 5, for instance, would be called Slugaway nowadays. It was 570 yards long and three man-sized pokes onto the hill-hemmed green from which the name Punch Bowl came.

Boy In a Boat

The Toboggan, then and still No 2, really is the best sled-riding hill on the course.

Sunset really stretched to the west.

Bunker Hill really was bunker-bound and plenty of hill.

The Beeches had the green set among beeches which still are on the grounds.

The Gateway got that name because the beeches guarded it like gateposts.

Church Hill was laid uphill, with Pleasant Ridge Presbyterian Church as a backdrop for the green.

A school building now is located on the site of the old green.

The green on Barn Yard (No. 16) actually was in the barnyard of the old Langdon Farm.

And Frank Gelhot, now pro at Clovernook, used to wait in a rowboat on the lake on Nos. 13 and 16 to retrieve "floater" balls which landed short and in the water in great numbers on days of heavy play. No. 18, then as now, is pretty much the same. It headed "Home," up a steep hill. Is there a golf course anywhere with the "home" hole downhill?

A 1946 *Post* article about the original Losantiville course. One of the many gems discovered during research.

The Joy of Discovery—Losantiville 1906

When writing this book, there are times when you make a real connection with history. Over the time span you read about a player starting as a caddy or young student and then follow many of them through to an obituary as you chronicle their achievements. They become as familiar as any present-day sports figure. The attached article published on May 9, 1946, in the *Cincinnati Post* appeared late one night while researching a different subject for the book. The happiness in writer Wally Forste's description of the finding of a locker room attendant who had "only" been there since 1924 was evident. It mirrored the many times for us when previously unknown names or places or accomplishments would surface from the dusty pages of archives, newspapers, books and magazines. So now Losantiville locker room attendant Cliff Bell is part of Cincinnati golf history as he should be. He represents a tie to a time of hickory shafts and Haskell balls and layouts of courses that had holes named more than numbered. And the reporting of those times is carried through the words of Forste for hopefully another seventy-five years.

In conclusion, we have traced the origin of the game of golf from Great Britain and on to Greater Cincinnati. We attempted to include the most interesting people, courses, and events that were influential in the development of the game here. There are over 100 golf courses, public and private, in the area and no doubt we have missed some of your favorites. It was not possible to include all of the research found on all golf related subjects that have happened over those first seventy years. This book was fun researching and writing and we hope you will enjoy the pictures and words that tell the story.

Geoff Hensley—PGA Master Golf Professional

Golf REACHES THE Seven Hills

CHAPTER 1
That Scottish Game

Cincinnati is a beautiful city: cheerful, thriving and animated. I have not often seen a place that commends itself so favorably and pleasantly to a stranger at first glance as this does.

—Charles Dickens, 1842

The earliest golf courses in the United States started to appear in the East around 1882. Foxburg GC in Western Pennsylvania has operated continuously since 1884 when Joseph Fox brought back some balls and clubs from Old Tom Morris and built an eight-hole course on his summer estate in

Golf being demonstrated at Yonkers, New York, in 1888 at one of the country's first golf courses.

Clarion County. But even before that, in the pre-history of American golf, there were times when individuals were introduced to "that Scottish game" while travelling to Europe or on college campuses back east.

William Cooper Procter was one of those individuals as the game was starting to be discussed as early as 1882 in his school newspapers at Princeton University. Procter would be among the pioneers delivering the game to the Queen City. They included business leaders and city fathers who organized country clubs and financed golf's beginnings. And it was accompanied by an emerging group of women athletes eager to try the new sport and who actually started two golf clubs still operating here today.

So, from a humble beginning of home-made golf courses on estates, dairy farms and in city parks and with flower pots and tin cans for holes, the area would boast sixty-five playing facilities by 1960. But with all of Greater

This *Cincinnati Post* article from September 4, 1895, indicates golf was also being played by the Procter family that year.

Cincinnati's energy and leadership, the sport still had to overcome its hot summers, a ring of hills hemming in the population, twenty years of bossism and bad local government, economic depressions, wars, and even Prohibition. But at the same time, the game was started during America's Progressive Era. That included outside influences with a national new can-do attitude from leaders like Teddy Roosevelt. And it was bolstered by successes on the world stage such as the building of the Panama Canal and inventions like the airplane, automobile, telephone and electric power. These spawned newer and bigger architectural projects that even spilled over to local golf courses and club houses at the time. That is golf's story here and it begins with the region's unique history.

Cincinnati was the first major city founded after the American Revolution and was also the nation's first "boom town." By the middle of the nineteenth century it was rivaling the larger coastal cities in size and wealth and was listed sixth in the country's population. It was the main hub for Western migration as settlers used the tributaries of the Ohio River for expansion inland and began to populate the Louisiana Purchase. In addition, there were daily stage coaches to Dayton, Columbus and Cleveland and a major canal connecting its river port to Lake Erie.

The city and state were situated well politically and financially. Three American Presidents (Ulysses S. Grant, Benjamin Harrison and William Howard Taft) were born within twenty-five miles of Fountain Square. And a fourth President, William Henry Harrison, moved to the area as a young soldier, became the city's Congressman in 1816 and lived here until his death in the White House in 1841. Only Boston

can duplicate that number in American history. Besides being a transportation hub, it had flourishing manufacturing, meat packing, soap, banking and service businesses. The wealth of Ohio, Kentucky and Indiana farms was stored, packaged and shipped from the port of Cincinnati using riverboats (made here in the world's largest river boat yard) and later railroads. And Ohio was the center of political America. From 1868 to 1920, an astounding eight Presidential elections were won by Ohio natives.

After the Civil War, Cincinnati was the third largest manufacturing center in the United States, behind only New York and Philadelphia. But it slowly began to consider itself more of a cultural center, calling itself "The Paris of America" as it drifted away from its focus on heavy industry and meat packing businesses. It began a Golden Age of architecture and the arts, as

Future U.S. President William Howard Taft was the first Chairman of the Cincinnati Golf Club in 1895.

the city built itself a great Music Hall, Zoo, the Roebling Bridge, Central Library, houses of worship and museums. The city's leaders and residents also formed symphonies and music and art festivals to improve the quality of life.

But the region still maintained manufacturing and entrepreneurial roots that were the fuel for the city's cultural expansion and its welcome for this new phenomenon called leisure. Child labor laws were well in the future and other worker abuses still existed but a new and expanding middle class was emerging that would eventually provide a population eager for new ways to spend their free time.

The city's standing was also a reflection of the first group of entrepreneurs and speculators that later would start the families that brought golf here. In 1803, a twenty-one-year-old Nicholas Longworth had arrived in Cincinnati with little more than the clothes

Nicholas Longworth produced grapes on Mt. Adams in his Garden of Eden and they were used to make champagne and other wines. Cincinnati was the leading wine producing city in the United States in 1850.

on his back. The Longworth name will be repeated in the sections on the introduction of golf into Cincinnati, but "Nicholas I" began with the city, and built a fortune on the practice of law, land speculation and other enterprises such as agriculture and wine production. He became the richest man in the city, and only William Astor of New York paid more realty taxes in the United States. Worth more than ten-million dollars at his death in 1863, his life was marked by his great philanthropy to the city and other causes. Eventually his grandson, also named Nicholas and who would become Speaker of the House of Representatives, would be one of the very first pioneers of golf in the city.

A few decades after Nicholas I, a large immigration of Germans and Irish had begun swelling the city's population. Fully 45% of the city were foreign born immigrants by 1851 and they came with skills and work ethic to build the city from the inside. They manned the many new manufacturing jobs with craftsmen and artisans that would form the beginnings of a strong middle class.

The son of one of those immigrants, Barney Kroger, invested his life savings of $372 to open a grocery store on Pearl Street near the Ohio River in downtown Cincinnati. He built this operation into what would be the world's second largest grocery chain in the world by the 1930s. An avid golfer, he was a founding member of Avondale/Hamilton County (Maketewah) Golf Club and actually located its property in Bond Hill while on a Sunday drive in 1910. He also helped the formation of the new Western Hills Country Club and was a founding member there.

Hungarian immigrants Charles and Max Fleischmann created the first compressed yeast, changing the baking industry worldwide. The Fleischmann family stayed active in local sports, including golf, and started the Fleischmann Cup, played at The Camargo Club. Charles' son Julius was one of the pioneer golfing members at Cincinnati Golf Club in the 1890s. New

Barney Kroger, founder of one of the nation's largest grocery companies, was instrumental in the founding of Avondale Athletic Club and its move to Bond Hill. He was also one of the founders of Western Hills Country Club.

businesses brought Cincinnati to lead in the world's production of playing cards, laundry machines, aluminum products, machine tools, sporting goods and office furniture (where Globe-Wernicke executives laid out their golf course behind the plant in Norwood in the 1890s and then helped found Losantiville Golf Club in Oakley in 1902).

The city was still a major national player in many other industries. Procter & Gamble (under the leadership of William Cooper Procter) had not only become the world's largest producer of soap products but also had instituted many plans such as profit sharing, paid vacations, and stock ownership which increased the wealth of the city's general population. Considered radical socialism at the time, it provided opportunity for the factory worker, bookkeeper and others to grab a handle on their future. It also benefitted the region immensely as the area's average wage was almost 50% more than the national number.

Cincinnati was still the *world's* leader in the production of wagons and carriages (in 1890 almost half the nation's production). Another son of German immigrants, Otto Armleder, was founder and owner of one of those carriage companies that eventually built trucks and automobiles. Armleder was a golfer and benefactor of golf who held mortgages on Maketewah Country Club and Kenwood Country Club to help them stay afloat during the Depression.

The city also was a world leader in the production of boots and shoes, leather goods, glass liquor bottles and distilled liquors. It was near the top in men's clothing, beer, metal products, soap and candles. By 1909 it also boasted the world's largest tannery, iron tube works and printing ink plant (where Cincinnati CC founder and golfer Frank Wiborg stood at the helm).

This diverse production continued until about 1921 when a new product was introduced that would spring Cincinnati into the Roaring 20s. In that year, a thirty-five-year-old Powell Crosley Jr. got interested in radio and by 1925 was the world's leading manufacturer of radio sets, producing 500 units per day. While building a broadcast empire, refrigerators, Crosley automobiles and owning the Cincinnati Reds he also co-founded Clovernook Country Club with his brother Lewis and both remained avid golfers through their lifetimes.

Radios, machine tools, soap, bakery products, shoes and automobile production kept Cincinnati workers active through the 1920s until the nation was caught off guard unexpectedly by the Stock Market Crash in 1929. Though Cincinnati weathered the Depression better than most cities, it was a devastating setback and many courses closed or reduced in size. Other industries, like insurance and light manufacturing, provided more energy to the city through the post-WWII period, and other civic leaders like the Williams family helped start the Coldstream Country Club at the end of golf's golden age here.

The beginning of golf in the region mirrored the successes of the city's business leaders and the resulting creation of a viable and educated middle class. The original spirit of a Nicholas Longworth, as he disembarked a barge at Cincinnati in 1803, and the industry leaders to follow, carried the city through its remarkable history and eventually provided a nesting place for "that Scottish game." And a bevy of immigrants with the skilled labor to man and manage the machinery, mills and factories would provide a source of players and spectators to grow the game.

In spite of this leadership and manpower, there were still impediments to the game's growth. The scenic hills of Cincinnati and Northern Kentucky also stood in the way of progress. If you stand on any tall building in downtown Cincinnati and do a 360-degree survey of the surrounding hills you can see at once the challenge to expanding the city. From Mt. Adams to Mount Auburn and over west to Fairview and Price Hill, you will see only the slightest opening as the Mill Creek Valley presents itself north of the West End. Similarly, the Kentucky hills also provide a barrier for traffic and the "Cut in the Hill" still represents the most direct route to the south.

Caricature of Otto Armleder who was a business leader and a member at both Maketewah and Kenwood Country Clubs. He held mortgages to both during the Great Depression to keep them solvent and in operation.

Powell Crosley, businessman and owner of the Cincinnati Reds, founded Clovernook Country Club in 1926.

The topography provided by the advancing and retreating glaciers for several thousand years had given Cincinnati its unique charm and famous seven hills, but also a landscape that hemmed it in on almost all sides. This would especially challenge local golf enthusiasts as they searched for sites to build their courses. By the middle of the nineteenth Century, some of the wealthier citizens had been building homes on those surrounding hills to escape the air pollution of over 200,000 residents. But the limits of horses to climb those hills and the treacherous roads and weather were still providing obstacles to city expansion.

The city was actually the most densely populated in the United States with over 37,000 people living in each square mile at a time before skyscrapers and high rises. By the beginning of the twentieth century, a

William Cooper Procter, President of Procter & Gamble, was the founding member of several golf clubs including Glendale Golf Club, Avondale Golf Club and Hamilton County (Maketewah) Country Club. (Photo circa 1915)

This 1930s photo of downtown Cincinnati shows how densely populated the city was.

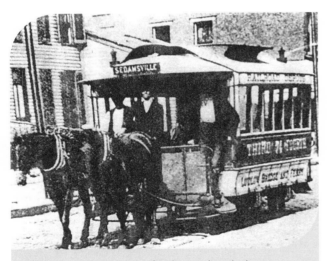

The Sedamsville horsecar. After the omnibus, the horsecars were introduced and rode on rails allowing more passengers and more comfort.

new class of merchants, doctors, lawyers and industrialists followed the lead to the high ground as they also sought cleaner air and water. They were feeling the encroachment of even more factories, breweries and mills squeezed against their downtown residences. But the region needed a transportation system that could conquer the hills and replace the horse drawn omnibuses that had limited range and capacities.

The omnibuses were eventually replaced by horsecars and metal tracks to improve efficiency and passenger comfort. Cincinnati was actually one of the first cities in the nation to install horsecar routes in 1859. The direction of roads and horsecar tracks still generally followed valleys and the paths of least resistance up the hills. Later viaducts would dot the city to span the distances between the hills and speeding growth further. In addition, by 1880 inclines had been built up the sides of four hills, providing escape from the basin, and expansion was on. Growth continued through the 1880s and 1890s as towns such as Avondale, Mt. Auburn, Price Hill, Westwood, and Glendale were formed.

The omnibus was the first mode of mass transport in the 1840s.

An 1899 *Enquirer* sketch of the original Pillars clubhouse.

Julius Fleischmann, businessman and Mayor of Cincinnati, made the famous bet with Longworth.

Nicholas Longworth played from the first tee of Cincinnati Golf Course to the Pillars (a little more than four miles) to win the bet of a chicken dinner.

The Pillars and "The Bet"

The Pillars was a very exclusive country club that had limited its membership to the city's top fifty businessmen and civic leaders. Located on Madison Road in Madisonville and near the present site of the Children's Home, it featured a beautiful mansion with tall pillars and a small golf course as early as 1895. Golf was soon abandoned because the site had too many trees but it did have a swimming pool and ball fields and was known as being the host club for the most important visitors to the city. It was also the finishing point on a unique bet made at Cincinnati Golf Club (CGC) between Cincinnati Mayor Julius Fleischmann and Nicholas Longworth, future Speaker of the House of Representatives. In 1900, Fleishmann bet Longworth a chicken dinner that he could not cover the five miles between the first tee at CGC and the front porch of the Pillars in less than 150 strokes. Over roads, around houses, through broken windows and 101 strokes later he covered the distance. With sixteen lost balls he also covered the bet with a total of 117 strokes. The Madisonville location would be destroyed by fire in 1905 and the club relocated to a thirty-acre site on Brotherton Road in Oakley in 1907. During the Depression, that site was sold in 1936

The new Pillars clubhouse was on Brotherton Road in Oakley.

along with the surrounding property bordering Hyde Park Country Club and today is a subdivision with over 150 homes. Thus, ended the most exclusive club in Cincinnati.

Gas street lights were replacing the oil lamps previously set out every seventh house to keep roads accessible at night. Streets were cleaned twice a month but they were still basically Macadam. This was a system developed in Scotland in 1820 and consisted of a roadway of small angular stones compacted with the dust of the stones. Unfortunately, each horse or mule on the streets dumped about ten–twenty pounds of manure per day and the gray macadam road dust soon turned into shades of tan and brown. Windy days could be very uncomfortable for pedestrians as the tan road dust went everywhere—clothes and open windows and doors and Reds games on occasion had to

be cancelled due to the dust storms. Fortunately, some main roadways and downtown streets were starting to use bricks, wood blocks or cobble stones as pavement especially where horsecar rails were installed.

Cheaper electricity and better electrical distribution also provided an opportunity for further city growth as the streetcar entered the scene in 1889. Streetcars replaced the horsecars completely by 1904. Newer neighborhoods like Norwood, Pleasant Ridge, College Hill and Mt. Airy benefitted by connection to downtown via streetcar. The city boundaries also grew through annexation. Starting as early as 1808 (Walnut Hills), cities like Price Hill and Mt. Lookout (1870),

Streetcars going up the Mt. Adams Incline. The streetcar and incline both helped Cincinnati conquer the hills and expand the city limits.

the 1930s) and eventually by diesel powered busses.

But it was the advent of the automobile changed everything. In 1899 in the United States, there were less than 8,000 total automobiles, cars of various makes and models and only two in Greater Cincinnati. One was owned by Jacob Schmidlapp, but he lived across the street from Cincinnati GC so a commute was not necessary. By 1905 there were enough of these new machines to have the Cincinnati City Council pass an ordinance with a seven mile per hour speed limit in the city as the national total had grown to 77,400 cars and trucks. When America went to war in 1917, the number of vehicles on roads increased to 6,160,000 cars and trucks (also resulting in 9,630 fatalities). Automobiles were now competing with horse and mule traffic on local streets and their numbers were growing exponentially.

Westwood and Clifton (1896), Hyde Park and Bond Hill (1903), Roselawn (1905) and Delhi Village (1910) joined Cincinnati. 1911 yielded ten more annexations including College Hill, Carthage and Mt. Airy. On the Cincinnati side of the river there were now 44 distinct neighborhoods downtown and in the new hilltop suburbs, and almost simultaneously some small golf courses were starting to appear.

Most of the early locations for courses were sited near the streetcar lines both for the members and staff to commute. A businessman or the groundskeeper could take the #21 or #22 car out to Cincinnati GC. Similarly, the #54 car ran through to Pleasant Ridge and Losantiville CC or the #2 or #34 cars made it up Reading Road to service Avondale GC or you could take the #12 car up to its terminus at Nebraska Avenue to play Elberon GC. Hyde Park CC moved from their first location on Marburg Avenue to Erie Avenue to access the street car.

Eventually there would be over 220 miles of streetcar track in Cincinnati and Northern Kentucky carrying over 100 million passengers a year and many lines ran past the early golf courses. The streetcars disappeared from the streets in 1951 and were replaced by street trolleys (electric busses with overhead wires introduced in

No longer was the traveler tied to the rails of the streetcars. Courses built in the 1920s and 1930s were now being located at properties that provided attributes other than being near a streetcar stop. Summit Hills CC, The Camargo Club and Kenwood CC were examples of new clubs not tethered by street car lines.

Cincinnati weather could also present problems. The game in Scotland was played in cool and damp conditions and it took a while for the game to adapt to the varied climates in the States. This was especially true in our region with hot and humid summers and sometimes frigid winters. The golf season at many clubs was spring, fall and winter and many players went to the tennis courts during the summer. Before Terrace Park CC moved to Milford, it actually shut down golf for the summer. That subsided as courses installed irrigation but that would not be until the 1920s and 30s, and then for only a few private clubs.

This affected not only the play for locals but also was a hindrance to getting major tournaments to come to town. Nationwide, most of the major tournaments

THE ENQUIRER, CINCINNATI, TUESDAY, JULY 21, 1925

NUMBER 5—WHY DOES THE MAYOR SMILE?

Another "splendid" example of what Madison road should NOT be, looking west from in front of 1849 Madison road. The loosened wood block and the entire disappearance of the surface of the street in some places illustrate the negligence of the City Hall administration in keeping Cincinnati streets in repair. Close inspection will reveal that the entire stretch has loosened and that a rain as heavy as that of yesterday easily can wash the wood block away and create other hazards of which Madison road already has enough. Mr. Mayor, the motoring public demands action.

Macadam (crushed stone), woodblocks, bricks, and cobblestones would have to be replaced as auto traffic became more prevalent. (Photo circa 1925)

were played in the summer and so it would be difficult to count on a course in the warmer latitudes to provide good playing conditions for a full week. The US Open, starting in 1895, was played on northern courses for the most part. Except for two tournaments in Maryland, it was 1941 in Ft. Worth TX before the tournament moved South.

Similarly, when the US Amateur landed at Kenwood CC in 1933, there had only been two other Southern tier sites (St. Louis CC in 1921 and Baltimore CC in 1932) in its previous thirty-eight-year history. The Kenwood tournament would be played during one of the worst droughts in Cincinnati history at that time confirming the weather risks when venturing too far South.

Before WWI, Cincinnati courses were not long enough for major tournaments. Hamilton County CC (Maketewah) was the city's first 6,000-yard course in 1910, and by that time venues throughout the country were building even longer courses to host major

The Greenup Street Trolley riding the rails in Covington. (Photo circa 1895)

Five barges of autos being offloaded for greater Cincinnati households. (Photo circa 1920)

events. After Donald Ross rebuilt and lengthened the Maketewah course, there was an unsuccessful 1926 attempt to host the 1928 US Open with an entourage led by Head Professional George Bowden. That same year, The Camargo Club built a world class course that could be used for any major tournament but there was no immediate desire by the members to host an Open. So, besides the climate, the area was also lacking sites to host majors in the early years.

On the Horizon

Despite geography, transportation, weather, indifferent city governments, wars, Depression and Prohibition, and no venue to host big national tournaments, the game survived here and flourished. It did that with great Amateurs and Professionals, courses, and a strong group of Women's players, all with the support of good organizations and media. The sum of that total is the history of golf here in black and white.

As the game moves to the Modern Period in 1960, there are new challenges. But Palmer, Nicklaus, Player, Trevino, Miller, and a host of others lead golf into a new arena, with brand new courses designed on CAD systems, new ball and club technology, TV channels devoted to sports and even one for golf—and all in living color. By 1961, only a period of fifty-eight years since the Wright Brothers' first flight, Alan Shepard had made the first American manned space flight, plans were being made for a moon landing by 1969, and soon thereafter a golf ball will be driven from the moon's surface.

But challenges remained. 1960 was the peak for the number of golf courses in America. The building boom after WWII added more courses, but by 1960 there were too many. There have been peaks and valleys since, but the game remains steady and vibrant and it is built on a foundation from the 1890s when our book begins.

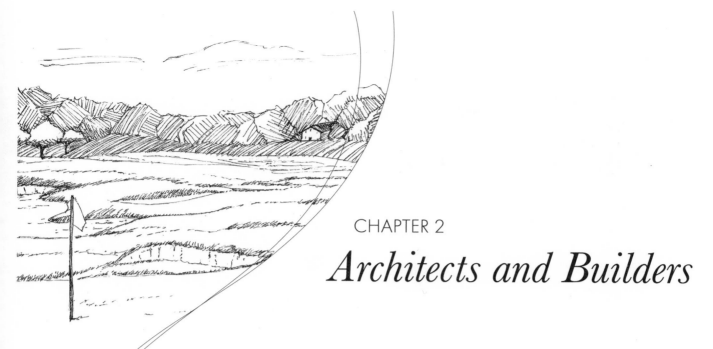

CHAPTER 2
Architects and Builders

The early players and designers were inclined to follow natural paths in the earth, rather than superimposing a routing plan, and that was the game pure and simple.
—Robert Trent Jones, *Golf by Design*

Introduction

A lot is taken for granted when standing on the tee. As the hole is presented in front of you, it is the product of someone's vision, skills, installation, management and maintenance. The experience can be breathtaking or mundane as it challenges the player. The hole might be simple as intended or it might be vexing with its risks and rewards. It is then combined with eight or seventeen other holes, each situated to complete the experience.

How each hole is conceived on sketch pad, how each obstacle, green and tee is marked by dropping stakes, how it is shaped to its final layout and how it is maintained is summed to provide that unique result. Some of these holes and courses have become hallowed in golfing lore. Some names have become familiar to everyone who tees the ball, courses such as Pebble Beach and St. Andrew's and individual holes like the seventeenth at Sawgrass or the Postage Stamp at Royal Troon.

Some holes are by happenstance, the pathways of Scottish shepherds. Others are merely the location of convenience by the builder. Still others are planned by months of surveys and revisions and site visits and mathematical calculations. And a few treasures are tinkered with and reviewed by experts and journalists and competitors to eke out the final perfection. Some courses and holes are never finished, though over a century old.

A whole new industry had to be built in America to allow golf to permeate every city and village that wanted to play the game. Eventually it created new professions—golf architect, course builder, superintendent, greens keeper—that had not existed here before. It

Chicagoan Charles Blair McDonald, the father of American golf Architecture.

Ten of the fourteen Charter Members of the American Society of Golf Course Architects meeting in Pinehurst in 1948; Cincinnati courses were designed by four men in this picture—Robert White (second from left), W.B. Langford (third from left), Donald Ross (fourth from left), and William Diddel (second from right).

took America from one little course in Yonkers NY in 1888 to over 16,000 total courses by the 1960s. This would represent a peak as the number has declined after the 60s. How did this amazing growth touch Greater Cincinnati and who made it happen?

The Golf Course Architect in America and Locally

The new profession known as Golf Course Architect started in the United States with the work of C.B. McDonald in Chicago. Locally, three architects—Tom Bendelow, Donald Ross and Bill Diddel—designed many of the early courses in the classic period in Cincinnati and there were also contributions by Langford & Moreau, Bill Jackson, Seth Raynor and Dick Wilson among others. But all can trace their American efforts back to McDonald and Chicago.

Before 1890 in Great Britain, course design had been the specialty of a select group of Scottish experts and especially Old Tom Morris. Before his death in 1908 he had influenced an unbeliev-

able group of great designers on his way to building The Old Course at St. Andrew's, Prestwick and Royal County Down among so many others. And his influence on that cadre of other designers, many who went on to their own great careers in the United States, helped build the game world-wide. C.B. McDonald, William Herbert Fowler, Harry Colt, Donald Ross, and a relatively unknown designer named Archie Simpson Sr.—worked alongside Old Tom at one time or another and did most of their design work in the States. Ross and Simpson would have an influence on designs and remodels in the Cincinnati area in the early twentieth century so some of our local sites have direct con-

Old Tom Morris of St. Andrews, Scotland (1821–1908), one of golf's early superstars was a course architect and greenskeeper. Many American architects worked under his direction and two (Donald Ross and Archie Simpson Sr.) built courses in Cincinnati.

nections to Old Tom and the origin of golf architecture itself.

In the Tri-State, the eight courses in place before 1900 were all originally designed by the club members. But in 1896 the Cincinnati Golf Club (CGC) hired Robert White, a Scotsman born in St. Andrew's, as their first Professional and the city's first course Architect. White proceeded to lay out CGC's first eighteen-hole course on Grandin Road. Eventually, he would also design the eighteen-hole course at Avondale Athletic Club, courses at Clifton GC and a private course in Terrace Park before moving on to Chicago and eventually becoming the first President of the PGA. White would also add to his design resume with almost twenty more courses in Eastern Pennsylvania, New York, Delaware and South Carolina.

Robert White Jr. between 1896 and 1902, designed the Cincinnati Golf Club, Avondale Golf Club, Clifton Golf Club and a private course in Terrace Park while in Cincinnati.

Scotsman Tom Bendelow designed over 600 courses in the United States and Canada, including seven in the Cincinnati area. He was considered "The Johnny Appleseed of Golf" for his widespread covering of the North American continent promoting all aspects of the sport.

The Johnny Appleseed of Course Designers

Meanwhile back east, while C.B. McDonald and others were laying out the nation's first courses, the career of another Scotsman began that would lead eventually to over six hundred of his designs being built nationwide. Sportsman A.G. Spalding had hired a thirty-year-old Tom Bendelow to promote the new game in the New York and New Jersey areas. Bendelow had been teaching golf and building a small course for the elite of New York society but Spalding had a different market in mind. Both Spalding and Bendelow wanted to bring the game to the American public and that included building courses that new players could enjoy and afford.

One of his first courses was the Van Cortland Park public links in New York City in 1898 where Bendelow introduced many of the foundations of today's game. These included public golf instruction, affordability and caddie training. He laid out designs for almost all of the private country clubs in the Cincinnati area before 1920 but his main interest still remained public access courses for the whole country.

Bendelow also used his contacts to provide job opportunities for young Professionals to move to new venues. Dave Mentiply at Wyoming CC and Richard Cass at Hamilton County CC were two local Professionals who were imported through recommendations

by Bendelow. Without Spalding, Bendelow, and the Official Golf Guide (see the chapter on "Media"), the game of golf would not have been the same in Cincinnati or in the United States. Spalding and Bendelow brought the game out from behind the walls of the country clubs and onto the national scene. And Bendelow earned the moniker of "The Johnny Appleseed of Golf" as he built new courses—public and private —from coast to coast.

He travelled almost constantly and sometimes he would design two or three different courses at the same train stop. Basically, he would walk the property for several days and then stake locations for greens, tees and bunkers. The stakes and measuring materials would be carried in his horse's saddlebags or maybe a wheel barrow. The final construction details would be left to the club and usually fell into the hands of the Club Professional or Superintendent. Most of the time local farmers were hired to complete the construction. The farmers would be paid a $1 a day and $2 if they furnished a horse. Normal charges were less than one-hundred dollars for Bendelow's design services.

In 1907 Bendelow became editor of *Spalding's Official Golf Guide* and his theories for course layouts were included in every issue he edited. At that time, the game was played close to the ground with hickory

Tom Bendelow supervising the location of a stake to be used to designate greens, tees and hazards. He wrote several treatises on the art of designing courses that were used by many clubs throughout the world.

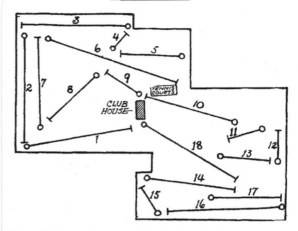

PLAN OF NEW GOLF COURSE.

Thomas Bendelow, of Chicago, the golf course expert who has been planning the lay-out for the new grounds of the Hamilton County Golf Club, yesterday submitted his plat and report. The plat provides for 18 holes, totaling 6,140 yards.

The report says that the grounds are "admirably adapted in every shape and way." Continuing, it says: "There will be no fewer than six short holes, the longest being a full drive of 230 yards; a cleek shot, two iron shots and two mashay shots. We also have two short holes, ranging from 300 to 390 yards. Taking this altogether, with the contour of your land, the many water courses, ravines and its general physical conformation, this will give you as sporty an eighteen-hole course as you will find in the state of Ohio."

After describing the work necessary to place the course in commission he says: "Teeing grounds I would suggest you do not elevate, but take the natural lay of the ground, if at all possible, and tee off that; of course, where the ground is not level enough for this purpose it could be made so quite readily, and thus conform more to the traditions of the game. There is no reason why the grounds should not be ready by July."

The following is the record of the new course:

Hole No.		Hole No.		Hole No.	
1	460 yds.	7	340 yds.	13	290 yds.
2	590 yds.	8	350 yds.	14	280 yds.
3	500 yds.	9	135 yds.	15	165 yds.
4	165 yds.	10	535 yds.	16	325 yds.
5	230 yds.	11	175 yds.	17	375 yds.
6	525 yds.	12	135 yds.	18	500 yds.

Plans for the new Hamilton County (Maketewah) Country Club course from a December 25, 1910, article in the *Cincinnati Post*. Designed by Tom Bendelow and built by Richard Cass, these types of sketches were typical of early Bendelow single line layouts.

shafted clubs and Haskell (rubber core) golf balls (see the chapter on "Equipment"). In an article in the December 25, 1910 *Cincinnati Post*, Bendelow wrote, "Teeing grounds I would suggest you do not elevate, but take the natural lay of the ground, if at all possible, and tee off that."

Greens were small and cut by hand. Early green sizes were recommended to be "at least sixty square feet." Irrigation basically did not exist so grass might burn out in the summer on most courses. Ground was hard and fast. Later in the century, courses (and alterations to the original Bendelow courses) would use more of the elevation changes frequently found in the Greater Cincinnati area.

The Spalding Co. had a branch office on 5th Street in Cincinnati where Bendelow would work when in the area and his first known visit to the Tri-State was in 1902 for Losantiville GC to lay out the course in the infield of the Oakley Park Race Track. He was not an exceptional player but did compete in the 1905 Western Open contested at Cincinnati Golf Club. Bendelow's architectural impact on Cincinnati would extend to the following projects while working out of Spalding's Cincinnati office:

- Ft. Mitchell CC (1904)
- Losantiville CC (Pleasant Ridge site) (1907)
- Hyde Park CC (1909)
- Hamilton County (Maketewah) CC (1911)
- Western Hills CC (1912) (plus remodel in 1925)
- Wyoming CC (1912)
- Highland CC (1915)

As *Spalding Golf* Editor, he also became an advocate of longer courses to neutralize the new Haskell type golf balls. The course he laid out at Hamilton County CC in 1910 was the area's first 6,000-yard routing in response to that need. Many courses across the country began to scramble to purchase adjacent land to add yardage to match the technology improvements.

Hyde Park CC was one club that had purchased additional property in 1909 and hired Bendelow to add to their nine-hole layout. But the remainder of the decade the club also experimented with different design revisions to the original as Head Professionals Alec

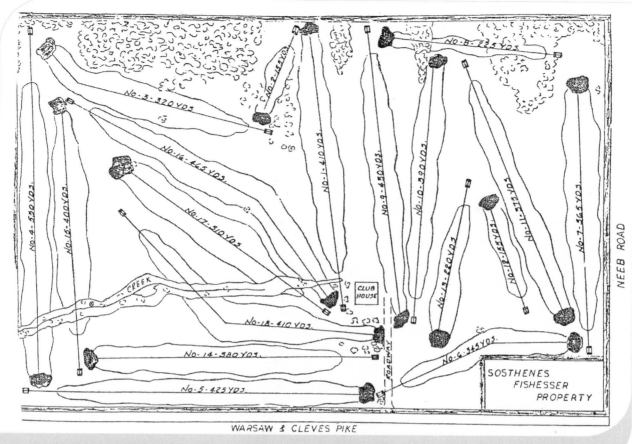

Western Hills Country Club layout before the 1925 remodel by Tom Bendelow.

Gerrard and Bob McDonald, both from Scotland, added many bunkers and other obstacles. Other Pros and members like William Harig also contributed design improvements before 1921 when the club eventually hired Donald Ross. Most courses in those days were 'works in progress' and were tweaked by members, Superintendents and Professionals even in mid-season.

When Bendelow visited Wyoming CC in 1912 it was still undetermined if it would be a nine-hole or eighteen-hole layout. After several property transfers in 1913 it was decided to build a quality nine-hole layout rather than an eighteen-hole course that lacked a challenge. Dave Mentiply came in from Nebraska and, as Golf Professional, basically built the new Bendelow course while adding many of the features seen today.

During that same trip in August, 1912, Bendelow revisited Hamilton County CC course that he had laid out two years previous. Many holes had been changed pretty radically—most likely by Irish Club Professional Richard Cass—and Bendelow declared it "one of

the best in the country." That theme would be repeated on many of the local Bendelow courses. Bendelow was always upbeat and complimenting of the club's property and final layout and considered it as part of his promotion of the fledgling sport. Everything was trumpeted as "the best" or the like to keep members' interest for each project.

Original Bendelow layouts became murky as adjacent property was bought and revisions were relatively simple. Tees and greens were very small and easy to move. Holes could be lengthened with a pick and shovel in many cases. And Professionals like Cass, Mentiply, Gerrard and McDonald were not hesitant to tweak and improve layouts for their members.

Western Hills CC was another Bendelow layout. The members of Elberon GC needed more room for their eighteen-hole course, chose a site on Cleves-Warsaw Pike and changed their name to Western Hills CC. This mirrored the previous moves of Losantiville CC from Oakley to Pleasant Ridge and Avondale GC from Avondale to Bond Hill to get larger properties. Western Hills CC eventually added more property and did major remodel work in the 1920s under the tutelage of Bendelow and Head Professional Ed Brophy and again in 1931 using Bill Diddel. Much of the original Bendelow layout has been modified.

There was one last Bendelow effort in the Tri-State. Inverness CC had shut down operations in Kentucky in 1909 and there was a growing demand in Campbell County to fill the void. In 1913 there had been movement to buy a site adjacent to the old club but it fell short and it took another few years to acquire a larger site at the end of the Alexandria Pike street car line and Highland Country Club was begun. Bendelow laid out the nine holes among the pear and cherry orchards and 112 members began play in 1916.

The impact of Tom Bendelow on Cincinnati and golf in general cannot be overestimated. For the period from when he emigrated to America in 1892 to his passing in 1936 he was a tireless advocate for golf and helped carry the game through the early beginnings when its future was in doubt. This required untold days on trains and visiting almost the whole United States all the time building, designing, competing, officiating, training caddies, running tournaments, teaching, mentoring and being the face of the game. Even though there are scarce remains of his original layouts locally, golf and Cincinnati owe a lot to Tom Bendelow.

Architecture Starts to Move Mountains

Meanwhile, George Crupp from Philadelphia was a harbinger of another school of American golf architecture in 1914. The country was feeling its oats after building the Panama Canal and architects in every field took on a new energy. Golf courses were now being built nationwide with a

new American spirit of conquering the elements and the property rather than letting the natural conditions of the land determine the routing. Crupp's masterpiece was Pine Valley in New Jersey. Marshes were drained and 22,000 trees were removed and almost very great architect of the day pitched in and helped this amateur designer on his first and only project. Crupp died before the effort was completed but, in many eyes, it is still America's greatest course. Robert Hunter's famous book, "The Links", did a meticulous study with pictures of the great course in 1926 and that book influenced others in this new school of golf architecture.

That new spirit was beginning to take on elevation and contouring and was embraced by Donald Ross locally. Like Bendelow a native of Scotland, he worked out of offices in New England and Pinehurst NC. There are literally hundreds of books written about Ross, his design theories and the list of his accomplishments. Courses like Pinehurst #2, Oakland Hills CC, Seminole CC and hundreds of others dot the North American continent. The two Ross courses in Cincinnati, Maketewah CC (1919) and Hyde Park CC (1921), were built with hickory shafts in mind but his core thinking was more intricate in its attempt to influence the playability of the hole.

Bendelow's bunkers were there to penalize a wayward shot and frequently located by a mathematical formula (one-hundred yards from tee, etc.). But new iron clubs and livelier golf balls were providing easier escape from the rough. So, Ross began to shape the hole from the tee to give the player options and risk-reward decisions for each shot. He

Donald Ross, apprentice to Old Tom Morris at St. Andrews and one of the game's great architects, designed two courses in Cincinnati: Maketewah Country Club (1919) and Hyde Park Country Club (1921). (Photo circa 1905)

Before the 1940s, the fairways were shaped by mule teams.

would hide features and require players to shape their shots from left to right and right to left.

Ross built tees and greens on hills or into the sides of hills and ridges to force shots into the air. And he began to move more earth to get the shape he wanted for the drainage of fairways, greens and bunkers. It must be noted that, like George Crupp, Ross designs had to use horse and mule powered equipment to move the dirt and shape the bunkers. Steam powered winches would be used to remove stumps but construction was becoming costlier and involved than the old Bendelow type courses. Bendelow moved almost no land in his designs. Seldom did Ross move more than 50,000 cubic yards whereas modern course construction can include earth moving of 3,000,000 cubic yards or more.

Ross's greens also had more features. Larger and designed for drainage, they also provided putting strategies and usually included an open entrance from the fairway and extreme trouble for shots over the green. But every layout was different and even though the principles remained there was no repeat as each property was dissected. For example, Mid-Pines CC and Pine Needles CC, located across the street from each other in Pinehurst, are different courses in feel and appearance though both were designed by Ross.

Unlike Bendelow, Ross also kept control of the construction at most sites. At one point in the 1920s he had over three thousand construction workers employed on course building projects nationwide. Normally, especially before 1920, he would visit the site and then "mark with permanent stakes on the property, the location of trees, line of fair-greens (sic), size and shape of bunkers, and the outline of (greens)." He would then have the club furnish a surveyor plan of the property so he could then return to his offices and begin his detailed construction drawings and sketches.

In 1916, he had expanded his business to hire J.B McGovern who worked quietly behind the scenes until Ross's death. Two years later he added Walter Hatch who assisted him through the early Depression and then Walter Johnson came aboard in late 1920. This expansion provided the ability to take on many more commissions. There were many great courses being built by other renowned architects in the Roaring 20s but not as many as Ross's team accomplished.

Architecture's Next Wave in the Queen City

In 1924 Clovernook Country Club was being built by the Chicago architectural firm of Langford & Moreau. Like Ross, they had no problems shaping the course to their need. Both principals were Civil Engineers. Langford began his business at age thirty-five and had already designed courses in Illinois, Michigan and Kansas when he arrived in North College Hill to begin the project for Powell Crosley. Moreau's specialty was the supervision of the installations and shaping greens complexes and bunkers and Langford had a knack for coming up with inspired routings that incorporated ravines, hills and valleys in a manner that was pleasing to the eye. It was a combination that would collaborate for such masterpieces as Lawsonia Links in Green Lake, Wisconsin. They also had consults at Avon Fields GC and Phoenix GC in Cincinnati during this period but were not involved in their final designs.

On the last day of 1925 Ralph Love, the golf writer of the *Cincinnati Post*, announced in his article, "Whenever a new golf course is planned, the promoters proclaim that when completed their course will be the finest in the city, state or country … " But eventually those promises are fulfilled and that may have occurred in that same year when it was announced that The Camargo Club would be constructed.

Seth Raynor, the architect selected, calmly mentioned that this new creation could be "even finer than the National course in Long Island"—at that time considered one of the greatest in the world. His resume already included Fisher's Island Club,

William Langford, with Theodore Moreau designed Clovernook and Phoenix (Hillcrest) country clubs in Cincinnati. The pair were known as "The Sultans of the Steam Shovel" for their use of heavy equipment to shape modern golf courses after WWI.

Seth Raynor, Architect of the Camargo Club was not a golfer. Nevertheless, he built three of his great courses, Piping Rock, Sleepy Hollow and St. Louis country clubs, before he ever played the game. He passed away at age fifty-one while completing the Camargo Club project.

William C. Jackson's graduation picture from Virginia Military Institute. He designed over thirty courses in the Midwest including parts of The Camargo Club and Butler County Country Club, Potter's Park Golf Course and Summit Hills Country Club locally; he also designed Olympia Fields #4 in Chicago and was a sought-out turf expert when local clubs had problems to be solved. He also served as Head Professional and Superintendent at The Camargo Club.

Shoreacres, and The Course at Yale. Bunkers were to be up to "sixteen feet deep" as he took on the project located on over 200 acres in Indian Hill.

Raynor, also a Civil Engineer, was a non-golfer but learned his design trade at the side of C.B. McDonald. He used many of McDonald's features in his designs—Redan, Eden and Biarritz greens complexes—at Camargo. Unfortunately, Raynor passed away suddenly in 1927 before finishing the project and W.C. (Bill) Jackson (eventually Camargo's Professional), and Charles Banks (Raynor's construction manager) completed the design and the construction.

A special note goes to Jackson who took over most of the Camargo design effort after Raynor's health began to decline. Like Raynor, he was an engineer and he was true to Raynor's

Bill Diddel worked on ten course design and remodel projects in the Cincinnati area; Kenwood Country Club and Sharon Woods Golf Club are in his design resume of over two hundred courses nationwide.

Louis Sibbett "Dick" Wilson was the designer of Coldstream Country Club that was built in 1959. His design resume includes NCR South in Dayton, Ohio; Bay Hill Country Club, Royal Montreal Country Club, The Blue Monster at Doral Country Club, and Cog Hill #4 (Dub's Dread).

design intent. He did make some changes to Hole #16 (making it a Par 4) and Hole #17 (making it a Par 5). He was so well thought of as a designer that Olympia Fields in Chicago had used his services as an expert on grass cultivation and chose him to lay out their fourth course on the site before his move to the Cincinnati area. Jackson originally came here to design the back nine at Butler County CC (later called Hamilton Elk's CC) and would also design the course at Potter Park in Hamilton OH (1925), Summit Hills CC (1930) and consult on a project at Ft. Mitchell CC. Jackson also had many other designs in Illinois and Wisconsin.

Close by in Terrace Park there was design activity too. Residents were getting tired of broken windows as the seventy local enthusiasts played on a six-hole course in the village. A thirty-year odyssey from the original layouts finally came to an end under the direction of Charles Lush. A large farm property was located in Milford and Bill Harig, a renowned architect/builder and very good player at Hyde Park CC, was selected to lay out the course. Harig, Al Joslin Sr. and Jim Muirden would later collaborate on the course at Ridgewood GC and Joslin would also design the Naples Beach and Golf Club in Florida.

Besides Harig and Joslin, there were many examples of quality layouts and remodels of existing courses being accomplished by local Professionals and excellent amateur players during this time period. These courses included:

- Avon Fields GC (Tom McCormack) 1914
- Cincinnati CC (Harold W. Nichols) 1923
- Three Rivers CC (Ed Brophy) 1926
- DeVou Park GC (John Brophy and Benny Weichman) 1927
- Mariemont GC (remodeled by Archie Simpson Sr.) 1927
- Homestead GC (George Bowden) 1927

Archie Simpson Sr. was Head Professional and architect at Mariemont GC as well as even-

tually serving terms at Ft. Mitchell CC (1924) and Clovernook CC (1932) where he performed modifications to their layouts. Called "The Pioneer" in a *Golf Course Architecture Magazine* article, he was runner-up twice in the British Open. His design resume in Scotland included Nairn GC, Cruden Bay GC, Royal Dornoch GC, the remodel of Carnoustie GC (working with Old Tom Morris) and Royal Aberdeen GC! After emigrating to the USA (Detroit Country Club) he moved around—back to Scotland for a while, Vincennes GC in Indiana and the above three Cincinnati assignments—before dying in 1955 in Detroit at age eighty-eight. His primary effort here, Mariemont GC, closed in 1938 after severe floods on the Little Miami River (see chapter on "Ghost Courses").

If there is any architect whose both number and longevity of designs has survived locally it is Indianapolis, IN native Bill Diddel. He was an excellent amateur golfer having won the Indiana Amateur five times. In his design career, he amassed a resume of over 200 courses with many in the Cincinnati area. The most famous is Kenwood CC, built after a preliminary layout from Donald Ross in 1929. He also built the California GC and Sharon Woods GC as WPA projects and designed Winton Woods GC for WPA before WWII although it was not built until after the war. His other designs and remodels in this time period in Cincinnati included:

- Dearborn CC (1925)
- Western Hills CC (Remodel 1931)
- Swaim Fields GC (1933)
- Avon Fields GC (Remodel 1933)
- Highland CC (Remodel 1954)
- Reeves GC (1955)
- Miami View GC (1959)
- Kenwood CC (six holes revised) (1966)

Diddel worked mostly in the Midwest on flat terrains. He did not move a lot of dirt in building

Archie Simpson Sr. was considered one of golf's most underrated designers. His resume in Scotland included Nairn and Cruden Bay golf clubs along with the remodels of Royal Aberdeen and Carnoustie. On the latter project he worked with Old Tom Morris. In Cincinnati he designed Mariemont Golf Club and the improvements at Clovernook and Ft. Mitchell country clubs.

Manpower as well as horsepower was utilized to build greens and bunkers in the 1920s.

the courses on flat ground and preferred North-South layouts to reduce effects of sun and wind. But many of his layouts like Kenwood CC, Western Hills CC and Sharon Woods GC locally show amazing creativity and ingenuity. He died in 1985 at the age of 101.

Louis Sibbett (Dick) Wilson was the last major architect to enter the region as in 1959 he was selected to build the new Coldstream Country Club on Asbury Road in Anderson Township. Wilson, born in 1904 in Philadelphia, already had a heady resume as he entered the project. He had completed the NCR South Course in Dayton OH, Bay Hill CC, Cog Hill #4 (Dub's Dread), Doral CC, and Royal Montreal CC among his projects on about every continent. He was a protégé of the great designer William Flynn and had worked as his construction supervisor for the overhaul design of Shinnecock Hills CC.

Wilson was a no-nonsense, outspoken Civil Engineer who was comfortable in a pair of muddy boots and facing up to a client if he felt he was right. He favored softly mounded fairways and large challenging greens and long tees. He believed that a course "should inspire you, keep you alert." Concentration for all 18 holes was paramount. Wilson's love for playing the game inspired him to design courses challenging for the scratch player yet making them enjoyable for all levels of ability. He designed seventy-four golf courses worldwide and died in 1965 at the age of sixty-one. Coldstream CC remains one of his masterpieces.

The Builders and Keepers

The day may not be far off when a horse will be a strange sight on a golf course.
—Tom Mascaro (1915–1997) inventor of the modern turf aerifier

Introduction

The building and maintenance of golf courses mirrored the progress and the mechanization of the American farm. During the period of this book from 1890 to 1960, the research and innovations of companies like Allis Chalmers, John Deere, Caterpillar and Toro plus other individuals and companies who worked in the fertilizer and irrigation businesses provided a quantum leap in the playability of courses and the ability for architects and builders to be more creative.

Turf grasses for recreation had been around for hundreds of years before golf came on the scene here. Europeans had played tennis, lawn bowling, croquet, soccer and cricket on manicured surfaces so there was a base of knowledge available. However, these skills had not previously been used on the sites of fifty or more acres needed for even the smallest of golf courses nor the varied climates found in the States.

Besides the turf design and management, there were changes to construction. The transition period that stated about 1915 and lasted until 1941—when many local courses were built—featured horse and mule teams and scraping tools for construction. For the most part, lakes and creeks were left in place and the course built around the major terrain features. However, Architects were now starting to build tees and greens into hillsides, creating deeper bunkers, and shaping greens and fairways for better drainage and challenges. In addition, trees and brush was easier to remove creating more flexibility for routings.

After WWII, the course builder had even more tools to create alterations to the property. More complicated irrigation plans, drainage, flood control and other civil engineering and environmental issues could now be handled. Many older courses were beginning to undertake remodeling and modernization of old layouts so these new tools and techniques could be used

TOWNSEND'S TRIPLEX LAWN MOWER
(PAT. PEND.)

The Greatest Grass Cutter on Earth—Cuts a Swath 86 inches Wide

Drawn by one horse and operated by one man, the Triplex mower will mow more lawn in a day than the best motor mower ever made, and cut it better and at a fraction of the cost.

Drawn by one horse and operated by one man, it will mow more lawn in a day than any three other horse-drawn mowers with three horses and three men. (We guarantee this).

One mower may be climbing a knoll while a second may be skimming the level and a third may be paring a hollow.

Floats over the uneven ground as a ship rides the waves.

Does not smash the grass to earth and plaster it in the mud in the springtime, neither does it crush the life out of the grass between hot rollers and hard hot ground in the summer as does the Motor mower.

Write for beautiful descriptive catalogue containing list of users. Free.

S. P. TOWNSEND & CO.

Orange, New Jersey

Innovation took a three-horse lawnmower and brought it to a requirement for only one horse. (Photo circa 1915)

throughout the region. The installation at Coldstream CC in 1959 was the last course in this time period built with old classical methods of design. Reeves and Miami View projects were also started at this time. And it had begun in Cincinnati with Robert White's layouts at Cincinnati GC before the turn of the last century.

Horsepower and Manpower—Literally

The mechanization of the American farm also hailed the improvement of golf course building and maintenance. The American farm family in the 1920s on average could manage about 100 acres with their horse driven equipment. Horses, oxen and mules provided fertilizer (manure) and the power for tilling, plowing, seeding and harvesting. But it also took about twen-

ty acres of that farm to provide feed for the animals, leaving a net of eighty acres for the produce. The same ratio also applied to golf courses that used horse and mule power to keep the course maintained.

The introduction of mechanical equipment to replace horses and the additions of effective irrigation, pesticides and fertilizers unleashed a multi-fold increase in productivity on the farm. Similarly, the golf course turf management business benefitted from this progress. Affordable tractor driven systems eventually could be used for grass cutting, fertilizer and pesticide application, aeration and construction projects but it took many years (the late 1940s) before it was used city wide.

When Camargo was built in the early 1920s, the local farmers would show up at the construction sites

Tractor and gang mower with steel wheels fitted with "lugs" for traction. (Photo circa 1920)

with up to twenty different mule teams to work on shaping the course to Seth Raynor's design. After WWII, heavy equipment designed primarily to serve the American farmers would be adapted for use on the ever-increasing numbers of golf courses being built at Coldstream, Winton Woods, and other large projects.

Tractors were not viable for golf course maintenance use until the invention of large pneumatic tires. Before that, tractor wheels were either tracked—like a military tank—or had steel wheels with cleats or lugs for gripping the turf. This was suitable for course construction but not for grass cutting and other work on finished fairways.

Horses and mules remained the main source of power for gang mowers before WWII. In 1910 the invention of the large reel mower by Charles Worthington dominated golf course cutting (with horse or mule power) for the next several decades. The horses would be fitted with special boots for their hooves to minimize damage, especially under wet conditions. Many times, crews worked at night to keep the horses from tiring. But the turf damage from horses was too much for many courses and encouraged the use of new hand-driven rotary mowers in the 1930s. One of the last vestiges of mule power was removed when two barns were torn down at Highland CC in 2007 for a course remodel.

In addition, many courses also incorporated livestock power. Avon Fields GC and Hamilton Elks CC used herds of sheep to keep rough and fairways manageable. Before Terrace Park CC moved to their present Milford location, their early courses used cows to keep greens at a manageable height. Livestock also grazed the links at Wyoming CC, Hyde Park CC and Cincinnati GC. Hamilton County CC and Three Rivers CC

Large pneumatic tires were introduced in the early 1930s making turf care much easier on the fairways. By 1940, 95% of the new tractors were fitted with rubber tires.

One-horse-power gang mower. (Photo circa 1915)

were easily built because they were on sites of dairy farms and needed only manicuring for tees and greens to be in business. But they also employed sheep for the roughs.

Turf and Irrigation

In our region, turf was usually limited to local grasses such as Kentucky blue grass or perennial ryegrass. By the 1920s, bent grass varieties were being introduced at many courses, especially in greens and fairways where they could be cut to shorter heights. Roughs usually remained with local varieties of rye or bluegrass because they do better in longer lengths and were also hardier. Bent grass now required better irrigation to maintain play through the summer so some clubs were beginning to install underground pipes to feed sprinklers on fairways and greens.

The push reel lawnmower became the mainstay for cutting around the greens. (Photo circa 1929)

Horse boots were placed on the hooves of mules and horses to protect the turf while cutting grass.

Greenkeepers were known for their skills of maintaining fairways and greens through humid Cincinnati summers. At the turn of the century, many courses shut down for the summer months when grasses died and ground became rock hard. In 1917 Western Hills CC made application for their site to be used for the Met because their greens were clover and withstood the July conditions plaguing other local courses.

In 1931 Dr. John Monteith wrote an article encouraging the use of new chemical fertilizers to replace the accepted method of turf feeding—animal manure. For those who imagine the old days of playing with hickory clubs and Haskell balls, you can add the experience of playing on a fairway top dressed with nature's own grass treatment. Actually, the development of the chemical fertilizer business was sped because horses were being replaced by machines and the sources of manure were disappearing. But until chemicals were universally accepted, the player was still burdened with bulky applications of manure on greens and fairways.

The Camargo Club was the first locally to install underground piping for irrigation. Large sprinklers on wheels would be attached to the piping system for use around a particular fairway or green. It would then be detached manually and moved on to the next site. Kenwood CC and Cincinnati CC would follow in the 1930s as their courses were built and remodeled. Hyde Park CC was the first to have irrigated fairways. It would be the 1950s and 60s before more local courses added their irrigation.

Aerification in the 1920s was a labor-intensive effort with hand forks. Most courses counted on their own earth worms but the importance of an aerification program was soon identified by USGA and a mechanical unit was designed in the mid-1920s and further improved right after WWII.

Bent grass was being introduced in the 1920s to improve the fairways and greens.

The Experts

Taylor Boyd was the Kenwood CC Greens Superintendent working under Bill Diddel on the 1933 US Amateur project. He was one of many well-known local experts in the field of turf management and would also serve at Camargo, Losantiville and Terrace Park clubs. In 1952, he was voted Vice-President of the Midwest Regional Turf Foundation, headquartered at Purdue University.

Other experts included Bill Harig of Hyde Park CC who was internationally known for development of local turf grasses especially for use on Greens. He worked out of an experimental station he built behind #2 tee at the club in 1930. That station was visited frequently by USGA turf experts who had formed their Greens Section in 1920. In his spare time, Harig designed Terrace Park CC, Ridgewood, GC and redesigned many holes at his home course.

Bill Jackson was also nationally known expert on grass types and especially seed application. He served The Camargo Club as Professional and Course Superintendent, one of the few experts who possessed both sets of skills. But he was usually the first person called locally when a course had a particular problem with turf that others could not solve.

There were scores of other excellent Greenkeepers and Superintendents who were able to maintain quality grounds through the period and provide the sites for all of the enjoyment and accomplishments by players. They included Charlie Tadge, Harry Mesloh at Clovernook CC, George Benvie at Maketewah CC, Clifford "Mickey" Forste at Losantiville CC, Joe Allen at the Public Recreation Commission and Bill Fruectemeyer at Hyde Park CC. Like Bill Jackson, Fruectemeyer also served in the dual role as Head Professional. Others who served a dual role as Pro and Superintendent included Bill Roach at Wyoming CC, B.J. (Bunny) Berning of Crest Hills CC and Bob Lindenschmidt at Hartwell CC. At the same time, the game was advanced by skilled people on Greens Com-

As courses moved from horse-driven mowers to tractors, they lost their source of fertilizer (manure) so manufactured fertilizer was applied. Most courses still used other supplies for manure (cows, sheep, etc.) to save money but this was uncomfortable for golfers due to the smell as they walked the course. (Photo circa 1931)

The invention of the Impact Arm Sprinkler in 1933 allowed Cincinnati courses to stay playable through hot summers.

mittees. Howard Dammel, ten years at Clovernook CC and thirty years at Kenwood CC serving on their Greens Committee, was an example of the team effort required between members and Superintendents to get the job done.

On the Horizon

The Cincinnati area's architectural heritage reaches back to Old Tom Morris and nineteenth century Scotland. Through Bendelow, Ross, Simpson and numerous club Professionals in the first wave of emigration to Cincinnati, many courses have their feet firmly planted in Scottish soil. Continued work through the classical period have added world renowned architects like Seth Raynor, Bill Diddel and Dick Wilson. The list of Classic courses in Cincinnati is well represented by the architects involved. After 1960 and golf's Mod-

Harry Mesloh, superintendent at Clovernook Country Club, receiving the 1967 LPGA Award for best conditioned course for their tour that year.

ern Era begins, architects such as Jack Nicklaus, Jack Kidwell, Arthur Hills, Greg Norman, Arnold Palmer,

Michael Hurdzan and Brian Silva would provide designs for the Tri-State. Very few regions can boast of the variety and depth of architecture as experienced here in Greater Cincinnati.

The Modern Era also introduced different design and building methods with courses built by construction teams of bulldozers, power shovels and other earth moving equipment. Eventually they would be fitted with GPS controls to shape fairways, bunkers and greens to exact measurements. Turf grasses would continue to improve to reduce water usage and provide longer playing seasons. Irrigation and drainage would be built as the course was installed and included coverage of roughs. Many new courses were built as parts of real estate developments so design alterations were made to fit roads and building lots. Design concepts moved from saddle bags, wooden stakes and sketch pads to CAD stations, Environmental Impact Statements and legal teams. But the ideas and thought processes for local courses were still anchored in their Scottish roots and Old Tom Morris.

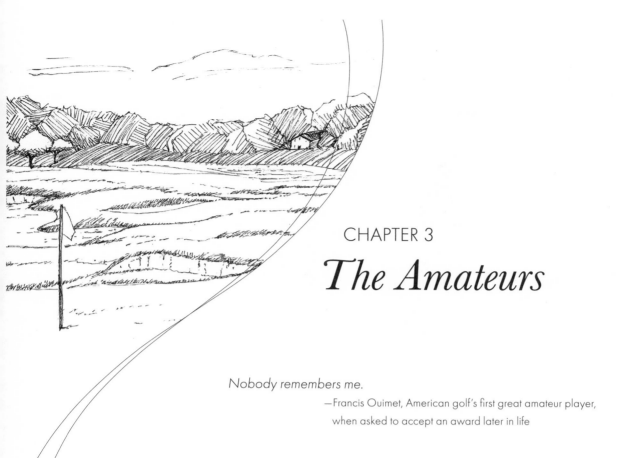

CHAPTER 3

The Amateurs

Nobody remembers me.

—Francis Ouimet, American golf's first great amateur player,
when asked to accept an award later in life

Introduction

In 1893, even the best players barely broke 100 on eighteen-hole courses that were a little over 3,000-yards in length. Technology changed as the ball design went from Gutta Percha to Haskell to improved covers of Balata (See "Equipment" chapter). Club shafts went from hickory and boxwood to steel. But courses also became longer and more challenging as architects took on nature and elevation changes and new types of grasses were planted on fairways and greens. So, to compare eras is difficult and it is probably best to rate a player and his or her accomplishments with those of their peers.

From 1890 to the mid-1930s, the amateur game compared favorably with that of the Professionals. Players like Francis Ouimet, Chick Evans and Bobby Jones competed just as well in Open Championships as in the contests only for amateurs. After the formation of the Professional Golf Association in 1916, there was a new breed of competitor who took the game to its highest level. Eventually the tour player would represent the pinnacle of performance but in the early days,

many local amateurs would play the game as well as anyone in the world.

On May 10, 1987, the *Cincinnati Enquirer* ran an article in anticipation of the USGA Public Links Tournament that would be held at Glenview Golf Course that year. It included a debate of who was the greatest amateur male golfer ever developed in Greater Cincinnati. Many names were included and it tended to feature more recent stars such as Tony Blom, Dr. Harry Duccilli, Taylor Metcalf, Jim Meuthing, Marion Scheibly and Don Niehaus. They included some champions in the 40s and 50s but the consensus seemed to feature the same four golfers and in the same order and all appeared in the period between 1890 and 1960. Since this book features players before 1960, the above-named players, however worthy, would be excluded. Who were the great local amateurs between 1890 and 1960 when the game was growing and building its legacy?

Individual Stars First Appear (1895–1915)

The last years of the nineteenth century were pretty much spent on rudimentary layouts with players of varied abilities scattered around the area. The best men's and women's players of this era were concentrated at Cincinnati GC on Grandin Road. Lucy Herron had already competed on the national level at the US Women's Amateur in 1899 as had Annie Harrison, Ethel Barnet and Clara Longworth. Some Cincinnati male Amateurs also started to show up in national championships, including Allen Reid in 1899 and Fay and C.H. Ingalls in 1900, but none made it past the first day of competition and local skills were not matching those of their counterparts in Chicago and back East.

A July 7, 1927 *Cincinnati Post* article by golf columnist Ralph Love (see "Media" chapter) offered another explanation about why the early golfers were not as good as their national rivals. His opinion was that the early games in town were more "drinking bouts with golf as a sideline." The first players did not welcome younger players into competition where they could gain interest and develop skills. To play in city tournaments and club competitions you had to be voting age (twenty-one at that time). Good young, competitive athletes turned to other sports like baseball, gymnastics and tennis rather than golf. The sport before 1900 remained the domain of older business leaders and those who had some leisure time to pursue the game and improve their ability to compete.

By the turn of the century there began a parade of players who would begin to stand out above their peers and they came from all over the Tristate. Some even began as caddies rather than club members. Five players from Northern Kentucky started to win more than their share of competitions locally and created some excitement when paired in matches. When Carl Piepho, Frank Thompson and Byron Trueblood from Inverness CC or Bradford Eldridge and Beattie Warner from Ft. Mitchell CC were scheduled to play, there was generally

Brad Eldridge of Ft. Mitchell Country Club, the area's first golf superstar and winner of 1911 and 1912 Mets. (Photo circa 1909)

a crowd of spectators following. Eldridge was premier on the south side of the river and would prove his mettle by winning the Greater Cincinnati Metropolitan Championship (Met) in 1911 and 1912. He would follow that up by a victory in the Kentucky Amateur before eventually leaving Cincinnati for California and Arizona.

Crowds of a thousand or more would show up on a Saturday afternoon when these and other key players were in action. Odds were given, bets were put down and sometimes admission was charged by the home club or participants. Spectator sports were also getting their starts nationwide and baseball players and boxers in particular had become celebrities on the local scene. Soon golfers would also be celebrated in the nation's and local newspapers. Visiting national stars like Willy Anderson, Chick Evans, Harry Vardon and others would guarantee a good turnout even when getting a quick exhibition organized during a train layover and some locals were beginning to hold their own in these matches.

The Cincinnati side of the river also developed some new "crack" amateurs like, J.W. Mackelfresh, George Ebersole, Neil MacNeale, L.C. Rose and others. Good scores were now in the 80s for eighteen-holes. By this time, there were American and Scottish courses over 6,000 yards but it would be 1910 (Hamilton County CC and Losantiville CC) before there would be a 6,000-yard course here. Early courses were also designed for the ground game and greens were extremely small.

The introduction of state competitions in 1904 and the first Cincinnati championship in 1910 (The "Met") presented

Holden Wilson of the Cincinnati Golf Club was consistently in the top five players in the city and, with Brad Eldridge, carried the city's lowest handicap. (Photo circa 1905)

Billy Groesbeck and Al Baumgartner won four of the first ten Met Championships. Baumgartner had a long and storied career starting as a caddy at Clifton Golf Course. He won three Mets and was runner up in one more. He won club championships at Western Hills Country Club, Hyde Park Country Club and Clovernook Country Club and was the runner up in the 1916 Ohio Amateur; he also won a National ABC Singles Bowling Champion in 1923 shooting a 723 for the title.

an opportunity to actually identify the best local players through head to head competition. William "Billy" Groesbeck of Cincinnati GC would claim the first Met crown and he repeated his victory in 1916. In addition, in 1912, the Western Golf Association published a list that identified the best local golfers and compared them by handicaps. Leading the local list were Eldridge at Ft. Mitchell CC and Holden Wilson of Cincinnati GC and

closely followed by Neil MacNeale, George Balch, Millard Mayer and Beatty Warner.

The First World War and Roaring 20s (1915–1929)
Just before WWI there was a new surge of young players that would pick up the yoke and carry their game well into the 1920s. In the 1914 Met, six of the final

Father and Son Started In Same Race For Title

R.A Holden was soon overtaken by son Ira at the Cincinnati Golf Club. Ira would go on to win the Ohio Amateur in 1916.

Junior Championship (considered the most elite junior event in the country) and had secured his place among the state's elite players. He would go on to more success in the Ohio Amateur with a win again in 1919 as well as more Met championships and Cincinnati GC championships. In 1927, he moved to The Camargo Club where he won their first club championship that same year and continued a stellar career that was capped with a Senior Met championship.

Cincinnati had been shut out of the first seven state titles but won four of the next nine (Russell Jones (1911), DeWitt Balch (1913 and 1919) as well as Ira Holden (1916) as local play improved. Part of the problem was that the contestant had to be from a member club of the Ohio Golf Association and only Elberon GC and Cincinnati GC had joined at first. Hamilton County CC and Hyde Park CC and other clubs soon joined, opening up opportunities for others to compete statewide.

To build on Ralph Love's assertion that Cincinnati golf was late in developing young players there were some exceptions starting to show. Young Balch started playing golf when he was eight and under the tutelage of his dad and Ira Holden started about the same age. Spencer Kuhn (twice a Met winner) began as a youngster at Avondale GC and Al Baumgartner (who would win the Met three times and was runner up once) started playing as a caddy at Clifton GC in Burnet Woods. Baumgartner had a particularly long run of great competitive golf that ran from his first

sixteen players were youngsters under twenty-one (Al Baumgartner, Harold Whitaker, DeWitt Balch (George's son), Holden Wilson, Steve Lahusen, and Bill Harig). By that time "Dewey" Balch had already won the 1913 Ohio Amateur (at age sixteen) and the 1915 Western

THEY ARE STRONG CONTENDERS FOR CITY GOLF CROWN

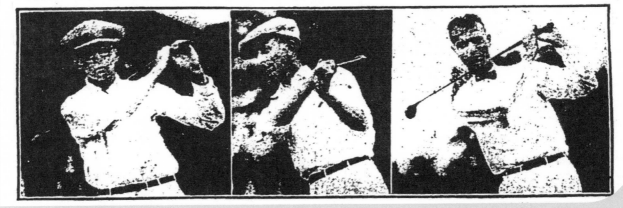

In the 1926 Met, Harold LeBlond (l) won the medal for low qualifier. Doug Hill (c) from Cincinnati Country Club defeated Hyde Parker Al Baumgartner (r) in the finals for the championship.

Met in 1914 and continued into the 1930s when he competed against Nelson Ruddy at Clovernook CC. Even more caddies were becoming the stars of the 1920s and that theme would be developed later when some tremendous young local talent (and maybe the best of all) came from the caddy ranks.

After WWI, the country clubs were furnishing a new wave of talent like Harold "Hop" LeBlond, Ernie Diehl, Dr. Fred Lush and Templeton Briggs but there were more young players also entering the scene from a new source—Avon Fields GC—the city's first major municipal track. Avon youngsters like Neil Ransick, Milt Cook, Bill Clensy and Don Gill had great success in the Met and would move on to play at other clubs. There they would garner more honors and gain a total of nine Met and two Senior Met crowns among them. Milt Cook would be the first winner of the Met while playing from a Public Course (Twin Oaks GC) in 1931. Bill Clensy, Pete Stuntebeck and Tom Nieporte would add Met titles from the Public Courses later on.

Some encouragement came from the country clubs and extended into the caddy and junior ranks to develop talent. Al Joslin Sr., with Jim Kenny and Irv Bauer, would start a trend to develop new young players including initiating a city-wide Junior Championship that would eventually become the Junior Met. The first tournament had over 150 players from all over the city and was not limited to country clubs so caddies could participate.

Nelson Ruddy, another young phenom, entered the arena in 1927 by beating Spencer Kuhn in the finals of the Met and claiming the title at seventeen years of age. It also included a 2-up victory over Kentucky Open winner Darwin Stapp from Highland CC that some claimed to be the greatest match play exhibition up to that time. When Ruddy was sixteen years old he had come on the scene and immediately shot to the top of amateur golf in Cincinnati. His family had moved in from Chicago and he had been playing the game for about five years to help him with some health issues. In 1926, he first grabbed the Junior Met at Ridgewood GC and then the Clovernook club championship by defeating outstanding player Oliver Perrin 10 and 9 in a thirty-six-hole final. The win in the 1927 Met made it three victories in his first three tournaments on the local stage. Match play victories included a big one

Bill Clensy starred at Avon Fields, Devou Golf Course and the Sycamore Club. He won the 1935 Ohio Publinx and 1938 Met and was the first player to win both the Met and Senior Met.

Milt Cook, one of the city's greatest match players won the Met in 1931, 1933, 1934 and 1937.

against fellow Clovernook player and three-time Met champ Al Baumgartner.

He then followed that up with another club championship. Ruddy's play continued at a high level through the rest of the decade as he starred in college at the University of Dayton and competed locally with the likes of Johnny Fischer and Neil Ransick. He continued his great play in the 1930s with a great finish in the Western Amateur and participation in the Western Open. Ruddy was very comfortable playing against the Pro's and he later moved over the river to win the Kentucky Amateur and also added a second Met title in 1942 while playing from Summit Hills CC.

While Ruddy was winning his first Met, another young player was moving up from the caddy ranks to arguably be the best of them all from Cincinnati. Johnny Fischer was a sixteen-year-old from Price Hill and caddy at Western Hills CC. 1927 had been a good year for him too as he followed Ruddy as Junior champion, won the city Caddy Championship and finished as low amateur in the Cincinnati Open—all at age fifteen. In that City Open he finished ahead of great amateurs like Doug Hill (1926 Met winner), DeWitt Balch and Nelson Ruddy as well as several Professionals.

In 1928 a third young player, Neil Ransick of Maketewah CC, became the next to enter the stage.

George Dunlap tees off for the final match play round.

The Main Stage—1933 US Amateur at Kenwood CC

Cincinnati's giant step onto the world stage occurred in 1933 when the nation's number one tourna ment—the US Amateur—came to the three-year old Kenwood CC grounds. In those days the Amateur was considered the greatest championship in American golf. Previous winners included Bobby Jones, Francis Ouimet and Chick Evans

Final match ends on the thirteenth green.

Dunlap putts out on the seventeenth green.

Harold Nichols of Cincinnati Country Club was one of the most influential persons in golf during the period between WWI and WWII. He was president of the Greater Cincinnati Golf Association, single handedly bringing USGA events to the city, and presided over the redesign of the Cincinnati Country Club course in 1923.

and over 600 players tried to qualify nationally. When the thirty-six-hole championship medal rounds started at Kenwood, Cincinnatian Johnny Fischer broke his own scoring record shared previously with Bobby Jones and others. Cincinnati was able to secure that championship jewel based on the hard work of Harold W. Nichols of Cincinnati CC. He was also President of the Cincinnati Golfers League (later called Greater Cincinnati Golf Association) and had led an attempt to bring the US Open to Cincinnati in 1932. The city had mobilized for the Open bid for the new Kenwood CC course and brought in course designer Bill Diddel as part of the presentation to a visiting Prescott Bush of the USGA. Sadly, Cincinnati was by-passed as the Open went to North Shore CC in Chicago.

This did not stop Nichols from trying to bring another National Championship to Cincinnati. After another

Program from the 1933 U.S. Amateur Golf Tournament at the Kenwood Country Club.

visit by Bush during the 1932 US Am Qualifier at Camargo coupled with a $5,000 guarantee (pledged partly by Kenwood CC members and the Chamber of Commerce), the city was able to gain the 1933 US Amateur. With all of the hard work and preparation, the tournament was a financial success and pulled off during one of the city's worst droughts. In preparation for the tournament, Kenwood CC applied 100,000,000 gallons of water to the grounds. Local papers equated this to filling the Coney Island Pool over 400 times. In addition, the club brought in 7,500 tons of sand to build and replace bunkers, three tons of grass seed and fifty tons of fertilizer and brought Bill Diddel back to manage the effort. In the finals of match play for the trophy, NCAA Champion George Dunlap from Princeton University would defeat 1923 US Amateur winner Max Marston 6&5.

Learning the game at Avon Fields GC he would go on to win three Met titles and the Ohio Amateur in 1934 as well as play in 1929 and 1930 US Opens. At one time, through two Met victories and a victory in the Ohio Amateur, Ransick had won fifteen straight matches against the top Cincinnati and Ohio competition. He would later play also at Hillcrest CC and Hyde Park CC. And the next year another former caddy, Ralph Shelton of Wyoming CC, took the Met title. Youth was definitely an asset as the Roaring 20s ended.

Post Sports

Ralph "Pete" Stuntebeck had an amazing career on both sides of the river. He started as a caddy at Ft. Mitchell Country Club and then became a golf Professional there. After regaining his amateur status, he won the 1944 Met and was the 1942 runner up from the Sycamore Club in Cincinnati. He also played at Highland Country Club and won the Northern Kentucky Amateur three times. In 1951, he became a Professional again and took the helm at Twin Oaks Golf Course for twenty-six years, winning the Kentucky State Senior Open in 1955.

Nelson Ruddy won two Mets (playing from Clovernook and Summit Hills country clubs) and was runner up once (playing from Maketewah Country Club). He also won a Junior Met and a Kentucky Amateur and was a golf star at the University of Dayton.

Neil Ransick, winner of four Met titles for three different clubs in 1928, 1935, 1936, and 1946.

Johnny Fischer was the last U.S. Am winner to play with hickory shaft clubs. He was an NCAA Champ at the University of Michigan.

The Golden Age of Queen City Golf (1930–1940)

An amazing record came from the links at Western Hills CC in 1930. Three of their caddies (Johnny Fischer, Eph Collins and Larry Hendrixson) all made the Match Play portion of the Met that year. All had learned the game under the tutelage of Ed Brophy, Head Professional. Brophy also protected their amateur status with the USGA by not allowing them to caddy for pay after age sixteen.

Fischer won the Met that year and from 1927 to 1937 the new guard of Ruddy, Fischer, Cook, Ransick and Shelton would claim all the titles. New local rules also allowed these youngsters to compete for private clubs in inter-club matches. Fischer was quickly invited (at age sixteen) to join Twin Oaks GC and he got after-school work at Hughes High School to help with expenses. Eventually he would transfer after his sophomore year and graduate from newly opened Western Hills High School.

Johnny was playing out of Highland CC and that 1930 season as an eighteen-year-old was really special by winning three major tournaments (Kentucky Amateur, Cincinnati Met and the Queen City Open). In the latter, he out dueled Nelson Ruddy and Professional Clarence Dapper to come back from a four-stroke deficit. That year he also established four course records (Highlands CC, Kenwood CC, Western Hills CC and Sleepy Hollow CC in Detroit) and was low score in three invitational tournaments. His seventy-one in the Western Open in Chicago was second to Walter Hagen's sixty-eight in the qualifying round. In all, he was low amateur at the Western Open (then considered a Major) in 1929, 1931 and 1935.

After his graduation from Western Hills, he entered the University of Michigan where he won the 1932 NCAA and Big Ten Individual titles and helped lead the team to the NCAA title in 1933 and 1935. He was also Big Ten Individual titlist in 1933 and 1935, missing only 1934 because he was on the Walker Cup Team.

The Post Sports

Five Years Ago Today: Cardinals scored three in 11th and Reds came back with two. St. Louis winning, 9-6 with Reds making 19 hits and Cards 15.

Ten Years Ago Today: Nine-game winning streak by Reds ended in day's second game when Braves scored two in seventh and three in eighth at Redland Field to win, 5-3. Nineteen players appeared in Red lineup.

Four Kings and Two Queens of Clubs Come Tramping Down the Fairway

1935 was a great year for Cincinnati golf. The champions from that year are pictured left to right: Al Joslin Jr. (Maketewah) Ohio College Champ, John Fischer (Highland) Big Ten Champ, Olga Weil (Hillcrest) Ohio Am Champion, Elizabeth Reid (The Camargo Club) Women's Met Champion, Bill Clensy (Sycamore Club) Ohio Publinx Champ, and Neil Ransick (Hillcrest) Ohio Amateur Champion and Men's Met Champion.

But what really sets Fischer apart from all of the competition was his record and accomplishments on the national stage. At that time, some of the greatest golf was being played by amateurs. Professionals like Walter Hagen, Gene Sarazen and Byron Nelson certainly were stars in their own right but this was also the age of great amateur golfers like Bobby Jones, Chick Evans and Francis Ouimet, all of whom won the US Open as amateurs.

After Bobby Jones retired from competitive golf in 1930 with his Grand Slam, there was still a demand for amateur heroes. Jones had won four of the previous five US Amateurs (only losing in the finals to George Van Elm in 1926) and Francis Ouimet returned to take the title in 1931. Chick Evans had won his last Amateur in 1920 and Lawson Little from Stanford

University would win in 1934 and 1935 before turning Professional and winning the 1940 US Open. This was a time before the Masters and there was only cursory interest in the British Open and British Amateur and most professional events. The US Amateur was as big as any tournament in America.

Fischer's record in the US Amateur golf had already been spectacular when he entered the 1936 tournament at the Garden City Club in New York. He had been medalist in 1932 (tying Bobby Jones' record score of 142 at Baltimore CC) and then followed it up the next year by breaking the record with a 141 at Kenwood CC in Cincinnati—medalist two years running. At the same time, he reached the Quarter Finals in 1932 (where he lost to Francis Ouimet) and made the Round of 16 in 1933. After two more years making it

Maurice McCarthy known as "Maketewah Mick," played on three Walker Cups, won an NCAA championship, three Ohio Amateurs, and made nineteen straight appearances in the U.S. Am Match Play, also won state amateur titles in New York and Michigan.

into match play he cracked through to the 1936 title as he beat Jack McLean of Scotland in the Finals. He continued his success by getting to the Semi-Finals in 1937 and Quarter-Finals in 1940—a total of one win and four other top Eight's in nine years. And Johnny Fischer was also the last player to win the Amateur playing hickory shafts.

In addition, he finished tied-27th in the 1932 US Open and tied-43rd in 1933 US Open while still at Michigan. This success provided the opportunity to play on the Walker Cup Team for the United States in 1934, 1936 and 1938 and he eventually led the team as Captain in 1965. Johnny also had the privilege of setting up the course every year for the Masters at the request of fellow amateur Mr. Bobby Jones.

The 1936 victory was also marked by the fact that three other Cincinnatians (Bill Deupree of Ft.

Mitchell CC, Wally Chadwell from Hyde Park CC and Harold LeBlond of The Camargo Club) made it into the Match Play competition. The following year was yet another great milestone for Cincinnati and the US Amateur when six local players qualified for the championship in Portland OR. Johnny Fischer, as defending champion had a bye into the tournament although he still had to qualify into Match Play. But five others (Maurice McCarthy (Maketewah CC), Spencer Kerkow (Ft. Mitchell CC), DeWitt Balch (The Camargo Club), Milt Schloss (Losantiville CC) and John Wood II (Cincinnati CC) also made it to the big show.

In addition, the three alternates were also locals—Dick Meinken and Billy Gilbert III (Western Hills CC) and Mort Olman (Hillcrest CC). Many of these had been competing against one another in high school and the Junior Met only a few year's previous. 1936 and 1937 displayed the depth of the quality golf being played locally.

The old guard in the person of forty-two-year-old Bill Clensy of Avon Fields GC, DeVou GC, and then Sycamore GC (nee Stoneybrook GC) won the 1938 Met after winning the Ohio Publinx Tournament in 1935. He was the second Met winner from a public course and would eventually be the first winner of both the Met and Senior Met. All this set the stage for another national class amateur golfer to play in Cincinnati.

Maurice McCarthy, the "Maketewah Mick", would win the Met three times. In addition, he won three Ohio Amateurs (1935, 1937, 1938).

He (like Fischer an NCAA Individual Champion while at Georgetown University) played in the US Open in 1928 after losing to Bobby Jones in the first round of US Amateur in 1927. He is also famous for the longest match in US Amateur history where he beat George Van Elm in the second round in twenty-eight holes in 1930. Tied for second after the first round of the 1933 US Open he faded in the third-round to finish in the pack behind Johnny Goodman, the last amateur to win the Open.

In 1936, he was transferred on his job to Cincinnati from Cleveland and was already a ten-year veteran of the US Amateur. He continued his stellar play after transferring to Hamilton County GC (Maketewah) and Wyoming CC and was runner-up in the prestigious Western Amateur in 1938. As the 1938 US Amateur

An eighteen-year-old Jack Nicklaus accepting the championship trophy from Al Joslin's widow for the 1958 Joslin Memorial Amateur Tournament. Tom Earls (left) finished second and Tony Blom (right) finished third.

Jack Nicklaus and Cincinnati

Most are aware of the Jack Nicklaus Golf Center built in Mason, Ohio, and originally designed by Jack. It hosted tournaments by the PGA (Ohio Kings Island Open from 1973 to 1977), LPGA (Women's PGA Championship from 1978 to 1989) and Senior PGA (The Kroger Classic from 1990 to 2001). Jack won the inaugural Kings Island Open in 1973 for his only Professional Tour win in the Cincinnati area. But before that he had a remarkable record here as

Seventeen-year-old Jack Nicklaus.

an amateur. It started with a win at the Ohio Jaycee Tournament at Sharon Woods GC and then a US Am Qualifying attempt at The Camargo Club at age fourteen. As a seventeen-year-old in 1957, Nicklaus finished in a tie for second place for the Medal and secured a trip to the US Am tournament in Brookline, Massachusetts. In 1959 it took two victories in Cincinnati to get him to the US Open at Winged Foot CC. First, he was Medalist at the Open Qualifier staged with a round each at Clovernook CC and Maketewah CC and returned to Clovernook to win the Medal at the Sectional Tournament two weeks later. In between he was the champion at the Joslin Memorial Invitational at Maketewah CC where he bested a field of Ohio and Kentucky's top amateurs. In 1960, he paired with Professional Bob Kepler (Ohio State Golf Coach) to win the Annual Pro-Am Tournament at Losantiville CC, beating a field that included touring Pro's Sam Snead, Tommy Bolt and Lionel Hebert among others. As an amateur, seven tournaments with three wins, two medals and a tie for second. He then topped that off with a victory as a Professional when he returned to win the 1962 Pro-Am Tournament at Losantiville CC.

approached, McCarthy and Johnny Fisher led a contingent of five other Cincinnati qualifiers to Oakmont CC. McCarthy took a first-round lead of stroke play in a rain shortened first day and both Fischer and McCarthy plus Northern Kentucky star Bill Deupree (another perennial fixture at the US Amateur) eventually qualified for Match Play. Unfortunately, this year was not kind to the locals in match play as Deupree dropped his first-round match and Fischer and McCarthy bowed out in the second round. The tournament was won by Willy Turnesa.

McCarthy was an alternate qualifier for the 1939 US Open as he won his first of the three Met titles. He also won the 1943 Queen City Open and capped it off by following previous winner Byron Nelson to the Ohio Open title in 1944 (the first amateur to win the championship). This body of work rewarded him with another Walker Cup berth in 1947 as he continued his streak of an eventual nineteen straight US Amateur appearances begun in 1926. He

John Wood II from Cincinnati Country Club always played in white flannel trousers and a white shirt. He won the 1955 and 1957 Mets and was runner up in 1939. He also qualified for thirteen USGA events.

Ohio Open Title Won by McCarthy

Maurice McCarthy wins the 1944 Ohio Open; Byron Nelson had won the previous two years.

Johnny Fischer of Highland Country Club, was considered the area's greatest golfer and was a 1936 U.S. Am Champion.

unbelievably qualified for match play each time. Mc-Carthy also won the State Amateur Championships in New York and Michigan.

Al Joslin Jr. (Maketewah CC) had been Ohio Intercollegiate Champion while playing for the University of Cincinnati in 1934 and 1935. UC also won the state crown in 1934. Joslin's early Met record was full of missed opportunities in Match Play. He lost the Finals in 1936 to Neil Ransick and although having been medalist several times did not reach the Finals again until 1950 when he finally succeeded. He won the medal again in 1952 but this time went wire to wire to win the crown and then followed it one more time in 1953. Bill Deupree won in 1954 breaking his string of wins but with Joslin's untimely death in 1955, the city also lost a good citizen. Later, an annual tournament was held at Maketewah CC in his memory and featured a young Jack Nicklaus as one of its first winners.

Other players came on the stage and competed at the highest level and then left the scene. Robert (Bobby) Baugh, playing from Ft. Mitchell CC in 1932, was a graduate of the University of Alabama and a Rhodes Scholar. While studying at the University of London he won their college championship twice and played in the British Open. He held the Ft. Mitchell course record for many years but was never able to get to the City or State Championship level.

Al Joslin Jr. of Maketewah Country Club was the State College Champion from the University of Cincinnati and was also a three-time Met winner in 1950, 1952, and 1953.

World War II and the Post-War Era (1940–1960)

As World War II began, the makeup of all professional and amateur athletics changed as men and women entered the military service. Some of the older veteran players started to reacquaint themselves with the few championships still being played. Some tournaments became opportunities for support of the war effort but many of the large tournaments like the USGA and major tour events were shelved.

Locally it also offered opportunity for high school players to get some experience against the veteran players like Don Gill, Tom Earls, Doug Hill and Cleo McVicker. At the same time, Junior Met winners like 1944 Cham-pion Gordon Leishman found they could not defend their crown because they had joined the military.

Names were starting to show up in high school matches at the end of the war that would carry on thorough the next decades. Tom Nieporte (North College Hill), Tony Blom (Roger Bacon), Tom Strange (Withrow and Country Day) and Danny Dell (St. Xavier) were getting a lot of attention in sports pages as the public still had a demand for good competitive golf. The 1946 Junior Met was special as it featured Nieporte's 8 & 7 victory in the thirty-six-hole final over Tom Strange. Both players were fourteen and the

Spencer Kerkow of Ft. Mitchell Country Club was one of six local players to make it to the 1937 U.S. Amateur; sadly, he passed away at age twenty-six after winning the Northern Kentucky Am and Central Kentucky Am.

future was bright for a new wave of great amateur players. Nieporte played mostly at Homestead GC at the time and also caddied at Clovernook CC. Strange (Hyde Park CC) returned the favor by winning the 1947 Junior Met, beating Joe McVicker of Maketewah CC in the thirty-six-hole final.

By 1948, the sixteen-year-old Strange went national as he made the Quarter-Finals of the first USGA Junior Amateur in Ann Arbor. That tournament included teenagers Ken Venturi and Mason Rudolph. But he did return home to win the medal in the US Amateur Qualifier at Camargo and a trip to Memphis but unfortunately went out in the Round of 32. In 1949, he played in the US Open at Medinah CC but, like four other Cincinnatians, did not make the cut. The same year he won the Met at age seventeen beating veteran Tom Earls. His Semi-Final match against Tom Nieporte was called one of the greatest in Met history.

Local papers were already comparing Strange to Johnny Fischer at the same tender age and he left right from the Met victory to win a nine-hole exhibition match with partner Olga Weil against Tom Nieporte and Louise Suggs. In August, he helped Ohio win another Tri-State Championship, partnering with WWII Army veteran and Purple Heart recipient Al Whaling of Hyde Park CC.

By 1950 Strange had been invited to the prestigious North-South Tourney in Pinehurst where he qualified for Match-Play and then qualified for US Open at Merion. He had still not yet turned twenty years old. By 1951 his number came up in the military draft and he spent the summer playing in some Florida tournaments and qualifying for the US Open again at Oakland Hills. By being medalist at US Amateur Qualifier he edged out a talented field that included Gay Brewer from Louisville, Kentucky.

In November, he enlisted in the US Coast Guard but was able to use some free time to keep up his skills and, while on leave, qualify for the Ohio Amateur and Virginia Open. By then he had also qualified for three straight US Opens. In 1955, with honorable discharge in hand, he settled down in Norfolk, Virginia, and returned

1946 Junior Met Quarter Final matchups included some amazing talent. Back row versus seated row and left to right: Art Stone (Avon Field) versus Danny Dell (Hyde Park), Tom Strange (Hyde Park) versus Bill McIntosh (Maketewah), Joe McVicker (Maketewah) versus Gene Seyler (Terrace Park), Tom Nieporte (Homestead) versus Herschell Bowyer (Homestead).

to competitive golf. There he won the Virginia State Open as an amateur and then turned professional in 1957. As a Professional he played in three more US Opens and won four Virginia and Mid-Atlantic Professional Open titles. Tom died at the young age of thirty-eight years and was the father of PGA Professionals Allan and Curtis Strange.

The careers of Tom Strange and Tom Nieporte collided many times in the Met and both came away with victories and both high school stars got a lot of press as many of the young players of the game served in the military. Until Nieporte went on to college at Ohio State and Strange left for the

Ft. Mitchell Country Club's Bill Deupree won two Mets, was runner up three times, played eight times in the U.S. Amateur and won both the Northern Kentucky and Kentucky Amateur titles.

Ernie Diehl—Cincinnati's Greatest Amateur Athlete

Jim Thorpe was considered the Greatest American Athlete of the first fifty years of the twentieth century. He was an All-American football player and played in the NFL, played major league baseball for the Reds, Giants and Braves and won two Olympic Gold Medals at the 1912 Stockholm Olympics. But Cincinnati had a similar story at the time and featured one of its best golfers of the early years. Ernie Diehl was a star football player at Walnut Hills HS in 1896 but also excelled in baseball, shotput and tennis. At the Tri-State Tennis Championship (forerunner of the Western-Southern and second only to the US Tennis Open) in 1900 he and his partner Nat Emerson finished second to the team that included Fred Alexander, considered the world's greatest Doubles player. By 1905 he was winning the city gymnastics competition and starring as shortstop for the Avondales, the city's premier semi-pro team. Diehl maintained his amateur status while playing baseball for the National League Boston Bees and Pittsburgh Pirates teams without signing a professional contract. Several times his hitting beat the local Reds team and they spent the next ten years trying to get him to sign to no avail. While taking over as President of Edgewood Distilling Co., he spent his spare time as a college football referee and became the UC baseball coach while still playing semi-pro baseball in Cincinnati and Toledo. Finally, in 1911 he picked up a golf club for the first time and joined Hamilton County Country Club in Bond Hill. By 1914 he won the club championship there and then beat Brad Eldridge, Ft. Mitchell CC star and two-time Met Champion, in the Met to get to the semi-finals. In 1922 he won his third Club Championship, in 1923 is medalist at the Met with the course record at Western Hills CC. He then sets course record at Maketewah CC in 1924 and plays in his first Ohio Amateur. And during all this time he was a Cincinnati Councilman. Diehl was still playing semi-pro baseball at age seventy in Miami, Florida, when he passed away.

Newspaper caricature of multi-talented Ernie Diehl.

Coast Guard they were always the two favorites entering any local competition.

At the same time, Nieporte was teaming up in other sports with North College Hill classmate and future LPGA official and NBA and NCAA Basketball referee Len Wirtz, especially in golf and football. In 1946, after leading his team to runner-up in Ohio High School golf tournament, Nieporte started his national competition by finishing as runner-up in the National Caddy Championship that included a semi-final win over Dow Finsterwald. Unfortunately, he could not play in the Ohio Junior Championship because Homestead GC was not a member of the Ohio Golf Association.

With his high school diploma in hand he captured the 1947 Met by beating Doug Hill in the finals and headed for Ohio State University and a berth on the

Bob Kepler's golf team. The next year Tom lost in the finals of the Met to Al Whaling in an all-Clovernook match. In 1951, he won the NCAA Golf Title. Paired with Tony Trabert (University of Cincinnati), Cincinnati held both the NCAA golf and tennis individual trophies that year. In 1952 Nieporte entered the Army Air Force and began military training. Fortunately, he was able to keep working on his golf skills and was able to win the Hawaiian Islands Army Tournament and lead the Army to a win in the annual Inter-Service Golf Competition as well as finishing second in the Hawaiian Open.

After his honorable discharge from the military in 1953, Tom turned Pro and began work first for MacGregor Golf and then as a Club Professional in New York. Eventually he went on the PGA Tour for five years

Tom Nieporte, Homestead Golf Club caddy, high school star at North College Hill, NCAA Champion at Ohio State and three-time winner on the PGA Tour; here he is flanked by his parents accepting the Navy Open Championship Trophy in Hawaii in 1953.

and won three events including the 1967 Bob Hope Desert Classic. He returned to being a Head Professional, first at Piping Rock CC for fifteen years and finally at Winged Foot CC for twenty-eight years. His best finishes in majors included The Masters (tied-26th), PGA (tied-5th) and US Open (tied-17th).

The decade of the 1940s ended with a plane crash killing Cleo McVicker (Maketewah CC) a perennial match play participant in the Met and Ohio Open and participant at 1948 US Open at Riviera CC. Bill Deupree's (Ft. Mitchell CC) long frustration at the Met (runner-ups in 1951 and 1953) finally ended in victory in 1954 shooting

8-under for the thirty-three holes it took him to beat Tony Blom at Western Hills CC.

The last decade leading up to 1960 featured more veterans as Nieporte and Strange both left for new opportunities out of town. Their high school peers like Danny Dell (now captaining Xavier's golf team to

Tom Strange Jr., after a stellar amateur career in Cincinnati that included winning the 1947 Junior Met and 1949 Met at age seventeen, enlisted in the Coast Guard in 1951. He would continue his amateur career in the Tidewater region of Virginia and eventually turned professional.

1957 St. X High School Ohio State Champions. Front row: W. Busemeyer, W. Schulten, J. Stahl, J. Moran. Back row: A. Fischer, P. Cunningham, J. Meyer, C. Schlotman, T. Savage, W. Wehrman, E. Tedeschi, Coach Austin. Missing: L. Zins.

Ohio High Schools and Championships

The first official Ohio State High School Golf Tournament occurred in 1927 and Hughes HS finished second by two strokes to Akron St. Vincent. Coach Charles Krueck had his team of Eph Collins, Herman Stoller, John Fischer and Larry Hendrixson back the next year and this time they lapped the field, winning by twenty-three strokes over runner up Upper Arlington. Collins and Hendrixson tied for Medalist as low individuals. 1929 was not as successful for the Hughes team but Fischer did capture State Medalist honors. It would be 1940 before another Cincinnati school would get on the platform as a Hamilton HS team coached by Harold Hutchison finished second to a strong squad from Toledo DeVilbiss. In 1942 a North College Hill team led by Odie Harper also won the runner-up trophy and John Zoller from Hamilton HS, now a senior, took the medal for low tournament individual score. NCH would repeat their second-place finish in 1945 as Len Wirtz and Tom Nieporte led the squad while a young caddy from Roger Bacon HS, Tony Blom, would win the Medal for individual scoring.

North College Hill HS, located so close to Clovernook and Homestead golf courses, must have had a steady supply of caddies who played well because they returned to state in 1946 under Coach Cliff Alexander only again to finish second to powerhouse Columbus North. However, 1948 and 1949 were great years for

The 1948 Hamilton High School State Championship Golf Team. Left to right: C. Griffith, H. Quinn, Coach Richard Goos, W. Johnson, J. Tewart, W. Barrett.

the locals. First Hamilton HS won the 1948 Championship with a team of Hugh Quinn, Jim Tewart, Bill Johnson and Wayne Barrett. In 1949 Reading HS Blue Devils took the crown featuring a team of Russ Fleckenstein, Roger Mize, John Sears and Dick Brune. Another drought started for the locals in 1950-1953 though Withrow HS and Hamilton HS both fielded strong teams and David Moore from Withrow was co-medalist in 1951.

1928 Hughes High School State Champions including E. Collins, H. Stoller, L. Hendrixson, J. Fischer and Coach Charles Krueck.

St. Xavier HS started to come on the scene in 1954. A fourteen-year-old Jack Nicklaus also started play for Upper Arlington HS the same time and their paths would keep crossing. In 1955 the Bombers with low scorer Paul Niklas got the State runner-up trophy under Coach Al Cavanaugh and then finished fifth behind Medalist Nicklaus and Upper Arlington in 1956. In 1957, they could not stop Nicklaus from winning the individual Medal again but finally took the State title with a team of Jim Stahl, Bill Busemeyer, Warren Schulten and Jack Moran under Coach Charles Austin. St. Xavier would send a couple strong teams to state as the decade ended.

Jim Stahl, leading scorer for 1957 St. X State Champions would go on to win the 1995 US Senior Amateur at Prairie Dunes Country Club.

The 1949 Reading High School State Champion Squad. Front row: Coach Ken Powers, Captain R. Fleckenstein; Back row (left to right): R. Scheidt, D. Sears, R. Brune, R. Mize, H. Lang, V. Barnes, C. Cromer, D. Bullock.

John Busemeyer Sr. won the Junior Met and Met as well as fifteen Club Championships at Wyoming Country Club. In 1948 he qualified for both the U.S. Open and U.S. Amateur, one of very few people to do so.

Roger McManus of Kenwood Country Club made it to the semi-finals of the 1958 U.S. Amateur in San Francisco; he qualified for the U.S. Open two times and the U.S. Amateur seventeen times.

the 1952 Ohio Collegiate title) and Tony Blom (Ohio Am winner in 1959 and again in 1962 along with three Met titles), Larry Kunkemoeller, Jim Beckjord, John Busemeyer, John Wood II and Jim Stahl were filling the sports pages with their accomplishments and scores through the 1950s.

And there is special mention of Roger McManus (Kenwood CC) who came on the local competitive scene in the mid 1950s and consistently broke par in local tournaments. McManus made it to the Semifinals of the 1958 US Amateur at Olympic CC in San Francisco where he lost to eventual champion Charley Coe. He qualified for the US Open twice, the US Amateur seventeen times and five times for USGA Senior events.

One player that is conspicuous by absence is Jimmy Woods. African Americans were not permitted to play in the Met until 1967 so there was no way to measure his ability strictly by championships won or official head to head competition. Woods was born in Nashville in 1920 and learned the game from his dad with hand-made clubs. He came to Cincinnati in the 1940s and worked as a waiter on the C&O railroad and eventually took the game up again in the 1950s.

Playing at Avon Fields, he did win the City Municipal Championships from 1951 to 1953 but most of his reputation was built playing high stakes games with the city's best players at Sharon Woods, Winton Woods and many local country clubs. One often-told story had him playing eighteen holes of golf with a visiting Arnold Palmer for some high stakes and then turning around and playing nine more holes left handed. PGA Tour multi-winner Bob Murphy also witnessed Woods playing even par left handed on one nine and turning around and shooting par right handed in the same match.

He did finish second in the 1968 Met at forty-eight years of age and second in 1975 at fifty-five years of age. He also won several Cincinnati Publinx championships, the Summit Hills Pro-Am and three local Met Seniors Championships. He also held the course record of 64 at Sharon Woods and won the Avon Fields Club Championship at age seventy-two. But his real talent was playing against pro's and great amateurs in Chicago, Detroit, St. Louis and other big towns where his reputation was known by all. Celebrities like Joe Louis, Bill Russell and visiting touring Pro's would contact Jimmy for a game when they came to town. He would continue playing competitively around the country well into his seventies and was named to the African-American Golfers Hall of Fame in 1993.

Conclusion

And what was the consensus of that 1987 *Cincinnati Post* article? The almost unanimous feelings among the experts: 1) Johnny Fischer 2) Maurice McCarthy 3) Tom

Jimmy Woods, playing from Avon Fields Golf Course and Sharon Woods Golf Course, was denied access to the Cincinnati Met because of race until age forty-seven when he finished second in his first start in 1968. He was nationally famous among visiting tour players and included in the local games when they visited. He played against them right-handed and left-handed.

Nieporte 4) Tom Strange. But there could be another twenty golfers based on their era and their accomplishments locally, statewide and nationally, that could easily fill out a top-ten list. And it would have been interesting to see Jimmy Woods play against the whole field in his prime. But the fact remains that the depth and talent of Cincinnati amateur golfers through the period could compete with the best anywhere.

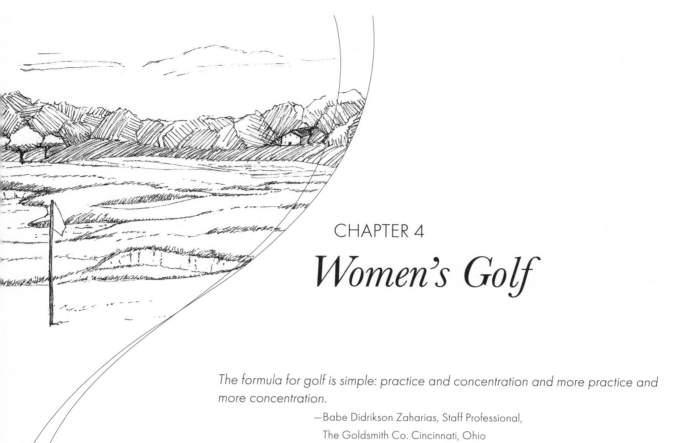

CHAPTER 4

Women's Golf

The formula for golf is simple: practice and concentration and more practice and more concentration.

—Babe Didrikson Zaharias, Staff Professional,
The Goldsmith Co. Cincinnati, Ohio

From Scotland to Cincinnati

When discussing women in golf in Cincinnati, it is important to start with the fact that for the first twenty-five years that the game was played here, they could tee it up at the country club but did not have the right to vote. The game was played from the same tees as men and they were encumbered at first by the Victorian dress in vogue at that time. In addition, they were not recognized with their given name but with their married name only. Olga Weil was always Mrs. Burt Weil in her accomplishments. Yet with all of these impediments, women fared very well here. Two clubs, Fernbank GC and Elberon GC (later to become Western Hills CC), were founded by women.

Women playing golf started almost from the game's beginning. Mary, Queen of Scots, was an avid golfer in the 1500s and there are news articles

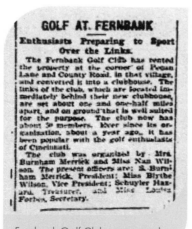

Fernbank Golf Club was started by female golfers in 1899.

of women's competitions in Scotland as early as 1738. Women's golf societies in Great Britain did not start until the latter part of the nineteenth century but by 1893 there were sixty-three Ladies' clubs there and a meeting that same year resulted in the founding of the Ladies' Golf Union (LGU). This was two years before the founding of the USGA in America and several years before the Royal & Ancient Golf Club of St. Andrews took control of the Rules of Golf.

In Cincinnati, women were also playing almost as early as the men. The by-laws of all the local clubs called for access to the courses by women players. An article in 1903 stated that the Clifton GC dues included playing privileges for "one woman player of a member's family. Other women and boys between sixteen and twenty-one would cost (extra)." In 1899, Clifton Golf Club listed 178 women players enjoying the links in Burnet Woods. But also,

Golfers at Western College for Women, Oxford, Ohio. (Photo circa 1910)

Score sheet for the 1897 U.S. Women's Amateur with two Cincinnatians in the top eight.

women were among the primary members in almost all golf and country clubs here from 1895 on. At the same time, women's golf was part of Physical Education training at many local schools and colleges.

Matches among the women players at Clifton GC, Cincinnati GC, Avondale GC, Ft. Mitchell CC and Elberon GC began right at the turn of the century although competition was informal until about 1905. That year the Cincinnati Golf league (CGL) was started for men's competition on Saturday afternoons. The CGL, later called the Greater Cincinnati Golf Association (GCGA), also did start informal competition among the women's clubs at this time but it was 1916 before they organized a city championship (the Women's Met).

Before that, good local women competitors had already stepped on the national stage using the skills developed at Cincinnati GC (CGC). When the USGA was founded in 1895, a national championship for women was included from the beginning. Clara Longworth from CGC played in the second US Women's Championship in 1896. In 1897, two Cincinnati women from CGC (Lucy Herron and Longworth) had qualified in the top eight in the nation and Clara made it to the semi-finals.

In 1901, Miss Herron would tie for medalist and reach the finals of match play only to lose the Championship to Genevieve Hecker at Baltusrol CC. That match was played in front of over a thousand patrons stretched ten-deep across the course. National papers congratulated Lucy for playing so well as she "had far surpassed the record of any Western woman." At that time, any place west of Buffalo was considered west.

Before WWI, CGC was still dominating the women's game locally with players like Ella Banning and Marjorie Dodd Letts. Ella won the first Women's Met in 1916 and repeated in 1919. She remained a strong competitor in that tournament even making it to the second round of Match Play in 1937 at the age of sixty-six! Tennis player Marjorie Dodd Letts, who took up golf at the request of CGC Professional Otto Hackbarth, won the 1916 Western Women's Amateur in Chicago before moving there and winning two more titles. At that time, the Western was considered the equivalent of the US Women's Amateur. While still a Cincinnatian, she also played in the US Women's Amateur in 1916. But Marjorie is just as famous locally for returning to Cincinnati in 1924 with twenty-year old Glenna Collett and beating Cincinnati GC stars Doug Hill and DeWitt Balch 2-up in an exhibition match.

The Roaring 20s

With the departure of Marjorie Dodd Letts for Chicago, more great competitors had entered the local stage. And

The Stymie

As the rules of Golf evolved for the first sixty-five years there were certain ones that had major impact on the game and its progress in the city. Subjects such as the 14-club limit, the rules of amateur status, club and ball specifications made the sports pages of the day. But one Rule, in effect for almost this hole period of time, seemed the most controversial. In 1897, Rule 31 of the R&A stated: "All loose impediments may be removed from the putting green, except the opponent's ball, when at a distance from the player's greater than six inches." This allowed for the stymie in Match Play where a ball closer to the hole could block a putt from farther away. (Stymies had been eliminated from Stroke Play by 1830.) The USGA had tried to modify the effect of the stymie from their own rules as early as 1920 and 1938 but the R&A did not follow and the American body eliminated it from their rules entirely in 1950. Two years later, when the rules were combined, the R&A agreed to remove it completely from their rules too. When the stymie was eliminated in 1952, not all golfers were happy about it. Bobby Jones, in particular and himself a great Match player, lamented the end of the Rule and lobbied for

Three strategies to defeat the stymie in match play. Figures one and two show cutting the stymie to the right and left. Figure three shows lofting the stymie. The rule allowing stymies was eliminated by R&A and USGA in 1952.

its return in his book *Golf is My Game* in 1959. But the old Scottish golfing term still remains in our everyday lexicon as a verb to describe "hindering the progress of."

like the previous decades, Cincinnati Golf Club (CGC) led the parade. Rhea Geilfus won two Women's Met championships (1920 and 1921) at CGC and then a third competing as Mrs. Jerome Johnson while playing at Avon Fields. Caroline Painter Wilson won two others at GCG in this decade (1922 and 1926).

Wilson's victory over Western Hills CC star Kate Brophy in 1922 still is considered one of the great Championship matches ever in Women's Met History. Waged over twenty-two holes at Cincinnati CC, it was followed by a large gallery that was on the "verge of hysterics" as the match tipped back and forth. Brophy took a three-hole lead at the turn only to witness an amazing comeback by Wilson on the inward nine. Brophy was on the ropes on the eighteenth when Wilson putted directly in line with Brophy's ball laying three feet from the hole causing a stymie. Brophy calmly used her Mashie (5-iron) to chip over Wilson's ball and her shot landed directly in the cup without touching the edge. The crowd went wild at seeing such a difficult shot under so much pressure. That carried the match to extra holes and by the twenty-first, Wilson had taken the victory. Brophy would go on to win three Mets of her own in 1927, 1928 and 1929 while playing from Avon Fields GC and Ridgewood GC.

Olga Strashun Weil (with her eventual twelve Women's Met Championships at Hillcrest CC and Losantiville CC) would be on the scene by the end of the decade but one other player stands out because of her successes at the state and national level. Martha Kinsey was the daughter of one of the founders of Wyoming CC. As a youth, she was an excellent tennis player and had a Women's' Single title in the 1908 national Tri-State Tennis Tournament (now the Western-Southern Tournament and the second oldest Open tennis tournament in the country). In fact, it was tennis where she first met and competed against Marjorie Dodd Letts. (Letts was also world class tennis player as she won the Tri-State Singles title in 1911.)

Kinsey started to play golf seriously in 1917 and, in her first year in the Women's Met, was the Medalist and Champion defeating Nina Freiberg from Losantiville CC. By 1921 she was getting to the finals of the Ohio Women's Amateur. She would finish second in 1921, 1922, 1924 and 1926 and won the tournament finally in 1925 at Dayton CC. She also won the Women's Met a total of three times (1917, 1925, 1931). The first victory was from Wyoming CC and the final two from Cincinnati CC where she joined in 1924.

Her career is illustrious enough but also is measured by the quality of opponents during her time in competition. With players such as Rhea Geilfus, Marjorie Dodd Letts, Kate Brophy, Caroline Painter Wilson and Olga Strashun Weil, she won against

In 1924, Marjorie Dodd Letts (l) and Glenna Collett (r) defeated Cincinnati Country Club stars DeWitt Balch and Doug Hill in a well-publicized match at the Country Club.

Cincinnatian Lucy Herron paired with Beatrix Hoyt in the 1897 U.S. Women's Amateur on the tee at Ardsley Country Club in New York. Hoyt was a three-time winner of the Women's Am before turning nineteen and was the granddaughter of Cincinnatian Salmon P. Chase. Herron would be runner up in 1901.

win the Mexican National Singles Championship!

An Amazing Saga (1930–1960)

As the Depression hit in 1929 many clubs were forced to curtail play, reduce from eighteen to nine holes or use other measures to stay open. But even with the reduced play, another ex-tennis player entered the arena as the best of the next decade. Olga Strashun Weil was listed #1 in Doubles and #4 in Singles in the rankings of the US Tennis Association Western Section as late as 1926. She had already won the Ohio State Tennis Tournament in Singles (1922) and Mixed Doubles (1923 and 1924) when she began her golf career in 1926.

By 1928 she was playing at Hillcrest CC and under the tutelage of Head Professional Clarence Dapper. In that same year, she made it to the Championship Flight in the Ohio Amateur at Cincinnati CC. Week after week she was in the headlines as she broke course records at Hillcrest CC (4 under Women's par) and Losantiville CC and battled Kate Cassidy Brophy and Martha Kinsey in all local invitational tournaments. Olga also won three consecutive Ohio Amateur tournaments (1934–1936) and was State runner up in 1938 as well as winning those record twelve Cincinnati Women's Met titles on a span from 1930 to 1954.

As Olga was entering the launch pad for what would be an unprecedented career in local championships, she ran into two road blocks almost immediately. The first was an amazing player from the Camargo Club named Elizabeth Cassatt Reid. Reid and Weil would meet in the finals of four straight Women's Mets from 1934 to 1937 and each would win twice. And amazingly the scores of those four finals were 1up, 2&1, 2up and 2&1. Reid later would be one of Cincinnati's first woman City Councilmen.

Then in 1939, a young Dolly Schildmiller came on the scene and was to win the next five Cincinnati Women's Mets while playing at Kenwood CC

the best of her era. Add her multiple appearances at the US Women's Amateur, numerous club scoring records, dominance in local golf league competitions, and Kinsey stands out in a decade of star performers. And in 1930 she returned to the tennis courts to

A 1929 *Cincinnati Post* headline about the strange ruling stopping Kate Brophy from competing at the Ohio Women's Amateur in Akron, Ohio.

1955. Left to right, Olga Weil, Kate Brophy and Dolly Schildmiller McCarthy at Brophy Invitational at Western Hills Country Club. Among the three they won twenty-two Women's Met Tournaments.

Catherine Cassidy Brophy, three-time Women's Met Champion and one of the nation's first female Professionals.

Catherine Cassidy Brophy—"Aunt Kate"

The stories of golf sometimes go beyond trophies or great shots under pressure or even long and illustrious careers. Some tales are of perseverance against odds off of the course and success in spite of barriers laid down. Such was the case of Kate Brophy for she had the trophies, shots and career but her story also had victory over discrimination. Cincinnati had issues during this period with exclusions based on race but also on other cultural aspects that were hidden below the surface. This extended to immigration and even to the social status of Golf Professionals.

Soon after Kate arrived from her native Ireland around 1902 to work as a nanny for a Cincinnati family, she met Ed Brophy. Ed had worked his way up from caddy at Cincinnati Golf Club and was trying to become a Golf Professional. He first worked at Elberon GC in Price Hill and when that club moved up the road and became Western Hills CC, Ed was selected as their Head Professional. In 1915 the couple married and Ed settled into running the operation on Cleves-Warsaw Pike. Kate started taking golf lessons from Ed and it was evident very early she had talent to take her game into city competition. At first, she entered from Western Hills CC but also played from Avon Fields GC and Ridgewood CC. With Ed as her coach, she quickly won the Avon Fields Club Championship and was ready for the city tournaments. At her first Women's Met in 1921 she made it to the Quarter Finals before being ousted. The next year she reached the Women's Met Final but lost to Carol Painter Wilson in what is considered one of the greatest matches in Women's Met history. By 1923 she held the Women's course records at Western Hills CC, Avon Fields GC and Hyde Park CC and was leading the Avon Fields team to great success against the private courses in league competition. She also competed in the 1927 and 1928 Ohio Women's Amateur as a member of Avon Fields GC and the streak continued as she captured the Women's Met in 1927, 1928 and 1929.

Fresh off that third straight Women's Met championship she traveled to Akron to play in the 1929 Ohio Women's Amateur. Kate was now also a member now of Western Hills CC, an affiliated club with the Ohio Women's Golf Association (OWGA). While looking for her name on the pairing sheet in the clubhouse, an official informed her that the USGA had declared her a Professional. She apparently had allowed Burkhardt's, a local clothing store, to use her name and picture in an ad during the 1928 Christmas season but had not been compensated. An anonymous complaint had been lodged back in January, though curiously it had not been made to the officials in Cincinnati where she successfully defended her Met crown that summer. Even though she was not compensated for the ad and was member at Western Hills CC, the ruling stood in spite of a rush of affidavits to prove her case to the USGA and the OWGA. Most of the tournament players and officials wanted her to play but it really was the protest of a fellow Cincinnatian and OWGA Secretary Lenora Kent that kept her from the first tee. Kate was then also told that wives of Professionals were not permitted to play in amateur events but that was easily challenged. It was apparent that someone or some group was doing everything to keep Kate from participating. Whether it was really that advertisement, the fact that she was a wife of a Professional, her affiliation with public courses, her success as an outsider in city tournaments and league play, or maybe that Irish brogue from the former nanny, we will never know.

Without recourse to the USGA decision, she returned home and Twin Oaks CC quickly snubbed the ruling and invited the ever-popular Kate to play as an amateur in their annual Invitational. Hyde Park CC followed suit right after and invited her to play in their Pow Wow Invitational and then she played in the Western Hills CC event. It was clear how the city felt about the ruling but, in effect, Kate was eliminated from any future events on the big stage. The Cincinnati press picked up her cause but questions to the USGA and OWGA remained unanswered and the ruling remained. She and Ed left for Miami, Florida for the winter to defend many of her championships there but was formally informed in February 1930 that she was banned from amateur events for three years.

The "Brophy Trophy" is proudly presented by two-time Women's Met Champion Jane DeGroff to the winning Terrace Park Country Club team at the 100th Women's Met in 2015.

Ed and Kate returned to Western Hills CC that following Spring and she opened a driving range at their home and began to teach. There was no LPGA tour or other ways to make money playing and opportunities for a lady Professional were limited. At that time there was only a handful of women in that role nationally. Her students were men, women and youngsters and she was especially adept at teaching people new to the game. Soon, an opportunity to become a Head Professional was made available when Bill Lewis Sr. built the Woodland Golf Course on Muddy Creek Road in 1931. Since Mrs. Brophy had been teaching both at her driving range and in Miami during the winter, it was an easy transition now to managing the pro shop and taking on even more teaching duties. She remained there a few years and eventually returned to Western Hills CC as Assistant Professional and Caddy Master and served into the 1950s.

At Western Hills, "Aunt Kate" and "Uncle Ed" raised two of Kate's orphaned nieces and her reputation as a teacher, mentor and advisor spread beyond the club's boundaries. Her competitive career had been cut short by the actions of others but she remained a giant influence on all she met and the game of golf in Cincinnati. Aunt Kate passed away in Sarasota, Florida, in 1977. Since 1955, the Greater Cincinnati Women's Golf Association has presented the "Brophy Trophy" to the club with the lowest four scores in the Stroke Play qualifying at the Women's Met and her legacy continues.

(1939–1943). This was added to her victory in the first Women's Junior Met in 1937 while playing out of Avon Fields GC. Before that she had won the Avon Fields Women's Club Championship at sixteen years of age while attending Hughes High School.

But it was her 1 up win over Olga Weil in the 1939 Women's Met at Western Hills CC that signified an apparent changing of the guard from Olga to Dolly. Weil was 3-up after nine holes but a strong back nine by Schildmiller captured the championship. In reality, though Dolly won the next five Mets, she had to beat Olga in the finals for three of those wins so Weil was far from giving up. Even more young players were on the horizon as Tippy Conroy (Cincinnati CC Champion at age sixteen) and a pair of Wyoming high school players—Carol Clark and Nancy Porter—came on the scene in 1943. Clark had already reached the 1942 Met semi-finals at age fourteen. The following year, the Met's youngest winner at age sixteen was Porter, beating Clark in the finals at Maketewah CC. It would seem that youth had taken the reins but neither Dolly and Olga were giving up.

In fact, Olga Weil would begin a string of Met success that will not be repeated. In the next ten years (1945–1954) of Met competition she won eight times including two wins over Schildmiller. Amazingly, Carol Clark of Wyoming CC finished second four times, usually to Olga. Only Dolly Schildmiller McCarthy (now married and playing from Maketewah CC and Ridgewood GC) and Ruth Heutle had Met wins during that period. Dolly would add one other win in 1955 to cap her career with seven Met victories. Heutle would repeat her Met crown in 1958 and another teenager—Janet McIntosh from Maketewah CC— would win a championship but no one would compete with the Olga and Dolly show that dominated three decades from 1930 to 1960 with a total of nineteen Women's Met titles between them.

A Brief Encounter—Marion Miley

In 1937 for a couple of years, Cincinnati flirted again with national prominence in golf. Fred Miley had been named Head Professional at Maketewah CC and with him came daughter Marion. Fred had been Head Professional at Lexington CC and his wife stayed behind to manage the operation there. Marion learned the game from her dad and had competed during the winter on the informal Orange Blossom Amateur Tour in Florida. There she played against the best of the era—Babe Didrikson, Glenna Collett Vare, Patty Berg and Betty Jameson.

As Kentucky state champion, Miley had already played in Greater Cincinnati in 1932 at the Summit Hills Invitational with Martha Kinsey, Kate Brophy and Olga Weil in the field. She not only won but also broke the Summit Hills CC course record. By 1935

Marion Miley of Maketewah Country Club, plays out of trouble during a practice round of the 1938 Curtis Cup at Essex Country Club in Massachusetts. Teammate Maureen Orcutt looks on.

Changing of the Guard. Olga Weil (r) beat Martha Kinsey (l) in the 1932 Women's Met Final at Western Hills Country Club.

Elizabeth Cassatt Reid in 1934 of The Camargo Club was a two-time women's Met winner and the first President of the GCWGA. She was also a city councilman; she later returned to competitive golf in the 1960s as Elizabeth Cash.

1934 Women's Met Preview featuring Elizabeth Reid, Virginia Jones, Olga Weil, Martha, Kinsey and Mrs. Walter Ibold; Reid would beat Weil in the Final at Kenwood Country Club.

she had already won the Women's Western Amateur and the Women's Trans-Mississippi and made her first berth on the Curtis Cup team. After coming to Cincinnati, she was added to the Maketewah team in the local golf league matches and tournaments.

In addition to playing locally, she continued playing in major tournaments nationwide. She won the 1937 Western Women's Championship again and took the 1938 Women's Southern Amateur Championship. Her closest chance at the US Women's Amateur came in 1938 when she lost to Patty Berg in a dramatic semi-final. On her third Curtis Cup Team in 1938 she eked out a Singles win to help the USA retain the Cup.

After the 1938 season she returned to live with her mother at Lexington CC while commuting back and forth to Cincinnati. 1941 would be another banner year of golf but it ended in tragedy. Marion and her mother were murdered that same year at Lexington CC during a robbery attempt. This ended a meteoric career that included six Kentucky Amateur championships. There is an annual tournament at Lexington CC called the Marion Miley Invitational and started in 1942.

It has been won by Cincinnatians "Loll" Theler (Clovernook CC) and Carol Clark (Wyoming CC).

Every year thru 1967 the WWGA presented the Marion Miley bracelet to the low total score in the Women's Western Am and the two first rounds of the Western Open. Margaret Jones (Ft. Mitchell CC) won the unbelievable double of claiming the Miley bracelet and winning the Miley Tournament in that same year of 1967!

Women's Golf Organizations

The USGA had a Women's Amateur Championship almost immediately after its founding in 1895 and Cincinnati women were competing the next year. The Women's Western Golf Association (WWGA) was formed later in 1900 to provide opportunity for competitions "west of Buffalo." Like the men's organization it had eastern and southern borders while the USGA and WGA remained in competition until the 1920s. Eventually the borders were eliminated in 1949.

The WWGA began running Women's amateur championships immediately in 1901 and the first Cin-

Left to right: Nancy Porter, Dolly Schildmiller and Olga Weil in 1946. Among the three of them, they won all of the women's Met titles between 1939 and 1949.

THE LADIES, BLESS 'EM, TEE OFF IN THE WOMEN'S METRO-POLITAN GOLF TOURNAMENT AT KENWOOD TODAY AND BACK TO DEFEND HER TITLE IS MRS. CHARLES HEUTLE THE 1958 CHAMP.

THAT'S IT! YOU CAN HAVE THE CLUBS!

AND YOU HAD TO STOP SHORT LESS THAN AN INCH!

THIS IS TO SUGGEST ANYONE WITH A TENDENCY TOWARD AN INFERIORITY COMPLEX STEER CLEAR OF KEN-WOOD THIS WEEK ...THE GALS REALLY BELT 'EM

MISSING A 25 FT. PUT BY JUDY ANDERSON (NOW MRS. BRUCE DIE) LAST YEAR GAVE M' HEUTLE THE SILVER'

wiese

Ruth Heutle of Kenwood Country Club. She was the 1950- and 1958-Women's Met Champion.

cinnati winner was Marjorie Dodd Letts from Cincinnati GC in 1916. The Western Women's Amateur was hosted twice in Cincinnati, at Cincinnati CC in 1936 (won by Dorothy Traung of San Francisco) and at The Camargo Club in 1951 (won by Marjorie Lindsay).

The rivalry between WGA and USGA was problematic for member clubs and this especially affected the women's competitions. Clubs like Cincinnati GC would be members of the WGA while also "allied" members of the USGA so that their male players could participate in the national championships. However, Cincinnati GC was not a member of the Women's Western Golf Association (WWGA) right away and only did play in USGA events.

In 1930, the WWGA added a Women's Open Tournament to their schedule. The Amateur tournament had been limited to member clubs and did not allow players from municipal or independent daily fee courses. By adding the Open championship, it provided a vehicle to welcome more players who were not members of the WWGA. It was not long until this also opened the door to lady Professional golfers and a first-place prize of $100 was added.

In effect, this became accepted as the virtual national Women's Open for many years until the USGA/LPGA created their Women's Open format in 1946. The Western Open tournament was played only one time locally—at Cincinnati CC in 1941—and Losantiville CC star amateur Olga Weil lost to Professional

Patty Berg in the finals. (This would be the first of seven wins for Berg in the tournament.) The WWGA also began a Junior tournament in 1920, almost thirty years before the USGA started their junior championship. Janet McIntosh of Maketewah CC did finish as runner-up to Barbara McIntire in the 1952 Western Junior Championship. It was not contested in Cincinnati until 1970 and then again in 1975 and 2012.

Women's state golf associations include the Women's Ohio State Golf Association (WOSGA) that has run state championship tournaments since 1920 but also originally limited competition to players from the member clubs. Winners from Cincinnati of the Ohio State Women's crown during this period included Martha Kinsey (1925, Cincinnati CC), and Olga Weil

Janet McIntosh Mueller (l), age twenty-four from Maketewah Country Club, defeats Margaret Jones, age seventeen, from Ft. Mitchell Country Club in the 1960 Women's Met; Mueller won her second of three Mets and Jones would go on to win Mets in 1962, 1963, and 1968.

Carol Clark of Wyoming Country Club wins the 1946 Marion Miley Memorial at Lexington Country Club in Lexington, Kentucky.

Marjorie Dodd Letts of Cincinnati Golf Club, Winner of the 1916 Western Women's Amateur at Kent Country Club in Michigan. She was a protégé of Cincinnati Golf Club Professional Otto Hackbarth.

three times (1934, 1935, 1936, Hillcrest CC) and Janet McIntosh from Maketewah CC was runner up in 1956.

Other competitions for low handicap players had been organized among Cincinnati, Columbus and Dayton as early as 1936. But they were halted by 1939 because of the lack of interest from the other cities. Similarly, a Tri-State Women's Tournament similar to that started by the men in 1940 among Ohio, Indiana and Kentucky was begun in 1948. Dolly Schildmiller McCarthy of Maketewah CC and Ridgewood CC won the event in 1950 and 1951. The Tournament was played once in Cincinnati at Maketewah CC in 1952 and won by Betty Rowland of Lexington, Kentucky. In addition, the prestigious Trans-Mississippi Women's Tournament was held at Kenwood CC in 1960 and won by Amateur Sandra Haynie from Ft. Worth, Texas at age seventeen. Haynie joined the LPGA Tour the next year and went on to forty-two wins and election to the World Golf Hall of Fame.

Greater Cincinnati Women's Golf Association

Even though the by-laws of the local clubs all gave equal standing to women players, it took years to get the clubs to organize competitive play among women on a citywide basis. Through the efforts of Emily Tietig and Lenora Kent, the Cincinnati Golf League (CGL) organized the first Women's' Met at Western Hills CC in 1916 (won by Ella Banning of Cincinnati GC).

Women remained as part of the CGL until 1936 when the Greater Cincinnati Women's Golf Association (GCWGA) was formed and Elizabeth Reid of The Camargo Club was named as first President. They would continue to run tournaments, provide organization and scheduling, manage handicaps and promote interclub play for over seventy-five years. The charter member clubs of the GCWGA were Cincinnati CC, The Camargo Club, Clovernook CC, Ft. Mitchell CC, Highland CC, Hillcrest CC, Hyde Park CC, Kenwood CC, Losantiville CC, Maketewah CC, Western Hills CC and Wyoming CC.

The GCWGA was instrumental in organizing a City Championship for Junior girls in 1957. Suggested by Mrs. James Patton Orr of The Camargo Club, it included the city's best young players. This was also a time to include the young players from Northern Kentucky and was suggested by Board member (and future GCWGA President) Loretta Jones. By inviting the youngsters over from Northern Kentucky, it also gave it true status as a Metropolitan event. Play was

Margaret Jones
Loretta Jones

Margaret Jones and Loretta Jones from Ft. Mitchell Country Club competed in several Women's Mets together. In 1960, Margaret won the Junior Met and was runner up in the Women's Met.

Mrs. Carol Johnson practice-putts in the dinning room of her Wyoming home as her children watch how mom does it. The kids are (left to right) Sally, 11; Carrie, 7; Jan, 13. and Jay, 10.

Carol Johnson Is First Local Member of LPGA

Carol "Keanie" Johnson was named the area's first LPGA member in 1967; she would be named LPGA Teacher of the Year in 1975.

nine-holes of Match play and ran simultaneously with the Women's Met at Camargo that year.

Northern Kentucky honored their invitation by winning the first four events as Lesley Franz of Ft. Mitchell CC won the first year by defeating club mate Margaret Jones. Jones then returned to win the next three Junior events in 1958, 1959 and 1960. In 1960 Jones won the Junior Met and was runner up in the Women's Met closing out the decade.

Ladies Professional Golf Association

For Women Professionals, it took a little more time to get organized. There were some op-portunities for exhibition matches, satellite tours and open tourna-ments into the 1930s. Eventually in 1944, Ellen Griffin, Hope Sei-gnous and Betty Hicks formed the Women's Professional Golf Association (WPGA). This was

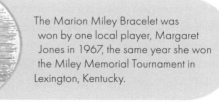

the first organization of any kind for women Pro-fessional golfers and open to all races and econom-ic backgrounds. It was only mildly successful and in 1950, after Babe Didrikson Zaharias and Shirley Spork proclaimed themselves Professional, the LPGA was formed in attempt to replace the financially failing WPGA. Founding members also included Patty Berg, Betty Jameson and Louise Suggs among others. The WPGA and LPGA ran the Women's Open for six years before turning the reins over to the USGA in 1952.

By 1959, the LPGA added a Teach-

The Marion Miley Bracelet was won by one local player, Margaret Jones in 1967, the same year she won the Miley Memorial Tournament in Lexington, Kentucky.

ing Committee to provide instructional services. Locally the first member of the LPGA was Carol Clark Johnson who joined the Teaching Committee in 1966 and was named national Teacher of the Year in 1975. "Keanie" Johnson, was preceded by Kate Brophy in the 1920s as she started with an illustrious amateur career before suddenly being designated a Professional due to the rules of amateur status in effect then.

On the Horizon

Cincinnati women's golf during the Classic period from 1895–1960 had been a history of growth and increased popularity with great individual performances on the local and state level and appearances on the national stage at the Western Women's Amateur and Open, US Women's Amateur and others. It included victories, finals and semi-final appearances and even selection to the American Curtis Cup team. Quite a record of accomplishment for the Queen City. But golf accomplishments had just begun.

As the 1960s started, some old and new names entered the scene and would compete at high levels too. Met winners in that decade would include Judy Anderson Diem (four wins between 1959 and 1976), Margaret Jones (winning three times and runner up a total of three times in the decade of the 60s), Janet McIntosh Mueller (Met wins two and three) and Joan Comisar (her first of four Met wins).

In 1961, former North College Hill golf standout Lenny Wirtz left his job at MacGregor Co. and took over as Tournament Director of the LPGA. This was only fifteen years after his NCH team finished second in the Ohio High School State tournament. Always known for his fairness in over twenty years as an NCAA and NBA basketball referee, he exhibited the same trait while playing golf and managing a golf tour. In the 1940s the Wyoming HS Boy's golf team featured two amazing female golfers, Nancy Porter and Carol Clark. Most boy's teams refused to play Wyoming but NCH, led by Wirtz and Tom Nieporte, had no problems with it and enjoyed the competition. Similarly, during his decade long stint with the LPGA, he fought many times to change venues when clubs refused to admit Black

Lenny Wirtz, was a North College Hill High School golf star and became the Tournament Director of the LPGA from 1961 to 1969. He's pictured sitting between LPGA stars Mickey Wright and Betsy Rawls.

Professionals Althea Gibson and Rene Powell to their facilities.

The LPGA held their Championship and one of their Majors at the Jack Nicklaus Sports Center in Mason OH from 1978 to 1989. Always well attended and popular with fans, it featured multiple wins by players such as Donna Caponi, Patty Sheehan and Nancy Lopez. Nancy would move to Cincinnati during that period of time. The LPGA membership also has grown locally with many Pro's competing, teaching and advancing the game of golf.

Meanwhile, the Greater Cincinnati Women's Golf Association grew from the original twelve-member clubs to over twenty-five organizations and now has a Scholarship Foundation for graduating female high school seniors to provide an award on the basis of academic achievement, excellence of character and involvement in the sport of golf. The tradition of great women's golf started in 1895 has continued to this day.

Judy Anderson, playing from Terrace Park Country Club, was runner-up in the Women's Met in 1957 and 1958 and finally broke through with a win as Judy Anderson Diem in 1959. Judy would win the Women's Met four more times in 1961, 1969, 1973 and 1976, playing from Coldstream Country Club.

CHAPTER 5
The Professionals

Make the hard ones look easy and the easy ones look hard.
—Walter Hagen

Introduction—The Experts

The story and evolution of the golf profession is coupled with the game itself. For a few years in Cincinnati, there was literally one person in the whole city who fit the description of what we now know as a Golf Professional. In some places he was known as a Professional but he also wore the moniker of Expert or Superintendent or even Greenskeeper. Typical of that time, he was a recent immigrant from Scotland, England, or Ireland and someone who had a knack for playing the game. But he also had other important skills like designing and building a golf course, building clubs (woods mostly but sometimes irons too), maintaining the property, and training members and caddies of every aspect of play including etiquette and rules.

After the first eight golf courses began operation locally in the 1890s it took a while to get organized. These clubs in all cases were loose confederations of neighbors and members of social or business clubs who were looking for exercise, competition and the enjoyment of this new game from Scotland. Some organizations might have a part time landscaper to manage the grounds. That person would keep the grass cut and build tees and greens but routings of the courses were performed by the members. But in 1896, the Cincinnati Golf Club recognized it needed an expert to expand and manage the course, provide instruction, make golf clubs and take care of all of the auxiliary services like caddies, water and supplies. It needed someone who would make their golf club in the style of the better facilities back east and in Chicago.

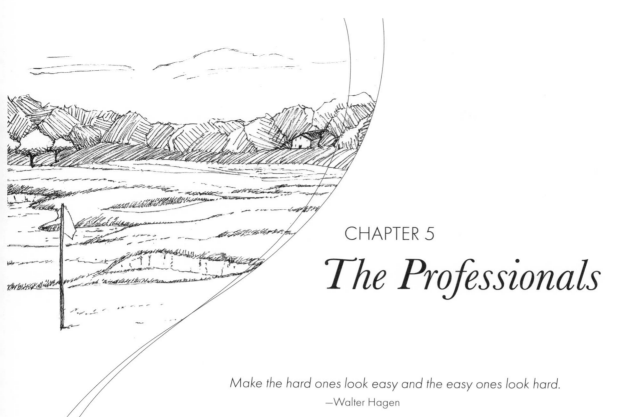

Robert White Jr., Cincinnati's first Golf Professional and eventual first President of the Professional Golfers of America (PGA). (Picture circa 1904)

The Robert White family portrait. Robert White Jr. (far right) worked with his father (center of picture, sitting) in Cincinnati starting in 1896; White Sr. was a blacksmith by trade but also an expert "cleekmaker," a builder of golf club irons, and worked for many years at MacGregor Golf in Dayton.

AFTER GOLF CRACK

The Losantiville Golf Club is making an effort to engage Willie Anderson, golf professional, for its new links in Pleasant Ridge.

In 1906, news about Losantiville Country Club's attempt to bring Four-Time U.S. Open winner Willie Anderson in as Head Professional.

The Region's First Professionals— Sons of Scotland

Cincinnati Golf Club hired Robert White Jr. White had been born in St. Andrew's, Scotland and came to Cincinnati GC at twenty-two years of age with his father and brother-in-law. He had emigrated to the United States to study Agronomy and worked in Boston for a short time before coming to Cincinnati. While at Cincinnati GC, he laid out their first permanent nine-hole course and shared the course record with member Nicholas Longworth. By 1897, White

was taking control of the Grandin Rd. links, playing in the US Open at Chicago Golf Club and building very good hickory stick golf clubs with his father and a partner. White's father (also Robert White) had been a "cleekmaker" in St. Andrew's where he forged iron club heads. White Sr. had come to Dayton, Ohio, in 1896 to discuss club making with the president of the company that would eventually be MacGregor Golf Co. Father and son also built clubs in Cincinnati during the son's career here.

Young White represented that first wave of Scottish and British immigrant golf experts. The younger ones like White Jr. usually came alone or with their parents. Some of the older ones, like Archie Simpson Sr., came with his wife and family. They had no safety net. They were usually hired by word of mouth. A fellow Edinburgh school mate or caddy friend from North Berwick would recommend someone in the old country or already working on the east coast to a member looking for an employee for his club. Poaching among clubs was prevalent. With a thick brogue they were labeled as immigrants and received no special favors. When reporting for employment they were left to their own devices to manage the caddies and staff, tend to the course, build new holes, make golf clubs, keep their accounts and provide to the needs of the club members.

The early club Professional sometimes was not welcome outside the club environs, especially if there were no nearby neighborhoods that took him in. They were normally banned from

Robert Dow of Montrose, Scotland, was the second Professional at Avondale Athletic Club and third in the city; he eventually moved to Siwanoy Country Club in Bronxville, New York, as their first Professional in 1901.

Almost all of the top fifteen Professionals took part in the match play round robin format.

MONDAY, JUNE 20, 1938.

Armour and Walsh To Arrive Tuesday For $5000 Tourney

Guldahl and Snead Due on Scene Wednesday, Day Before Professional Round-Robin Opens; Cooper Is Current Leading Money Winner

BY WALLY FORSTE

ADVANCE guard of the all-star professional golf brigade of 15 scheduled to compete in the Palm Beach match play round-robin tournament starting Thursday at Kenwood was to arrive in Cincinnati Tuesday. First on deck will be Tommy Armour, former U. S. and British Open champion, and Frank Walsh, mop-topped and oversized Irishman. Both will come here from Chicago, where they have courses.

A 1938 *Post* article about arriving Professionals playing in the Palm Beach Invitational at Kenwood Country Club.

The Palm Beach Match Play Round Robin

In 1938 Kenwood CC was the scene for a unique event for Professionals. Sponsored by the local Palm Beach Clothing Co., the Palm Beach Match Play Round Robin included a field of the top fifteen Professional players all playing an eighteen-hole Match against each of the other players. The field included Sam Snead (eventual winner), Ralph Guldahl (fresh off his win at the US Open), Gene

Sam Snead wins the inaugural Palm Beach Invitational at Kenwood Country Club.

Sarazen, Tommy Armour, Lawson Little, Harry Cooper and Henry Picard among others. The $5,000 purse for only fifteen golfers was one of the year's biggest and almost the same size as the US Open. The tournament was eventually renamed the Goodall Invitational and played three more years before it was stopped during WWII. The Palm Beach Company was a real success locally as it came on the scene in Cincinnati in 1932 as an offshoot of the Goodall Company and eventually brought thousands of jobs here and helped employment during the Depression. By the 1950s they were making 25,000 men's summer suits a week and opened a 250,000 ft2 plant in Erlanger, Kentucky. By 1982, sales were $500 million annually and employed over 8,000 people.

club facilities like restaurants and locker rooms. In addition, many lived at the club year-round, sometimes above the caddy shed or behind the horse stable. Yet they needed to know immediately about local grasses and watering and drainage and routing of courses.

In 1898, White left Cincinnati GC to take over the Professional/Superintendent position at nearby Avondale Athletic Club. There he also laid out a new nine-hole course to replace the one routed by their members. Harry Reddie replaced White at Cincinnati

Alex Taylor, Professional at Losantiville Country Club and one of the nation's best players at the time; he won the Professional Golfer's Championship of Ohio in 1912.

Phil Honeyman, Head Professional at Cincinnati Golf Course and Phoenix Country Club; he was the second local Professional to enter the U.S. Open.

GC (CGC) and doubled the number of Professionals in the city. White later left Avondale AC (replaced by Scotsman Robert Dow) for Clifton GC in Cincinnati and eventually to a resort course in Old Sweet Springs, WV before arriving in 1902 at Ravisloe CC in Chicago. There he served for twelve years, studied more agronomy at the University of Wisconsin and eventually moved back to the east coast to design courses and become a Club Professional. In 1916 he was elected as the first President of the Professional Golfers of America (PGA) in New York City.

Annual employment renewals were at the whims of the Greens Committee or a key club member. Reaction to a bad drought or a prolonged caddy strike or any malfeasance by a staff member could throw the Professional back on the street. Some early experts jumped from club to club for even small salary raises or more opportunity. In the *Harper's Annual Golf Guide* in 1901, there was a listing of all courses in the United States including their officers and the name of the Greenskeeper (Professional). But that was also a book that could be used for poaching another club's expert. One club in Plainfield, New Jersey, listed the name of their Greenskeeper as "a worthy Scotchman (sic) who need not be spoiled by being set on a pedestal" so his name would not be known to other clubs. Job changes were frequent, each time starting new at a different venue. Tom McCormick eventually replaced Harry Reddie at CGC in 1901 and then McCormick left in

1905 to take the post at Losantiville GC in the Oakley Race Track infield. That was one of many positions locally for McCormick, who would end up building the first course at Avon Fields GC. Tenures were short and there was a lot of movement from club to club.

When McCormick left Cincinnati GC, a new face appeared on Grandin as Phil Honeyman arrived from Florida and had Bob White's course completely refurbished by 1907. In the meantime, McCormick went back to the course in Burnet Woods run by the city and Jimmy Watson was hired at Losantiville CC. Losantiville had made a play to bring four-time US Open winner Willie Anderson in as Head Professional for their new course in Pleasant Ridge but hired Watson instead when Anderson decided to stay in Philadelphia. The number of experts were increasing as each club realized it needed outside help to build the courses and teach the game to the members. Honeyman and Watson were the class golfers locally and would spend the next few years in competition as club members would put up purses and make bets. But there was one thing common to the Cincinnati Pro's: White, Reddie, Dow, McCormick, Anderson, Watson and Honeyman—Scotsmen all.

In 1909 another Scot, Alex Taylor, took over as Losantiville Professional and quickly was placed in matches against Honeyman as the club competitions continued. Hyde Park CC (Scottish) and Avondale GC (Irish) also had foreign-born Professionals by this time so the employment opportunities were expanding. And as many of the Professionals were trying to compete at the Western and US Opens and Ohio Open events, they were also rebuilding, improving and expanding their course layouts. For example, in 1911, Honeyman came upon an idea to use Lake Erie sand instead of Ohio River sand to dress the Grandin Rd. greens and protect them from severe rain storms and flooding. Eventually this was soon used by other local clubs. Everyone used their own devices and experiences to improve the game for their members.

By 1912, four Cincinnati Professionals made it to the US Open in Buffalo. Besides Taylor and Honeyman, Bob McDonald of Hyde Park CC and Peter Hendie of Ft. Mitchell CC qualified and all were Scots. Nationally, the first sixteen winners of the US Open were from the British Isles and the same was happening in Cincinnati when it came to hiring Professionals. But as WWI approached, there would be

Scotsman Peter Hendie, Head Professional of Ft. Mitchell Country Club and a U.S. Open player. (Photo circa 1912)

Bill Jackson, golf architect and Head Professional at Butler County Country Club and The Camargo Club shown in the center with Ted Ray (1912 British Open Winner and 1920 U.S. Open Winner), Harry Hampton (seven-time PGA tour winner), Harry Vardon (six-time British Open Champion and 1900 U.S. Open Champion) and Fred McLeod (1908 U.S. Open Champion). (Photo circa 1920)

indications of a new trend as Americans, primarily from the caddie ranks, started to work their way up into the profession.

The First American Professionals

George Ensminger became Head Professional at Elberon GC (eventually Western Hills CC) in 1907 and was the first American hired locally. Losantiville CC meanwhile still maintained the Scottish connection when they chose first to hire Scotsmen Edward Townes and then replaced him with Alex ("Nipper") Campbell in 1920. Campbell would last only three years before moving on to Miami Valley CC in Dayton. Meanwhile, in 1913, John Brophy, barely 18-years-old and a looper (caddy) at Cincinnati GC, took the job as Head Professional at Portsmouth (OH) Country Club. After six years in Portsmouth and Bowling Green (KY) CC, he returned to take the job at Ft. Mitchell CC. John's brother, Ed Brophy, had taken the post of Head Professional at Western Hills CC in 1914 and so the brothers became the first Cincinnati-grown Pros. These were signals of things to come for the profession as well as a sign that the game itself was becoming an American sport.

Americans who learned the game as loopers were now filling the Professional slots throughout the country and carried new skills learned at their home courses. The type of game they played was different than their Scottish Experts had learned from the links courses in Europe. The American game featured more driving skills whereas the Scottish game depended on the second shot and accurate irons played close to the ground. America was still a country where baseball was the main sport so their caddies and home-grown Experts were more athletic and tended to hit the ball farther.

At the same time, American courses were being built longer, tended to be more forgiving off the tee and had more elevation changes than their counterparts in Britain so the game evolved

Otto Hackbarth. His time at Cincinnati Country Club from 1916–1951 signaled a trend of long tenured Professionals in the region. He was a winner of the first Ohio Open in 1917 and won the 1940 PGA Seniors Championship.

differently. The introduction of the Haskell ball (see "Equipment" chapter) that could travel farther also forced courses to get longer. When former caddies John McDermott, Francis Ouimet, Walter Hagen, and Chick Evans won six of the next seven US Opens, it was apparent that American-made talent on American courses, with its athleticism and gamesmanship, had matured. Starting in 1911 and until Gary Player's victory in 1965, there would be only four more US Open champions from outside the United States. Included in this new group of young American Professionals were the likes of Walter Hagen and Gene Sarazen.

After ten years at Cincinnati GC, Phil Honeyman left for Phoenix GC to help build their new course on Reading Road in Golf Manor and American-born Otto Hackbarth came to Grandin Road in 1916 to take the Head Professional post and signaled yet another trend in the game and the profession of golf. Hackbarth was the perfect choice to replace Honeyman at Cincinnati GC. A 6' 2" native of Wisconsin with three brothers who also were professional golfers, Hackbarth had that special combination of playing and innovative club design skills and was the consummate Pro.

He was well known nationally and had good records in the US Open (T-7th in 1912) and PGA (T-9th in 1919). In 1917 at Hamilton County CC, he won the first Ohio Open. He eventually proved his longevity as a competitor when at age fifty-three in 1939 he led the Ohio Open for two rounds before succumbing to former US Open winner Billie Burke. He capped off his playing career by winning the 1940 PGA Seniors championship in Sarasota, Florida, at the Bobby Jones Course

Walter Hagen, "Sir Walter," was comfortable around royalty and in any venue and is credited with bringing the golf profession into a position of respectability at private clubs and was a frequent visitor to Cincinnati for matches and exhibitions.

and Sara Bay CC (beating former British Open winner Jock Hutchison in a playoff).

Otto was also famous for his special design putter, "The Hackbarth." Used by Chick Evans for his US Open and US Amateur victories, it featured a hickory shaft and forked hosel. The putter was later banned by the Royal & Ancient Golf Club of St. Andrews (R&A) and the USGA soon followed but it still remains in demand by golf club collectors for its unique design and historical significance. But another significant change to the profession was evident with Hackbarth. He would stay at Cincinnati CC until 1951. That was a trend that would be repeated by many local Professionals as the merry-go-round of short tenures during the 1890s and early 1900s would eventually come to a stop.

Stability and continuity became more important as businessmen sought to run their country clubs like they ran their own affairs. Ray Derr took over for Campbell at Losantiville CC for a couple years but his assistant, Harry Boyer, eventually replaced him and retired from the post after twenty-six years. Derr's other assistant, Red Strauss, spent forty plus years as a local Professional, mostly for the city courses.

George Bowden stayed at Maketewah CC for nineteen years before leaving with health issues and eventually returned to the post at Terrace Park CC. Ed Brophy, Art Smith, Bill Jackson, Frank Gelhot, Bill Fruectemeyer

Frank Gelhot started as a caddy when he was eight at Losantiville Country Club and had a long career as Head Professional at Ridgewood and Clovernook country clubs. He opened his own driving range in Fairfield. (Photo circa 1933)

THREE BROPHY TRAINED BOYS REACH TOP FLIGHT OF CITY GOLF CHAMPIONSHIP

Ed Brophy with three Western Hills Country Club caddies who were the anchors of the 1928 Hughes High School state championship team. Left to right: Eph Collins, Johnny Fischer, Brophy, Larry Hendrixson.

CINCINNATI LAD ONE OF FEW AMERICAN GOLF PROFESSIONALS

JOHNNY BROPHY.

A 1908 *Cincinnati Post* article announcing eighteen-year-old Johnny Brophy taking the Professional's job at Portsmouth Country Club.

The Brophy's—Cincinnati's First Family of Golf

Golf in the early days was many times a family affair. Wisconsin native Otto Hackbarth, the long-time Professional at Cincinnati Country Club, was one of four brothers who all had long and illustrious golf careers. The seven brothers of the Turnesa family from New York were nationally famous and six were Golf Professionals. The youngest, Willie, was a premier Amateur who won the US Amateur twice and the British Amateur. And Cincinnati had their own version that began with three brothers as caddies at Cincinnati Golf Club in the 1890s.

John, Ed and James Brophy were eager youngsters who very quickly became mainstays at the Grandin Road course. They did odd jobs around the club and became the caddies on demand by the best players. And they helped their fellow caddies from O'Bryonville protect their golf territory from kids from other neighborhoods. Their money made caddying, shagging golf balls and doing odd jobs at the course helped the family finances in those tough times. They also developed playing skills using old discarded golf clubs and found balls to compete in caddy competitions. And they all had a notion to take their involvement in the game to a full-time vocation.

John was the first to take the opportunity in 1908 when he took the Head Professional's post at Portsmouth (OH) CC at age eighteen. After stints at Ashland (KY) CC and Bowling Green (KY) CC he finally returned home to take the job at Ft. Mitchell CC in 1914. He would stay there until 1922 when he began an odyssey that took him to Melbourne (FL) CC, Miami Beach CC, Ft. Mitchell CC a second

Jim Brophy at the driving range on Section Road. (Photo circa 1934)

time in 1925 and finally taking the Head Professional position at the exclusive Montauk Downs CC on the eastern tip of Long Island. There he would stay until returning home to take the Twin Oaks CC helm in 1934 and 1935. All this while he would winter at Bayshore (FL) CC. As the American Depression deepened, he would join back with his brothers—first with Jim at his Driving Range on Section Rd. and then as an Assistant to Ed at Western Hills for one year in 1942. He then returned to Ft. Mitchell CC for one brief time as he died suddenly in May of 1943. He served a total of twelve years at Ft. Mitchell CC and eighteen at Bayshore CC.

Ed was the Assistant Professional at Elberon GC in 1912 and first Head Professional at the Western Hills CC in 1914, a post he held until 1952. Starting in the early 1920s he and his wife Kate would travel to Florida each winter and Ed would take a position running the Miami CC course, teaching and competing on the winter circuit. He befriended Carl Fisher who was an entrepreneur and one of the partners developing a new Florida resort called Miami Beach. Ed was given the opportunity to move his winter position to the new Miami Beach CC and Kate was women's club champion there for three years. Ed was the first offered the new position at Montauk Downs on Long Island, New York, by Fisher but turned it down and his brother John took the job. By 1922 all brothers were wintering in Florida and were head Pros in Miami, Ft. Pierce and Melbourne. By 1926 all have moved to Miami Beach and held a lucrative and steady position teaching and competing there. At that time there was a strong movement to put playing Pros into these positions to add notoriety to their brand but Carl Fisher came through and promised all three brothers a job for life at his property. Unfortunately, Fisher lost most of his fortune in the Stock Market crash of 1929 but Ed and his brothers remained in good positions for most of the Depression. Ed died in 1973 in Sarasota, Florida, and Kate followed in 1977. Both were still teaching golf almost to the very end.

The youngest brother, Jim, also started young as a Professional when he took the head job at Ashland, Kentucky, CC in 1915 at age nineteen. After two years out of town he came back and took the post at Avon Fields GC in 1917. When the new Phoenix CC was built on the corner of Reading Road and Seymour Avenue in 1919, Jimmy took that opportunity and stayed through the club's name change to Hillcrest CC and then moved to Ridgewood GC in 1927. Also wintering in Florida, he became close friends with Gene Sarazen and Sarazen would make stops at Hillcrest CC for exhibitions when in the area. Jim was both a competitive player and teacher and, as the Depression hit, he made several other stops as clubs were having financial trouble. First, he took the Twin Oaks GC position in 1931 but decided this new opportunity called a Driving Range was the way to make it through the tough financial times hitting the industry. He opened an operation on Section Road in Roselawn and soon his brother John joined him as well

Heavyweight Boxing Champion Gene Tunney (l) watching the Brophy brothers on the green at Miami Beach Country Club. Left to right: Jim Brophy (putting), Ed Brophy and John Brophy. (Photo circa 1930)

as other teachers. It was there that he developed the game of a young Dotty Schildmiller who went on to win seven Women's Met's. Jim was also teaching at Driving Ranges on Madison Road and Tennessee Avenue. Eventually, he went back to Club positions at Dearborn, Indiana, CC, Sycamore GC on Reading Road and finally at Swaim Fields in Blue Ash. Jim died in Miami, Florida, in 1968.

There were many trials and tribulations faced by the family during their varied careers. John and his family were missing temporarily during one of Florida's hurricanes in 1926. Ed's Florida Pro Shop burnt down on New Year's Eve 1927 and he lost all of his stock and a year's revenue. Ed's wife, Kate, was declared a Professional in 1929 and this shortened her amateur competitive career. All three of the brother's wives played well and especially Ed's wife, Kate, who won three Women's Met's and ended up as a Professional herself. But they all had careers that carried them all over the eastern seaboard from Miami Beach to the tip of Long Island. And they played and taught golf to the movie stars and celebrities that frequented Miami, Florida, when it was the place to hide from the winter. Not bad for three caddies from O'Bryonville.

and many more started to represent the increased respect for the position as a key element in the success of the club and its programs.

Again, the profession was going through changes as country clubs became larger and golf clubs were now available from manufacturers like Spalding, Wilson and MacGregor. Most private courses were also hiring specialized Superintendents and Greenskeepers. Professionals could then concentrate on managing the golf affairs of the club such as running tournaments and Pro Shops as well as teaching and promoting the game. By the end of the

1920s, all new Professionals being hired locally were American born.

But there still was a stigma about being Professional in the early years. The USGA controlled the status of all players and determined who would be considered Professional and Amateur. Being classified a Professional obviously made prizes available in Open events but it also restricted the ability to play in all other tournaments. And Professionals were still considered to be the "servants" or instructors to the rich in many circles and forbidden entrance to the club houses and dining rooms of many country clubs.

The Golf Professional as teacher has been one of the skills required from the earliest play of the game. Here Ben Hogan, MacGregor Staff Professional, is taking instruction from Henry Picard in 1940; the change of grip catapulted Hogan's career. Pickard was a frequent player at Cincinnati exhibitions and tournaments including the Palm Beach Professional Round Robin Invitational at Kenwood Country Club.

But then along came Walter Hagen—"Sir Walter"—winner of the 1914 US Open at age twenty-one. He had a personality that would allow him to unnerve the snootiest among the world's royalty. He was always dressed to the nines and acted like he owned the mortgage at any club he entered. Few dining rooms or locker rooms were off limits to him and it lent a new swagger to many other Professionals of the day who were tired of the previous treatment. Coincidentally this was a start to longer tenures by the Experts as the clubs started to value the Club Professional as an asset to the operation. It started with Hagen nationally and Hackbarth in Cincinnati.

Keeping the Game Afloat— The Great Depression and the Teacher

That does not mean it was all easy. After the Stock Market crash in 1929, there were increased pressures on every club to keep the doors open and many courses did not make it. Some courses that did survive went from country club to public access format after members continued to leave. Staffs were cut, courses were reduced from eighteen holes to nine holes, sand bunkers were allowed to disappear, greens got smaller and many clubs installed illegal slot machines to gain revenue. Every strategy imaginable was tried to cut expenses or increase income and there was no end in sight for the Depression.

Ironically it was one of Cincinnati's greatest eras of Amateur golf. The decade of the thirties would feature Johnny Fischer and a cadre of great amateurs like Milt Cook, Neil Ransick, Maurice McCarthy, Ralph Shelton and Al Joslin Jr. Similarly, the Women's champions included Olga Weil, Elizabeth Cassatt Reid, Marion Miley, Dolly Schildmiller and Martha Kinsey. The group represented National and State Champions, Walker Cup and Curtis Cup players, NCAA champions and untold numbers of Met victories and club championships.

What this new cadre of great players had in common was expert instruction coming from the Golf Professional. As the role had evolved away from Club Maker and Greens Superintendent, many Club Professionals became extremely proficient at teaching. This included another former hometown caddy and Caddy Master at Losantiville CC. Clarence Dapper, had worked his way up through the ranks to Professional and had moved to western Indiana. He won the 1922, 1923 and 1924 Terre Haute Opens while Head Professional of the Phoenix (IN) Country Club. After a year in Michigan, he returned home in 1927 to replace Head Professional Jimmy Brophy at Hillcrest CC. He promptly won the Queen City Open Medal Play championship and established himself as one of the best

Clarence Dapper, Head Professional at Hillcrest Country Club and Avon Fields Golf Course was an extraordinary player and teacher. He mentored many great players including Olga Weil.

Group Lessons at Avon Fields. (Circa 1935)

players in the region. But it was reputation as a teacher that set him apart from his peers.

Hillcrest CC was in a fight to stay in operation as the Depression deepened. It was an offshoot of the Phoenix CC started in Golf Manor in 1916 and had reorganized and taken their new name in 1919. They had many good players including a great woman tennis player named Olga Strashun Weil. As a twenty-year-old she had been awarded the Best Female Athlete at the University of Cincinnati where she played basketball and tennis. By age twenty-four she had already won one Ohio Amateur Tennis Singles and two Mixed-Doubles titles. In 1926, Dapper had witnessed her just winning the Western Tennis Championship and persuaded her to hit a few golf balls "just for fun." After that and under Dapper's tutelage, her focus changed to golf.

Weil's record is unmatched in local competition. She would go on to win twelve Women's Met titles and three Ohio Women's Amateur titles. In the 1941 Women's Western Open, as an amateur, she lost to

One of the nation's best Instructors, Art Smith of Summit Hills and Hyde Park country clubs, was sought out for his teaching skills and provided lessons for a young Curtis Strange, a two-time U.S. Open winner. Smith also taught Curtis's dad, Tom Strange, at Hyde Park Country Club.

Professional Patty Berg in the Finals. At that time, it was considered the greatest Women's Open championship in the world. Dapper would provide the lessons and direction but he also would take every opportunity to play competitively with her as a partner or against her in Singles matches and exhibitions. As a great tennis player, she already had competitive skills but building on those attributes with golf pressure experience took her game to a different level.

Dapper's ability as teacher and mentor got Weil to a top level and many other players to their best performance level but Weil eventually left Hillcrest CC

Tom Strange Jr. (shown here with twin sons Allan and Curtis Strange, both of whom would become PGA Professionals) turned Pro in Virginia in 1958. He served as the Assistant Pro to Sam Snead and Resident Professional at the Greenbriar. Tom tragically died of cancer in 1969 at the age of thirty-nine.

Walter Hagen, New York...	143	144—287
Jock Hutchison, Chicago.....	143	149—292
Emmet French, Youngstown.	140	154—294
•Bobby Jones, Atlanta.........	139	156—295
Joe Kirkwood, Australia....	148	147—295
Bob MacDonald, Chicago.....	147	152—301
George Bowden, Cincinnati..	157	144—301
Laurie Ayton, Chicago.......	149	153—302
Bob Peebles, Peoria.........	142	161—303
P. O. Hart, Marietta.......	146	157—303
Gene Sarazen, Titusville.....	153	150—303
Jim Barnes, New York.......	149	155—304
Otto Hackbarth, Cincinnati.	152	152—304
William Melhorn, Shreveport	148	156—304
Charles Mayo, Chicago......	151	155—306

Leaderboard of the 1921 Western Open. At the time it was considered the strongest field in any tournament in the world and for many years after. Cincinnati professionals George Bowden (T-6th) and Otto Hackbarth (T-11th) displayed the quality of play locally.

George Bowden, originally from Boston, was one of the city's best golfers in national competitions. He appeared in twelve U.S. Opens and had a best finish of T-9th; he was Head Professional at Maketewah and Terrace Park country clubs and designed Homestead Golf Course.

in 1937 and moved on to Losantiville CC. Hillcrest was losing more members and was not the playing challenge of other country clubs. It was flat and fairways were wide and the real estate was becoming more valuable for subdivisions and development. As other members left under the pressures of the continuing Depression, the second floor of the clubhouse was turned over to a rental hall for weddings and meetings. By 1940, the north half of the Hillcrest property was sold to build a subdivision and the handwriting was on the wall for Dapper. With Weil's departure, Dapper left soon after to concentrate on teaching at Eastwood Driving Range. Dapper would eventually

take the head Professional's post at Avon Fields GC in 1942 but always did stay in contact with Mrs. Weil providing coaching tips during her career.

Before Dapper's departure from Hillcrest, he and thirteen other teaching Professionals had banded together to provide free lessons to new potential golfers in 1935. Some of the game's elite teaching Professionals at the time, including Bill Jackson, Bill Fruectemeyer, Harry Boyer, Jim and Ed Brophy and others

Tom Nieporte, former Homestead Golf Course and Clovernook Country Club caddy, winner of three PGA tournaments, and long-time Head Professional at Winged Foot Country Club.

listed Neil Ransick, Bill Deupree, Spence Kerkow, Tom Strange Sr., Dow Finsterwald and Janet McIntosh among his pupils. He also ran an Indoor Practice Range at the Brendamour Sporting Goods Store on Main Street in downtown. In 1976 in an ultimate compliment to his teaching skills, Smith was approached by a young PGA Tour rookie named Curtis Strange (Tom Strange Sr.'s grandson) to help him prepare for Q-School. Besides Dapper and Smith, other renowned teaching Professionals included George Bowden, Ed and Jim Brophy, Dave Mentiply and Otto Hackbarth.

Post War and the Golf Professional

Like most professions, the golf business went through even more changes during and after the war. There were many course closures and cut backs and the normal feed system of good young players from the caddie ranks was diverted to military service. Staffs were cut back and jobs were hard to come by. Tour events were also stopped or formats were changed and purses reduced everywhere. But with the sudden end to the war in 1945, there was a large influx of veterans looking for jobs and restarting their lives and golf was on the upswing again. There were also opportunities from the GI Bill that provided college education and there were other programs to get soldiers and sailors back into the workplace.

For golf this meant new demand. Public access courses were quickly taken from the drawing board and built around the country and Professionals were needed to fill slots. Immediately after the war this meant quick opportunities for those too young to have been in the military but also there were now chances to go to university and perhaps play at the college level and enter

worked the program through the City Recreation Commission and the Cincinnati Post. They used their teaching skills in an attempt to get more people back into the game. Almost all of the public access courses and some country clubs like Hyde Park CC and Western Hills CC, participated and provided the sites for teaching. The program continued as the Depression deepened but disbanded as the War approached.

Art Smith was another local Professional whose reputation as a teacher was also well known. An article in a 1954 issue of the *PGA* magazine listed him as the "Maker of 15 Champions." Besides Olga Weil, they

Dick Plummer, caddy from 1947 to 1951, assistant to Bill Ferriel and then Head Professional at The Camargo Club from 1961 to 1998.

the profession from a different direction. At the same time, merchandizing and advertising was coming to the fore. Like many businesses, Madison Avenue and mass marketing techniques were hitting the golf market as radio and TV provided more exposure and golf was becoming financially stable. But it also added the need for business education to run the Pro Shop.

There were holdovers from the pre-War days and old traditional career paths still there to be followed. Experienced Professionals like Marty Kavanaugh, Art Smith, Red Strauss and Hank Wilms were still in demand for new assignments. But another direction also seemed to surface when younger Professionals like Stanford educated and Tour veteran Art Doering took over the Cincinnati CC post in 1951. Freeman Haywood, himself a graduate lawyer, replaced Doering after four years and spent eighteen years at the helm on Grandin Road. Young caddies and junior players still turned Professional after the war and included excellent players like Tom Strange Jr. and Tom Nieporte. Both would succesful careers as Club Professionals out of the city. There were many paths to getting the Head Professional position.

Open Events and Local Professional Players

Open tournaments (to include amateurs and professional men) were being held as early as 1895 by the USGA. Lo-

cally, Ohio and Kentucky started with their Open tournaments in 1917 and 1920 respectively. In addition, the local area also provided the Queen City Open that was attended by players from throughout the region.

At the beginning, the foreign-born Professionals had a distinct advantage of competitive experience. But nationally the American skills began to show as caddies, collegians, and other young players honing their game at country clubs began to create a cadre of great young American players. Many of these players turned to golf as their profession. This new wave of Professionals was expert at their skill of the game and competed in tournaments worldwide. They still did compete against great amateurs like Bobby Jones, Chick Evans and Francis Ouimet in Open events but they also would be able to earn a living by their own playing skills at tournaments, playing exhibitions, writing instructional books and teaching.

Frequently, Cincinnati club Professionals like Otto Hackbarth (Cincinnati GC), George Bowden (Maketewah CC), Clarence Dapper (Hillcrest CC) and others would also be able to make it to the US Open, Western Open, PGA or other large national tournaments. Bowden was tied for second and Hackbarth tied for sixth after first round of 1919 US Open (with Bowden eventually finishing tied for 9th with Chick Evans and behind winner Walter Hagen) and he finished T-6th at the Western Open in 1921.

Bowden also went on to co-win the 1922 Houston Open and made it into the final round of twenty in the 1923 US Open won by Bobby Jones. He was also selected to the first team to play against Great Britain in what would become the Ryder Cup. He declined to play while taking the Head Professional post at Maketewah CC instead. Besides Bowden and Hackbarth at the 1940 Senior PGA, the local winners of national tournaments included Art Doering in the 1951 Greater Greensboro Open and Tom Nieporte in the 1967 Bob Hope Classic.

On the Horizon

Teaching would remain as a primary job responsibility for the Cincinnati area Professional and many would obtain national honors for this skill. Carol Clark Johnson from Wyoming CC would be named 1975 LPGA Teacher of the Year. Jim Flick from Losantiville CC received PGA Teacher of the Year honors in 1988. Coca

Cola was very involved with golf education nationwide and locally and driving ranges became locations for instruction to enter the game or improve skills. Local SOPGA professionals annually present the Teacher of the Year honors and Dick Plummer former caddy and Head Professional of The Camargo Club won its first award in 1986.

In the decades after 1960, there still were opportunities from the caddy ranks but more Professionals were coming from college golf. It was a major change from those first ten or so immigrant Scotsmen who defined the profession in Cincinnati before WWI.

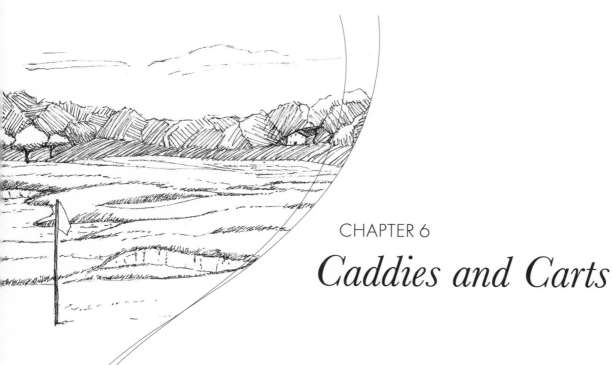

CHAPTER 6

Caddies and Carts

*The Caddy is the lifeblood of the game of golf, a great companion, a friendly
conversationalist and a smiling face. This is what the game of golf is truly about.*
—Charles "Chick" Evans, Founder, Evans Scholarship Program

Introduction

It was tough getting a caddy job in the early twentieth century in Cincinnati. There were only eight or ten places in town to find work and the sites were protected by neighborhood kids. O'Bryonville and Hyde Park boys protected their turf at Cincinnati GC while Bond Hillers took care of the Maketewah and Hillcrest clubs. The lads from Pleasant Ridge and Golf Manor caddied at Losantiville while Avon Fields was handled by the boys from St. Bernard and Elmwood. In the beginning, sometimes fisticuffs were involved but even after caddies became more mobile on street cars and busses (or by thumbing a ride) they generally kept to their own neighborhood courses.

Back in Scotland and Ireland, the caddy was generally an older fellow who made it his life's work but here the job immediately gravitated to inexperienced young men and boys. This was not the first time that young men had filled the role. Military cadets had been employed by Mary, Queen of Scots, to carry her clubs while in France in the 1560s. The term "caddy" or "caddie" had been around since the 1700s as an Anglicized term for cadet and the name had continued on and became part of the game's tradition. When the game came to the States, the name came with it.

The American Caddy

There were other reasons the young were chosen for these positions. The pay (generally about ten cents per

Caddies in the British Isles traditionally were older men.

Mary, Queen of Scots with her cadets.

four-hour round) could not sustain a household but was handy when provided by a youngster to help pay the family bills. And for the young caddy it was also a good alternative to working the ten-hour days as a helper in the city's dirty mills and factories.

At first in America, players and caddies were learning the game together under the tutelage of the first wave of immigrant Scottish Professionals. Caddying was the easiest and usual first step to be part of this new game. Like many sandlot baseball players who dreamt of making it to the majors, golf also piqued the interest of many early athletes who would first learn the game as a caddy.

Later, into the 1920s, the job was also becoming a good opportunity for many youths to earn fair income while learning life skills and getting even closer to the game. A good caddy could make more money and a bigger tip by doing a better job, exercising

Typical American caddy in 1915.

good manners and providing extra help to the player. If your hard work was recognized, there were further chances to work in the Pro Shop, cut grass, clean clubs and maybe become a Caddy Master or even a Professional. And the playing opportunities given to caddies on Mondays when the course was closed helped develop a new cadre of players and spawned many great professional and amateur careers.

The grounds and the caddies worked through the Caddy Master. Employed by the club or the Professional, he managed the caddy shack, kept the caddies trained and managed and would ensure the members got responsible boys to assist in their game. At some times, a hundred or more boys would be at the course waiting for a "loop" (carrying the player's clubs and bag for eighteen holes).

In the 1890s the caddy might carry only six or eight clubs in a canvas bag. But by the 1920s that number ballooned to several dozen clubs for many players

Caddy Eddie Lowery with Francis Ouimet at the 1913 U.S. Open.

Hilliard 'Honey Boy' Wingate

The most famous Caddy of the era was Eddie Lowery, the diminutive ten-year-old Boston looper during Francis Ouimet's victory in the 1913 US Open. There were other local youngsters who gained notoriety as caddies but the most famous was Hilliard "Honey Boy" Wingate. In 1933, he wandered into the Summit Hills CC parking lot in an old jalopy after hitch hiking from Florida. There he claimed to be Summit Hills' Professional Art Smith's caddie down South and asked for a job. Quiet and confident, the seventeen-year old soon became a celebrity among the city's caddies and he would chauffeur them to the caddy tournaments in a beat-up Model-T Ford. Wingate used his last $2 to enter the Junior Met while borrowing some clubs from a Summit Hills member. He promptly beat a field that included John Busemeyer, Bill Deupree and Billy Gilbert III (all future US Amateur participants) for the championship. Too old to play in another Junior Met, he won the city Caddie Championship the next year and the following year began work as Smith's Assistant Professional at Summit Hills. Hilliard lived in Covington for many years and passed away in Riverside, California in 1991.

A player and caddy leave the Avon Fields caddy shack for the day's round. (Photo circa 1935)

until the USGA finally set a limit of fourteen. It meant getting up before dawn, walking or riding a bike to the course and hoping for a loop or maybe two. Or if the Caddy Master was friendly, maybe a youngster could get a set of "doubles" (carrying the clubs and bags for two players during the same round).

By the 1920s the eighteen-hole rate had increased to twenty-five cents but it did not come without a lot of conflict. Strikes at Cincinnati GC had occurred as early as 1899 with the boys from O'Bryonville demanding a pay raise. That same year Clifton GC caddies struck for a pay increase to $0.15 per loop. In 1906 a Clifton GC strike was started to protest girls being permitted to caddy. Avondale GC had problems in 1907 because members were bringing their sons to caddy and by-passing the staff.

Further strikes up to and during the Depression did increase rates slightly but into the 1950s the cost for a loop had still only made it to $1.25 to $2.00 based on the caddy's experience. When the new Social Security laws were put in during the Depression there was a temporary hitch as to the status of caddies and whether they had to pay into the system. Also, there was a time when the liability for the caddy's safety was considered the player's and not the club's responsibility. In particular a $10,000 lawsuit against a golfer in 1943 as a result of the death of a caddy struck and killed at Hyde Park CC forced changes to regulations and liability.

After a round at Spanish Bay's golf course, ASGCA honoree John Zoller, left, relaxes with, from left, new society member Jack Nicklaus, outgoing President Robert Trent Jones Jr. and past President Pete Dye.

A 1990 photo of John Zoller at Spanish Bay Country Club with Jack Nicklaus, Robert Trent Jones and Pete Dye. Zoller was being honored with the prestigious Donald Ross Award that year.

John Allen Zoller, Hamilton High School class of 1943.

Zoller's 70 3rd In NCAA

John Zoller led the Ohio State golf team Monday with a one under par 70 in the qualifying round of the NCAA tournament over the Stanford University course at Palo Alto, Calif. Zollar fired a 34-36 to finish in a three-way tie for third behind Fred Wampler of Purdue and Tom Lambie of Stanford who carded three under par 68s.

Other Ohio State golfers finished as follows: Alex Polli, 38-36—74; Don Schook, 40-37—78; Bob Hamrich, 40-42—82; John Winters, 41-42—83, and Pete Sohl, 43-43—86.

Zoller competed in the 1948 NCAA Championship at Stanford University.

John Allen Zoller—"Renaissance Man of Golf"

There are many wonderful stories of youngsters who have used the game of golf as a career path from caddying to exciting and productive lives inside and outside the sport. Some of John Zoller's earliest memories were walking to Hamilton Elks Golf course where his brother herded the sheep that helped keep the grass cut. John caddied and helped around the property and developed a skill for the game that led him eventually to captain the Hamilton High School Squad. In 1942 he was the Medalist (lowest individual score for all players in the State tournament) on a team that finished fifth in the State. His high school career was strong enough to earn him a scholarship to play golf at The Ohio State University where he entered Engineering School in the Fall of 1942. At age nineteen, his school career was interrupted as he enlisted in the US Army and John would eventually serve as a Warrant Officer in Europe in the 103rd Division. His unit saw combat through France and into Austria and was involved in the liberation of the concentration camps around Dachau. Upon returning home after the war, John continued at Ohio State, lettered on the golf team in 1946, 1947 and 1948 and eventually received his Engineering degree.

John got into the golf career going slowly but eventually moved West and took over as Superintendent of the Eugene Country Club in Oregon in 1958. He moved on to the Monterrey Peninsula Country Club in California in 1974, working first as Superintendent and then the General Manager. In 1979 he was hired as Director of

ASGCA honors John Zoller as 'Renaissance man of golf'

BY MARK LESLIE

Cited as a "Renaissance man of golf," John Zoller symbolized superintendents, club managers and golf association administrators when he accepted the Donald Ross Award from the American Society of Golf Course Architects on March 26.

While ASGCA Past President Rees Jones classified Zoller with Herb and Joe Graffis as "Renaissance men of golf," outgoing President Robert Trent Jones Jr. said the recently retired senior executive director of the Northern California Golf Association has "literally done it all" in golf and "ev-

ery golf course architect appreciates what John has done personally to enlarge and enhance our profession."

Pointing toward Zoller's supervision or advisory work on all seven golf courses within the Del Monte forest on California's Monterey Peninsula, Bobby Jones said development of Poppy Hills Golf Club marks the first time in North America that a golf association of volunteers, with its own finances, has bought the land, constructed a course and operated it for its own members and the general public.

"What better way to meet the ex-

ploding demand for our grand and glorious game?" he asked.

United States Golf Association President C. Grant Spaeth, of Palo Alto, Calif., told the ASGCA members gathered at the Inn at Spanish Bay: "Your selection of John Zoller is consistent with my theme," which is to provide "playable golf at reasonable prices" for all golfers.

"There are an awful lot of happy golfers in this part of the world because of John Zoller," Spaeth said.

Zoller, an Ohio State University graduate who worked first as a course superintendent, then as a club man-

Zoller was known as golf's Renaissance man.

Golf by the Pebble Beach Company and then moved to the Executive Directorship of the Northern California Golf Association with its 140,000 members. In that capacity he developed and managed the building of the Poppy Hills Golf Club in Monterrey. He was also a tireless proponent of managing water on golf courses and was nationally published and ahead of his time on reducing water consumption. In 1990 after his retirement, he was presented with the Donald Ross Award by the American Golf Course Architects of America and doing so joined a list of honorees that included President George H. W. Bush, Jack Nicklaus, Robert Trent Jones and Arnold Palmer. After retirement, the man known as "Big Z" worked on the development of the Tehama golf property with Clint Eastwood and was one of the founders of First Tee in Monterrey. For his contribution of effort and time to the First Tee organization, the John Zoller National First Tee Scholarship is offered in his name. John passed away in 2007 in Monterrey, California, survived by six children and his wife of fifty-nine years.

Because of the job scarcity, caddy positions were sometimes handed from older to younger brothers. But even after getting through the gate, the chances

for a loop were still not guaranteed. Different methods for determining who got the loops were employed at each club and the Caddy Master always had the opportunity to get his favorites out and there were many players who demanded their own favorite caddy.

In 1921, Losantiville instituted a classification system so the older and more experienced caddies would garner a higher pay rate. The rookies would also get the poor tippers and those with bad tempers that sometimes bordered on cruelty. But if you did not get out for a loop you might still make a few cents shagging golf balls. Before the days of the course driving ranges (most did not get them well into the 1960s), the player would warm up by taking a bag of shag balls out onto a remote part of the property (see the chapter on "Driving Ranges"). The "shagger" or "shag boy" would stand out in the field and retrieve the balls and perhaps make a nickel or dime for his effort.

But a typical day also meant waiting hours in the caddy shack until the Caddy Master would give you an assignment. Some clubs had a ball field to occupy waiting time but in the early days it took a lot of summers of playing marbles, pitching pennies, or pulling out your pocket knife to play 'mumbly peg' to work your way up to better money. With the advent of golf carts after WWII, there was a decrease in caddy positions and the pay dropped but that has recovered and conditions today better recognize the importance of caddies and their contribution to the game.

The Caddy as Player

The Francis Ouimet victory in the 1913 US Open changed a lot of things. Gene Sarazen, at one time a caddy in Rye, New York, wrote in his 1950 memoir, "(Caddies) received a new lease on life after it was circulated that Ouimet started as a caddy." Caddies were starting to look like a possible resource for American golf to be preeminent in the world.

A caddy with some athletic ability might be able to get a few golf clubs handed down by a member or maybe buy some used. He might even get to play the club course on caddy day (usually a Monday when the course was

A 1914 photo of the caddy shack at Elberon Golf Course. Later that year the operation would move up the road to Cleves-Warsaw Pike and become Western Hills Country Club where Head Professional Ed Brophy would run one of the area's best caddy programs.

closed to members) or, more likely, beat old golf balls around the neighborhood with his buddies. He would learn the game by watching his players and soon many started to show real promise and started to compete. Some clubs would have a Professional, like Ed Brophy at Western Hills or Harry Boyers at Losantiville, who would recognize talent and provide extra mentoring and instruction. In 1922, Arthur Boggs, Professional at Losantiville CC and Hyde Park CC, could count five local golf Professionals that he had already developed from the caddies at his courses.

It did not take long for the American competitive nature in sports to reach into the caddy ranks and by 1900 the caddies at Clifton GC had an informal tournament among the caddies. In fact, bare foot caddies from Clifton were known to engage in matches with their counterparts at Cincinnati GC. Locally, the first published club caddy championship was in 1907 at the Inverness Club, located in the hills above Newport, Kentucky. By 1918, caddies were

Typical pose of a caddy from the 1890s to the 1960s, toting bags, tending pins and cleaning equipment.

Bill Jackson (c), Head Professional at The Camargo Club, with Jerry Purdy (l) 1947 Cincinnati Caddy Champion and Darrel Reed (r) the co-medalist. Jackson gave group instruction to all caddies and individual instruction to the six most promising caddies.

CADDY MAKES GOLF SCORE OF CRACKS

Caddies at the Inverness Club golf links Monday held a tournament to decide the "caddy championship." There had been a great deal of dispute, and a few fights on the quiet are said to have resulted from arguments over their playing abilities.

Edward Arnold came to the rescue by offering three cash prizes, and the tournament was immediately started with all of the caddies participating.

The final scores showed that Byron Erb had won first place with a total score of 45. As bogey can only go the course in 35, and some of the crack players play it in 40 when they are in their best form, Erb is a star, unless he forgot to count a few strokes every now and then.

Elmer Brockmeyer finished second with 44, but he was scratch man, and was allowed no handicap, as was Erb.

Windfield McCoy finished third with a score of 48.

A 1907 *Post* article about one of the earliest caddy tournaments in the area. This one at the Inverness Golf Course in Ft. Thomas indicated caddies were already shooting scores similar to the best golfers at the club (called "cracks").

actually setting course records at some courses and it was not long until matches and competitions were arranged between the caddies of one club and another. In 1922, there finally was a city wide individual and team Caddy Championship organized.

The early Rules of the USGA had actually designated any person over sixteen years old and working in the golf business (like a caddy) as a Professional. In fact, many early caddy championships had a Professional Division. This would obviously get complicated for players eventually wanting to play competitively as an Amateur and the USGA rules were properly changed.

Caddy tournaments were big news and reported in all the local papers. A fifteen-year-old could be toting bags one day and the next have his picture in the local paper right alongside Babe Ruth or Bobby Jones. Some of the area's greatest golfers, including John Fischer, Tony Blom, Ralph Shelton, Dick Plummer and Tom Nieporte, came from the caddy ranks. Plummer, three-time city Caddy Champion, served as both a caddy and eventually Head Professional at The Camargo Club.

Caddy championships also spawned larger more inclusive Junior Golf programs. Young members at the

Dick Plummer the 1951 City Caddie Champion at Camargo. He eventually became Head Professional there for thirty-four years.

country clubs could not compete with the adult members until age eighteen so there was no path to develop young players locally. Al Joslin Sr. solved that problem by organizing the first Junior Met in 1926 at his new Ridgewood GC in Amberly Village. The daily-fee club was actually built with young people in mind.

Ridgewood provided a new venue for competition and practice facilities for all players including club members and caddies from the region. Many caddies would ride their bike or hitch rides to Ridgewood to play the game after caddying all day at their own local course. Later in 1955, the Cincinnati Public Recreation Commission would also organize their own Youth Golf Association (YGA) to increase youth involvement in the sport. The evolution of many caddies into competitive players was built upon these efforts.

The Caddy and Club Programs

For the thousands of other boys who worked as caddies from the first days of golf in Cincinnati there are also were programs and help from other caring individuals. The great Charles "Chick" Evans, a US Open and Amateur champion and former caddy, had received royalties for a golf instruction book and re-

Proceeds from Chick Evans' golf training recordings in the 1920s were used to start the Evans Scholarship Program for caddies; the company making the recordings (Brunswick Balke Collender) was headquartered in Cincinnati.

cordings of golf instruction. He would lose his amateur status if he accepted the money and, at the suggestion of his mother, decided to donate it to a national scholarship effort for caddies. Many Cincinnati area caddies have benefitted from this scholarship assistance and it is one of golf's great success stories with over 12,000 college graduates from the program.

Ells Widerman of Kenwood CC introduced the Evans program to Cincinnati in the 1950s and remained a mentor to hundreds of caddies who received the Scholarship and volunteered to develop other caddy programs in the region. Known as the "Four O'clock Ranger" for his station at the forteenth hole at Kenwood to kibitz with the players participating that day, he was a 1-handicap who played in the 1954 Western Open. Chick Evans was Wideman's mentor and developed his passion for the welfare of caddies and the Evans Scholarship program.

Even before Evans started his program in 1930 there were Cincinnatians who also recognized the off-course needs of the caddies. Using the YMCA and other service organizations, many local golf clubs worked together to build baseball leagues, organize swim meets and stage informal golf matches for their caddies. For many years there was an annual excursion on steamboats to Coney Island to celebrate a Caddy Day with games, rides and a picnic. Individuals like Dr. J.W. Kirgan at Cincinnati CC, James J. Reis at Losantiville CC and Carroll Peterman at Maketewah CC also organized outside programs for caddies to help them through times when they were not on the course.

Carts as Competition for Caddies

After WWII, golf carts and trolleys (pulled or pushed by a walking golfer) hit the scene. Their early appearance was seen as an obvious threat to caddies. Battery powered golf cars had actually been seen as early as the 1930s but soon proved to be unworkable on

the course terrain. After WWII, a California inventor named Merle Williams built a cart that worked on a thirty-six-volt drive system that had originally been designed to power wing flaps on the B-17 bomber. His innovation gained early control of the market with his Marketeer model. However, the concept of riding while playing still moved slowly through the golf community. Caddies' jobs were secure going into the 1950s.

But soon, other companies like Harley-Davidson, Cushman, Linkmobile, E-Z- Go and Club Car entered the market place and the first gas powered units were making the scene by 1957. Most of the early models were tricycle designs with a tiller steering bar, no roof and a single front wheel. Many carts operated long before paved cart paths were installed. Golf's traditionalists considered these paths a blight on the course and that slowed the movement toward powered carts. But when President Eisenhower was seen riding in a golf cart, that changed the perception to the playing public and the evolution to playing the game while riding was unstoppable.

Trolleys or golf bag carts (or push carts) also were not popular until after WWII. Till then there were usually plenty of caddies available at country clubs and even public access courses. But in 1945, an inventor

SPIRITED STYLING, RUGGED POWER...
performance you can take for granted!

Link-mobile . . . this golf car scampers across hilly terrain, grades up to 35° — delivers speeds to 10 mph! Automotive muffler makes operation quiet. Foam rubber seats, exceptional stability assure passenger comfort . . . and easy-handling controls, automatic transmission make driving a breeze! Best of all, maintenance is held to the barest practical minimum. Husky 7 hp gasoline engine assures low-cost, uninterrupted service — no battery recharge nuisance, up to 72 holes on a 2-gallon tankful of gas! Caddy Master tires protect valuable turf. And the car keeps its good looks! Spike-proof matting protects dash and floor . . . easy-to-clean fiber glass body retains its handsome appearance, color is molded in. Wide choice — both standard and special colors. Write, wire or call for details.

Link·mobile®
DIVISION
NORTHWESTERN MOTOR COMPANY, EAU CLAIRE, WIS.

Linkmobile golf cart ad from 1960s.

A 1947 pull cart made by Bag Boy Co., it was one of first to hit American golf courses.

named Bruce Williamson from Portland, Oregon, fashioned a simple pull cart from some lawn mower wheels and a simple folding chassis. Eventually, after some acquisitions and mergers it would become the Bag Boy Golf Cart Company and they are still building carts today. Many other companies now make pulling and pushing models and are integral to the game on most courses today and used by most players in the British Isles.

On the Horizon— 1960s and Beyond

With the advent of golf carts after World War II, there were fewer courses using caddies. The local city Caddy Championship lost attendance and eventually drifted away. In its hay day it provided the city with champions of the highest quality and one, Johnny Fischer, even made it to the pinnacle of national golf with a US Amateur Championship. By the 1960s, almost all new courses were built with cart paths and the sport changed to a riding game for the golfing public. The design of courses with carts also provided the opportunity to locate holes where the next tee was remote from the previous green and so made it more difficult for players to walk. But even with the pressures of these new course designs, today's caddies remain a valuable part of the game at all playing levels, as they learn communication and work skills and command a front row seat to the game of golf.

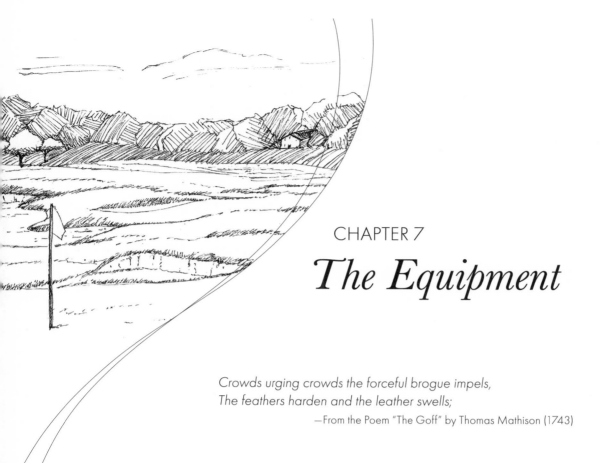

CHAPTER 7
The Equipment

Crowds urging crowds the forceful brogue impels,
The feathers harden and the leather swells;

—From the Poem "The Goff" by Thomas Mathison (1743)

Cincinnati and Golf Equipment

For a period, our city was the center of golf club manufacturing for the entire world. Two local companies were players in a growing market as technology improved from the hand-made clubs made by our first Scottish immigrant Professionals like Robert White and Archie Simpson. The country's golfers turned from hickory shafts to more predictable and durable steel. And the increasing golf population required mass production while still maintaining quality and performance. Meanwhile, golf ball technology improved, accessories like bags became lighter, clothing became more durable, casual and comfortable and new fabrics and designs for equipment were introduced. Cincinnati was in the middle of all of these changes and eventually was chosen to make the one of the most coveted symbols of golf championships.

The Golf Ball

The game of golf was on its heels by the mid-1850s. Shepherds and townspeople were still playing with golf balls made of beechwood but the better play-

ers needed the control and distance available from the "featherie." Prices of these special golf balls had risen to half a crown as fewer experts had the skills of stuffing a small leather pouch with duck feathers, and then soaking, stuffing, sewing, drying and forming until a ball was available for use. Because of the costs, by the middle of the nineteenth century interest in the game had shrunk and there were only seventeen golf clubs left in the British Isles. But a new material arrived on the scene by accident and saved the game.

There are many stories about who discovered Gutta Percha as a material for golf balls. After much debate, it centered on three possible Scotsmen and the evidence finally determined it was Dr. Robert Patterson in 1845 and a statue he had shipped from India packed in chips of this gummy material from a tree in Malaysia. Dr. Patterson had the forethought to mold this material

Featherie golf ball, leather and filled with duck feathers from 1700–1880.

Dead Ball May Cause St. Andrews Club To Lose Grip

The golfing world now is all aquiver.

The Royal and Ancient club of St. Andrews, regarded as the parent golf body of the world, intends to standardize golf balls. It hopes to return to the days of the floater, a ball which at the most can be driven 120 yards, altho the great Vardon at one time drove one 150 yards.

The floater, a ball generally used in England, has not been known in America for many years. In this country various brands of rubber-cored balls are used, which carry twice as far as the English floater. Canadian and American golf clubs usually follow the rules of St. Andrews, but if that club adopts the floater as its standard ball there will be a parting of the ways and St. Andrews will commit golfing suicide as far as its influence on this continent is concerned.

The American golfer wants distance to his drives and the cry is for balls that can travel far.

American pros are a unit in denouncing the St. Andrews attempt to standardize the golf ball. Arthur Bogrs of Losantiville, Alec Gerard of Hyde Park, and the [Bropny] brothers join their brother pros in favoring the rubber-cored ball. They ridicule the attempt of St. Andrews to adopt the floater as the standard ball.

NORTHSIDE'S BIG JOB

The Elmwood football team, which has been defeating all comers, will play the Northside eleven at Senate Park, Cumminsville, Sunday.

Several new players will make their debut with Northside, including Aherns, fullback, who is touted as a star. Northside will practise at Hoffner field Friday night.

In 1919, the R&A at St. Andrew's proposed a return from the Haskell ball and to an old design called "the floater" that could only be driven a little over 100 yards. This found a lot of resistance in America where players wanted more distance which put pressure on courses to get longer and buy more adjoining real estate.

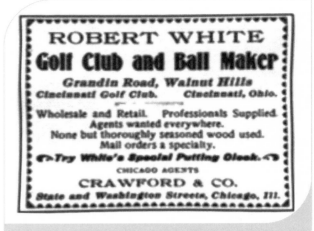

An 1896 ad for Robert White clubs and balls at the Cincinnati Golf Club.

erties to add length to particular holes or alter layouts to squeeze 6,000+ yards to hold the Haskell ball. As the golf ball saved the game it also changed it at the same time and by 1919 the R&A was proposing going back to the old golf ball and its 100 yard drives. The conflict of technology versus the physical limits of the courses was just beginning.

The Golf Club

The development and manufacturing of the golf club also has a distinct local flavor. During the day when the featherie ball ruled the game all the clubs were hand-made and most had wooden heads. An iron headed club or two might be in the bag but it was mainly used to get out of ruts or other bad lies. These early iron heads were crude and heavy and very tough on the featherie so they were used infrequently. With the advent of the gutta percha ball, an iron was becoming the club of choice for approaches to the green and when accuracy was needed. The new guttie ball could take the beating and the irons were becoming more durable too. When furnished with grooves or some other face pattern, the iron could impart backspin on the guttie and make it travel farther and more accurately.

The wooden clubs in early days had shafts of ash, greenheart or, the pre-

Early Haskell ball, circa 1900–1960s.

into the shape of a golf ball and the rest was history. It was inexpensive, more durable and more playable than the featherie. The reduced cost of gutties had helped spur a growth of the game for the rest of the century.

But as soon as the guttie ball was getting comfortable on Cincinnati's earliest courses, more innovation was arriving on the scene and this time from northern Ohio instead of Scotland. A couple of employees of the B.F. Goodrich Tire company in Akron, Ohio, came upon the idea of starting with a rubber core and then adding rubber band windings. Coburn Haskell and Bertram G. Work secured the patent for the company and the game would never be the same. The new ball was quickly called the Haskell ball and even though prices were higher than the guttie, the advantages were overpowering. The gutta percha cover was soon replaced by tree sap tapped from a South American tree called balata. This was the ball of choice well past 1960 in Cincinnati.

The net effect of the Haskell ball (forty yards farther on average per shot than the guttie) as it became prevalent in the early part of the last century was that golf courses in general were too short. All country clubs were scurrying to buy adjacent prop-

ferred, hickory. Ninety per-cent of the clubheads locally were dogwood but beech, and hickory were also used and persimmon was just starting to be the wood of choice. The United States was a major exporter to Great Britain of hickory and persimmon logs so most of its raw materials left the USA and returned as finished clubs. As the American market grew, it was a matter of time before local companies started to make the clubs themselves rather than exporting the wood. In 1898, the *Spalding Golf Guide* advertised that their woods were "made by Scotch (sic) and English club makers and entirely hand-made." Clubs were priced between $1.00 and $2.00 each (guttie balls sold for $3.00 per dozen). By 1904, Spalding no longer made any references to the hand-made craftsmanship of the British Isles as manufacturing had moved back to America and now clubs were being exported instead of raw materials.

After WWI, persimmon wood heads, brass plates on bottom, back weights and other features made woods more in the image we know today. Irons, made by drop forging techniques used in the automobile and other industries were now made with more precision and cost effective. Costs for woods about $4.00 to $8.00 and irons about $4.50 each.

In the evolution of the golf club, one local company stayed on the front lines for decades. When golf club manufacturing was brought to the States, there were three companies that built most of the clubs. One went out of business quickly, Spalding was the second and the other company started up I-75 in Dayton, Ohio. The Dayton Shoe Last Company began in 1829 in response to the need for new shoe manufacturing industry forming in Cincinnati and St.

Early club making operation.

Louis. Shoe lasts were the molds, modeled from a human foot, over which a cobbler or shoe maker would build shoes. They were made of persimmon or other local woods and the business grew quickly as Cincinnati in particular became a center for the shoe industry. The Dayton company also designed and built the first lathe machine to manufacture the lasts and this would be very important to another business. These same lathes would still be in use a hundred years later to make golf club heads.

In 1874, more partners were added to the Dayton company including a Scottish gentleman named John McGregor and a local businessman and sportsman named Edward Canby. Soon McGregor longed for the weather of his homeland and sold his shares but, before doing so, convinced Canby to go to Scotland

A shoe last as made by the Dayton Shoe Last Company.

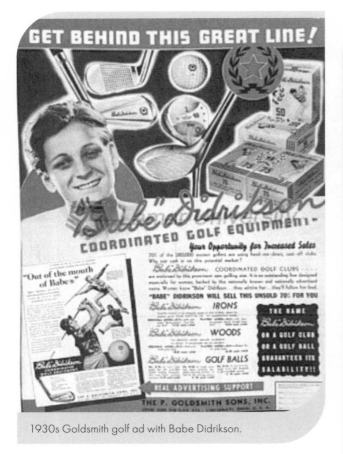

1930s Goldsmith golf ad with Babe Didrikson.

Toney Penna was the Professional who was the first MacGregor rep on the tour. He was also an innovator in bags, shoes and other equipment designs for the company.

play the game of golf. The net result was that Canby returned to the United States addicted to golf and convinced it had a real future in America. Canby had been searching for a product that could alleviate the ups and downs of the shoe last business while using their particular woodworking skills and marketing. Ironically, they had tried to diversify into the bowling business to build lanes and pins but ran head on into another Cincinnati company, Brunswick, that was already dominating that business. Eighty years in the future those companies would merge.

In 1897 the renamed Crawford, McGregor and Canby Company made its first golf club. At the same time a blacksmith and "cleek maker" from Scotland named Robert White Sr. visited the offices to show them the iron clubs he made. White's son (also named Robert White) at that time was the Professional at Cincinnati Golf Club. Canby's company added a forge shop to make iron clubs also.

By 1910, they were the world's largest maker of shoe lasts but now also exported over 100,000 wood heads and hickory shafts to Great Britain. There they were then assembled under different company names and many resold to America. But now the heads and shafts were also being sold direct to American Club Professionals who would assemble them in their club Pro Shops for sale to the members.

As WWI approached, their golf business shrank but the need for shoes increased and the company was able to survive. In the 1920s, MacGregor (with a new spelling for the name) did introduce the first set of matched finished clubs with steel shafts. By 1929 the meteoric growth of golf in the United States had resulted in 5,000 more golf courses being built right before the stock market crash in October and MacGregor's business soared. But almost as quickly, the Depression

MacGregor Plant on Spring Grove Avenue, 1947.

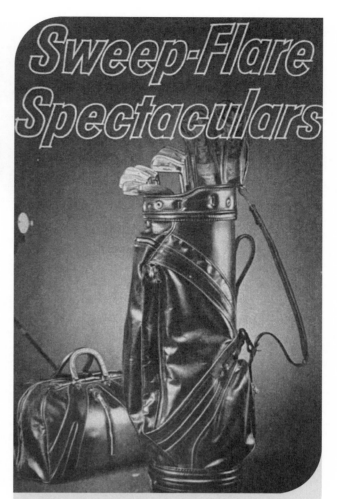

Sweep-Flare Spectaculars

Ad for MacGregor's innovative sweep flare bag with ball pouch built in.

deepened and the golf market floundered. By 1934, MacGregor was close to bankruptcy and was sold to a Cincinnati company, P. Goldsmith Co. The Goldsmith Company was one of the Big Four of the athletic goods industries. Goldsmith had their own small golf club making business and their advertisements featured a great woman player, Babe Didrikson. Unfortunately they had had little marketing or sales success. They were led by Phil Goldsmith who was playing golf at Hillcrest CC in Bond Hill.

Phil Goldsmith's father (also Phil Goldsmith) had been a Bohemian butcher who emigrated to the United States and tried to start a dry goods store in Chicago. He later moved to Covington, Kentucky, and started a five and dime store and eventually shifted to making toy dolls. Finally, in 1897, he picked up some scraps of leather from his doll factory and sewed them together to make a baseball. He was convinced that baseball would eventually be the national sport. They started making about six balls per day by hand and soon the doll business was forgotten and they made only baseballs. That led them to being a major athletic goods company. When they purchased MacGregor, they were one of the country's leaders in the sales of leather athletic equipment—football helmets and pads, baseball gloves, athletic shoes, etc. They were also known as the "Tailors of the Major Leagues" as they provided the uniforms to twelve of the existing sixteen teams, including the Reds.

The merger of the MacGregor and Goldsmith businesses eventually provided the financial strength to support the technical skills of the club making experts. This acquisition by Goldsmith also opened a new direction in marketing and promotion. Mac-

Gregor had fallen behind Spalding and Wilson and needed a jolt. First, they hired Tommy Armour, at that time the Head Professional at Medinah in Chicago, to design a new top of the line professional set of clubs called the Silver Scot Tourney. Then they hired another Chicago Club Professional, Toney Penna, to represent MacGregor on the Tour. Penna in turn then recommended three young, promising Professionals—Ben Hogan, Byron Nelson and Jimmy Demaret—to their staff. The three were signed for a total of $5,000.

MacGregor's young playing staff started cashing checks immediately as Nelson won the 1939 US Open and 1940 PGA. Demaret, a fan favorite with his easy demeanor and flashy wardrobe, won the 1940 Masters. Unbelievably Hogan was the last one to win his first Major but many more were to follow. This coup of the MacGregor Big Three was only facing

Johnny Miller at the 1973 Open.

MacGregor, Johnny Miller and the 1973 US Open

When Johnny Miller won the 1973 Open with that amazing 63 in the final round, in his bag he carried a 1961 MacGregor MT Driver, a 1945 MacGregor Tommy Armour 3-wood, a 1941 MacGregor Tommy Armour 4-wood and 1945 Tommy Armour 915T 2-7 Irons. In addition, he played the MacGregor Tourney 101 Compression ball also being played by Jack Nicklaus. Imagine playing and

Johnny Miller's golf bag for the 1973 Open contained some MacGregor clubs that were over thirty-two years old.

winning the US Open with a twelve-year-old Driver and some clubs as many as thirty-two years old in the bag! Such was the quality of MacGregor clubs at the time and still coveted by collectors today.

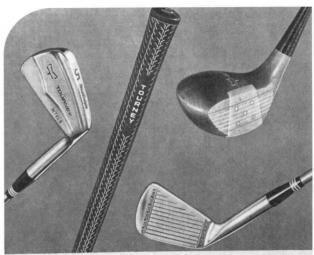

MacGregor MT Tourney Ladies' Clubs

The very finest ladies' golf clubs available. Fitted with MacGregor's Tourney Action shaft . . . made in your choice of 2 special ladies' patterns to give just the right amount of flex for extra distance performance. Top grade persimmon woods in rich Golden Oak finish are impregnated and weather sealed with 5 coats of special sealer. Irons give extra yardage, because club head weight is centered throughout the hitting area. And you get greater accuracy and improved hand action with "Built-in Forward Press," which automatically places hands ahead of ball at address, in "Power Position." Grips are all weather premium Tourney rubber.

And next time you tee up, make sure you're using the distance champion, MacGregor's DX Tourney golf ball, winner of 6 consecutive PGA distance driving contests. The DX Tourney will improve your game, too.

These prominent L.P.G.A. players are members of the MacGregor Advisory Staff—Kathy Ahern • Marlene Hagge Lesley Holbert • Ruth Jessen • Sharon Miller Barbara Romack • Louise Suggs

MacGregor
THE GREATEST NAME IN GOLF
CONSUMER DIVISION • BRUNSWICK CORPORATION
I-75 AT JIMSON ROAD • CINCINNATI, OHIO 45215

MacGregor also added a line of women's clubs very early and had many great players like Babe Didrikson Zaharias and Louise Suggs on their staff.

competition from Sam Snead at Wilson. Slowly the company began to turn things around through the years of WWII in spite of cutbacks in tournaments and course closings.

After the war, MacGregor moved to Cincinnati and occupied a plant on Spring Grove Ave. They started marketing their own golf balls, bags and other related products and the golf business exploded as the WWII veterans returned to civilian life. On the tour, Professionals were using more MacGregor woods and irons than all other manufacturers combined. In addition, Toney Penna was a force on the local and state Open events and MacGregor catapulted to the top of the golf world. Penna proved to be an innovative manager as well as he introduced the MT line of clubs (still in demand today by collectors) and the new Sweep Flare bag design that became number one for many years and still in use today.

Eventually there were a few hiccups as their golf ball was not up to modern standards and eventually

Jack Nicklaus and Johnny Miller sporting MacGregor clubs, bags and shoes.

touring Professionals like Ben Hogan quit playing it. Soon Demaret, Doug Ford, Dow Finsterwald and others followed. By 1957, MacGregor was acquired by Brunswick, the bowling company, as part of a big expansion. Under the new management, MacGregor moved their Headquarters and some manufacturing to Evendale, near the GE plant, and opened several other plants nationwide. This rapid growth had its own problems as Toney Penna left to start his own business

in 1964 and quality became an issue for clubs built in the other locations.

But after all of the years, the MacGregor Golf Co. still remains a beacon for American golf club manufacturing. Today the irons and woods made in Dayton from 1939–1942 and in Cincinnati from 1947–1955 remain some of the most sought after and valuable items on the classic club marketplace. Under the craftsmanship of Howard Delaney and his fellow clubmakers, the

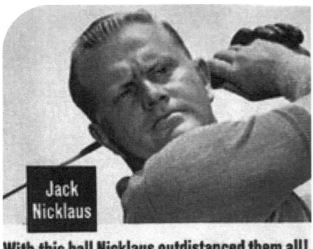

MacGregor golf ball ad with Jack Nicklaus.

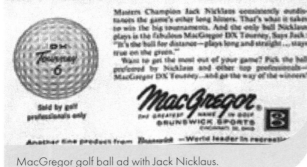

A 1900 Spalding ad for golf shoes.

Jack Nicklaus presents the Green Jacket to Gay Brewer, former Assistant Pro at Cincinnati Country Club, for his win at the 1967 Masters.

The Masters and Hamilton Tailors

In 1967, Cincinnati clothing firm Hamilton Tailoring Company would become the primary supplier for the green wool blazers that are emblematic of the Master's Champion. The company started in 1909 and from their operation on East McMillan Street, they would take about a month to tailor the coat that is worn only by Augusta National club members and winners of the tournament. Gay Brewer's one stroke victory earned that first Cincinnati-made Hamilton Tailoring jacket in 1967. Ironically, Brewer had been an Assistant Professional at Cincinnati Country Club in the 1950s and is presented the jacket by 1966 winner and Ohio native Jack Nicklaus.

persimmon wood was optimized for density and feel. Their innovations in oil-hardening of the persimmon heads, adding the first synthetic and rubber grips, designing special forging equipment for better irons and dampening of steel shafts and face inserts on wood clubs placed them at the top of club design and manufacturing in the United States for several decades.

A total of thirty-nine Majors were won by Mac-Gregor staff players between Tommy Armour in 1927 and Bob Rosburg in 1959, including twenty-seven after the company moved to Cincinnati in 1947. And there were ten top tour money winners during that period. Under the innovation and leadership of people like Toney Penna, Hugo and Phil Goldsmith, Clarence Rickey, amazing craftsmen like Howard Delaney and Art Emerson, consulting players like Jack Nicklaus, Byron Nelson, Ben Hogan, Tom Weiskopf, Tom Watson, Curtis Strange, Johnny Miller, Ben Crenshaw, Louise Suggs and others, MacGregor and Cincinnati were the center of the world's golf club manufacturing from 1947 through the 1970s.

Accessories

Any bag or device to hold clubs did not appear in early photographs and paintings of golfers and it was not until the last decade of the 1800s that a patent was

Women's golf attire in the early 1890s.

Women's summer golf attire at Clifton Golf Club, 1905. Showing the ankles eliminated the problem of mud staining the skirts.

taken out on what we would now call a golf bag. Before that, a caddy would carry a handful of clubs or wear them loosely in a strap over his shoulder or maybe in a burlap sack. The first golf bag patents in Great Britain appeared around 1892 and included a pouch for golf balls and even a tripod attachment much as seen on today's carry bags. The first golf cart (or trolley) that could be pushed or pulled was patented in 1897 but it would take another fifty years for that concept to take hold on both sides of the Atlantic.

Most golf bags in the early twentieth century were simple and about 4" diameter and, like the cars of that era, they were limited in color selection. For golf bags it was usually tan or brown. By 1920 or so, the diameter increased to 6"–9" to carry more clubs. Most were made from canvas and duck though there were some made with leather.

In 1939, the USGA limited the number of golf clubs in the bag to fourteen. Before that there was no limit so it was difficult to build a standard bag size and this change allowed for more standardization. The same innovation that was a hallmark of the Goldsmith and MacGregor companies spilled over to golf bags and other products.

When the two companies merged, Goldsmith was a premier uniform maker and so color and style were important to their design team. During a visit to a Goldsmith plant, Toney Penna noticed how they used colorful jockey silks and nylon to fashion football uniforms and he immediately ordered some brightly colored bags for himself as well as tour players Louise Suggs and Jimmy Demaret. They were an immediate hit on the tour and with experimentation on lighter materials like kangaroo leather and a brand-new Sweep Flare shape, MacGregor became the preeminent bag. The design has stood as the classic in shape, with the bag pouch built into the bag rather than being attached, and still used today for almost all golf bags.

Golf shoes also were slow to develop with the game. Early players wore boots and brogans but an article in a Scottish magazine in 1857 suggested that small nails or similar materials be added to the soles for more traction. When spiked shoes were introduced in the 1890s, Greenskeepers immediately reacted to the damage to greens and other turf. But that did not stop most golfers and advertisements for various

Harry Vardon in knickers in the 1900s.

GOLF CAPES.

Charming Creations, in Chic and Dashing Effects and Original Designs.

$7.50, $8.50, $10, $12

An 1898 Mabley & Carew ad for women's golf capes. Some ads for golf capes appeared five years before golf was played in Cincinnati.

corduroy with woolen caps and probably tackety boots with nails or similar nubs to gain traction. This dress was basically copied by the American counterparts though the early red coats of Cincinnati Golf Club were evidence that some classical dress had made it across the Atlantic.

The mentions of golf in Cincinnati newspapers in the early 1890s actually featured the new fashion of women's golf capes. Almost five years before the first golf ball hit the bottom of the flower pot buried on Grandin road, the local women were buying the fashionable long coats for fall and winter. Broader at the shoulder and more room in the sleeves it was suitable, if not manageable, for the early woman golfer. Men were also in tweeds with knee-breeches, stockings—some with argyle plaids, and coat tailored for shoulder movement. With the prescribed starched collar shirt and tie, it was the knickerbocker suit, called nickers for short.

Harry Vardon was the first Professional to sport the suit and soon nickers, coat and tie were the accepted dress for the American player. Later in the 1920s the Plus-Fours were introduced as a variation of the knickers. They were called that because they were bloused four inches below the knee and gave more freedom of movement for the golfer. Later, Payne Stewart revived the wearing of Plus-Fours during his career.

Comfort moved slowly on the golf course. With the Depression in the 1930s, woman players were finally wearing pants and even shorts though this was not prevalent until after WWII. Most women's attire leaned to classic skirt/blouse combinations or a shirt dress and both usually worn with a cardigan sweater. Men also moved from the nickers into flannel trousers, usually white or gray. Men were slower to accepting shorts on the course. Actually, men in shorts started during WWI in Bermuda but it took a little time for

rubber or metal studs that could be added to normal street shoes or the special shoes with thicker soles to take the screw connections. In Cincinnati, MacGregor also was a major supplier of golf shoes including the familiar saddle shoes worn by Nicklaus, Watson and Miller at the time.

Apparel

By the time the game had reached Cincinnati, the proper golfer had become more casual than his original Scottish predecessor. In the days of the featherie ball, the game had become mostly played by the aristocracy and top hats, swallow tail coats and breeches were the norm. Professionals and other commoners of the time would play in the traditional tweeds or

In 1916, women's golf attire was stylish and slightly more comfortable.

The athleticism of Arnold Palmer became the style in the 1960s.

The golf dress for which Martha West is famous. Washable pure silk in white, aqua, petal pink or maize. 10 to 44. 16.95 Mail orders promptly filled.

Martha West
SPORTSWEAR ORIGINATOR

Women's fashion for the golf course in the 1930s and 1940s.

that concept to work its way through society and onto the golf links. Tennis players were quicker to shorter women's skirts and men in shorts for play in the 1930s but golfers remained almost always in street wear with minor adaptions for athletic comfort.

During WWII, shorts became more in vogue but men mostly played in polo type shirt and light weight slacks. The snap brim or Panama hat as worn by Sam Snead also came into vogue and more flamboyance with colors as worn by Jimmy Demaret. After the war, the knitted golf shirt as invented by Lacoste for tennis and in all colors with golf shoes dyed in all colors for players like Doug Sanders were in vogue. But soon the Arnold Palmer look of cotton shirt, khaki or other colored trousers and oxford shoes emphasized athleticism.

On the Horizon

In the mid-1960s, a new synthetic resin, named *Surlyn*, was introduced by du Pont, as were other new *urethan* blends for golf ball covers. Because of durability, these new materials soon displaced balata. Golf balls came to be classified as either two-piece, three-piece, or four-piece balls according to the number of layered components. These basic materials continue to be used in modern balls, with further advances in technology creating balls that can be customized to a player's strengths and weaknesses, and even allowing for the combination of characteristics.

MacGregor would enter a contract with Jack Nicklaus in 1962 to produce the dealer line of Golden Bear woods and irons and eventually the exclusive Pro set called the Jack Nicklaus VIP model. Jack Nicklaus and Clark Johnson took the reins of the company in 1978. From 1973–79, MacGregor Tour Pros won many majors as Tom Weiskopf, Tom Watson and David Graham were on staff. In 1982

Howard Delaney, MacGregor's master clubmaker would leave and start Cincinnati Golf where he would continue to build quality persimmon clubs. He was elected to the Professional Clubmakers' Hall of Fame. For almost two decades the skill of club makers like Howard Delaney made Cincinnati the center of golf club technology and sales for the whole world.

CHAPTER 8

The Private Clubs and Courses

Cincinnati as a golfing center is up to standard with ten courses in good shape and patronized by enthusiastic golfers. The membership of these clubs amounts to about two thousand.

—L.C. Rose, Elberon Golf Club, 1905 *Spalding's Official Golf Guide*

Introduction
Country Clubs and Pioneers

The word "club" is Old English in origin and dated back to the seventeenth century. It mostly described a gathering place for those of common interest. Members would use taverns and coffee-houses as meeting sites on any number of subjects. Eventually one of those early common interests was golf and the first golf club house was formed (with attached golf links)

Skeet and trap shooting were popular at most early country clubs. Maketewah Country Club removed their trap shooting facilities to build a driving range in the 1950s.

in Leith Scotland in 1768. The oldest surviving club-house is at St. Andrew's and built in 1854. In Cincinnati, the first introductions to golf were in private clubs and called golf clubs or country clubs. The latter were a new phenomenon that involved a remote location—usually for day trips—and included recreation facilities like hiking, swimming and other outdoor sports.

Though the country clubs were new on the scene in the 1890s, Americans had historically gravitated to organizations to help solve problems, improve society and to socialize. Organizations of all types were able to enhance American individualism. There had been secret societies and guilds and other organizations in Europe but nowhere were clubs and societies so prevalent as in America. The clubs could be political, social, athletic, musical, religious or ethnic in nature. The fact that golf required a collective effort to acquire large tracts of real estate and hire support staff, the formation of country clubs was a natural part of the evolution of the game in the United States.

At the same time, the only other vehicle capable of building and investing in the game would have been local governments but most park boards and city councils were slow to recognize golf as a recreational sport and concentrated more on gardens and space for picnics and outings. The City of Cincinnati did maintain the golf links at Burnet Woods and Fernbank for a while after the initial private efforts failed in 1905 but it would be 1914 before there was a commitment to public golf with the construction of Avon Fields.

The country club was also a new vehicle for an expanding segment of the population. This growing group of entrepreneurs, businessmen, lawyers, and others were sporting new wealth created by an expanding economy in what was called the Progressive Era (1890–1920) in America. Members of this new middle class searched for space away from cities and stale air and where this new phenomenon called leisure time could be enjoyed. Golf did not create country clubs in the beginning but both arrived on the scene about the same time and it was a perfect fit.

The country clubs usually offered opportunities for games of all types and golf was only one of many available. But it was not long before golf itself became the catalyst for the founding of the club rather than vice versa. In Cincinnati in the 1890s, groups of players would start a club by convening in a nearby pasture or other open area and start—normally without any formal instruction—to play the game. Later, into the twentieth century, organizers no longer needed the pasture but would plan the club like any other business endeavor and acquire land and build a staff. Sometimes it would be the leadership of one person and sometimes a group but the country club and golf would remain partners as the game grew in the region.

The Game Begins
Cincinnati Golf Club (1895)

Thomas Mack, a representative of a metals company, moved to Cincinnati from Scotland and interested a group that included Nicholas Longworth, Charles Hinkle and Edmund Harrison in "the Scottish game." Together in 1893 they laid out a five-hole course and then a nine-hole course on Edwards and Grandin Roads in the suburb called East Walnut Hills. Many others joined them and future US President William Howard Taft, then a local judge, was named the first Chairman of the Cincinnati Golf Club (CGC) in 1895.

The members immediately began a search throughout the city and Northern Kentucky for a suitable

Cincinnati Country Club clubhouse. (Photo circa 1908)

site for their permanent course. The next year they hired Robert White, a Professional from Scotland, to run the operation and he laid out a new nine-hole course farther up Grandin Road and then expanded the course to eighteen-holes in 1897. When Cincinnati Country Club (CCC) was organized in 1902 it built a beautiful clubhouse at the site seen today at the course. CCC also owned the former dairy farm where the CGC course was situated and then continued their lease so play and improvements could continue for the golfing members.

The golf property had its own small improvised clubhouse that included "an annex in the back for chickens." It also served as a shelter house for caddies, a stable for the horses and other varied needs until eventually replaced in 1916. During that time buckets of water were brought in for bathing and lighting was from oil lamps and candles. Play was on what appeared to be "forty acres of hopeless hazard" and it would be a few years before players could clear all of the brush, plant seed and rid themselves of the dairy cows still grazing on the property.

The Cincinnati Country Club and Cincinnati Golf Club eventually merged in 1924 after a tenuous relationship that included a threat by CGC to move to Mt. Washington. The merger was a welcomed relief for those who were members at both clubs. During this early period Cincinnati Golf Club was the main communication between the city and the rest of the golfing world. Matches were arranged with country clubs in St. Louis, Pittsburgh, Chicago and Columbus. The members would board trains for their matches and either spend the night or take a night train back home. Then the club would return the favor and host their opponents. Nationally, the

Play at Cincinnati Country Club. (Photo circa 1930)

game was spreading quickly as more clubs were being formed and the competitive nature of the game lent itself to matches between clubs and cities.

Before the turn of the century, three CGC members (Lucy Herron, Clara Longworth and Mrs. R.I. Carter) were playing in the US Women's Amateur in Philadelphia. Other players from the club would play in national events and almost of all the great amateur players in the city at the turn of the century were playing at CGC. And when the great players from the international and national golfing world visited the city they headed first to Grandin Road. The facilities made great headway and the club was ready to think bigger and become a factor on the national scene.

In 1900 the great Harry Vardon visited for an exhibition match with former Club Professional Bob White and local amateurs. During that visit, Vardon set the new course record of 66 at CGC. He had already won three British Opens by then and would add a US Open title later in 1900. In a day when a 200-yard drive was memorable, Vardon could hit his tee shot 240 yards with the old hickory shafts and the new Spalding golf balls he was representing. Endorsement deals started early in the game of golf. Vardon would return in later years along with Ted Ray and other famous golfers of that era and Bobby Jones and many great players were frequent visitors to the Grandin Road links.

That first main eighteen-hole course was built on ninety acres and totaled about 3,800 yards. In those days, the holes each bore a name so Walnut Grove (Hole #6) paralleled today's Hole #2 and measured 333 yards. Other hole names included Hyde Park Corner, Esper-

anza, The Alp and Rookwood. The course expanded to about 4800 yards in 1908 when more property was added north to Observatory Road. Some of those holes are similar to the present layout with a couple of the familiar tee shots across Bedford Avenue.

Cincinnati GC was blessed with three exceptional Professionals of their own in their early years. Bob White was the first and, though only there a few years, laid out the first course at Cincinnati GC as well as building another course at Avondale Athletic Club and most probably at Clifton Golf Club. He would leave Cincinnati for Chicago and eventually become the first President of the PGA in 1916 and his design resume would include over twenty more courses in Pennsylvania, Maryland and Delaware. Harry Reddie replaced White in 1898 and Tom McCormick was Professional in 1899 until Phil Honeyman brought his playing skills to Grandin Road in 1900. He also designed and led that first expansion of the eighteen-hole layout in 1908.

In 1916 Otto Hackbarth became the fifth Club Professional bringing world class playing and club making skills. He would remain at Cincinnati Country Club until 1950. Otto was one of the new wave of American players coming to the fore in international competition and won the first Ohio Open ever played. One of four brothers who would become professionals, he was born in Wisconsin and would also go on to win the Senior PGA Tournament in 1940. He was also renowned for his invention of the "Hackbarth Putter" used by many players including US Open and US Amateur winner Chick Evans in all of his victories.

The course would go through another major redesign in 1925 and that effort was led by member Harold W. Nichols who expanded the routing to 5,900 yards. The course has always provided many challenging shots to the small greens where chipping, pitching and putting skills were especially needed. In the 1960s, property acquisitions expanded the course close to its present configuration. And from a single clay flower pot sunk into the turf on Grandin Road in 1895 for Hole #1, the city had its first and oldest golf facility firmly in place. And a membership that would persevere and continue to build the game in Cincinnati.

Cincinnati GC and Cincinnati CC have hosted two Majors. These include the 1905 Western Open and the 1941 Women's Western Open. The Women's

Barbed wire kept cattle off of the greens of the Wyoming Country Club before the Tom Bendelow course was built; similar barriers were in effect at many courses especially those where livestock kept the grass managed.

Western Open was the de facto women's national championship as the first USGA Women's Open did not occur until 1946 and the WWGA event remained a Women's Major until 1957. The year's previous winner, Babe Didrikson Zaharias, did not participate but the field included all of the other great women professionals and amateurs of that era. Amazingly, eleven Cincinnati women headed by Met champion Dolly Schildmiller, made it into Match Play. In the 1941 finals, Professional Patty Berg won the first of her seven Women's Western titles by beating Losantiville CC amateur Olga Stashun Weil 6&5 in the finals.

William Groesbeck of Cincinnati GC won the very first Men's Met championship in 1910 and won again in 1916. Other Met winners include Templeton Briggs (1915), DeWitt Balch (1920, 1921), Douglas Hill (1926), John Wood II (1955, 1957) and Dave Hall (1960). Lucy Herron was runner-up in the US Women's Amateur in 1901 at Baltusrol CC in New Jersey.

Women's Met winners include Ella Banning (1916, 1919), Rhea Geilfus Johnson (1920, 1921), Caroline Painter Wilson (1922, 1926), Martha Kinsey (1925, 1931) and Sally Christensen (1965).

Finding a Foothold—Success at the Turn of the Century

As the calendar turned to 1900, so did American vision and energy. The controversial Spanish-American War was over but it yielded more territory for expansion and the country was getting up a head of steam as the automobile was starting to push horse and mule carts off the road. Teddy Roosevelt became President in 1901 and the country followed his lead for more exercise and outdoor activities. The first manned flight by the Wright brothers would be in 1903, and American engineers and builders would take on the Panama Canal in 1904 after failures from the French.

Golf was still rudimentary at all of its local locations. Terrace Park CC tied a cow overnight on the 'green' and depended on the bovine's grazing skills to get ready for play the next day. There was finally agreement in USGA Rules that the cup should be 4 ¼" diameter and at least 4" deep but this was conveniently the dimensions of a 32-oz. tin can and that was still used at many locations. Barbed wire was used at Wyoming CC to keep cattle off their greens. A herd of sheep was used to manage the rough at Avon Fields GC and the Pillars. greens had to be cut every day rain or shine or else grass would be too thick for play. The USGA minimum size for greens was 120 ft^2 so a grazing cow or hand lawn mowers could handle most locations.

The game still continued to compete for real estate. The original 1880 idea for the traditional country club was a remote site in the country for day trips. But it was soon found that golf was a game was well suited for mornings or afternoons away from work and so players needed better and quicker access. Transportation except on trains was slow so courses needed to be located near work centers and close to the city. Unfortunately, golf also required large tracts of land and there was a conflict for playing space as

Wyoming Country Club clubhouse. (Photo circa 1920)

the city grew in area and began to annex its suburbs. Farms that had been located on the city's boundaries were prime potential locations for golf courses but country clubs had to compete with new subdivisions and factory sites as the city expanded.

With only the Cincinnati Golf Club in its permanent location by the turn of the century there would still be other sites required to cement golf into the local environs. Some of these early sites would move down the street or up the road or buy extra adjacent land but for most purposes they were the next wave of solid locations still in place today.

Wyoming CC and Golf in the Valley

Courses located out a little farther from the city center like Wyoming CC were immune from that first twentieth century wave of urban expansion. Wyoming was an offshoot of the efforts by William Cooper Procter and George Kinsey to build a club in Glendale (see Ghost Courses). By 1897, Kinsey had organized Wyoming Golf Club as a six-hole layout near his little farm in the village and then the next year began play on twenty-two acres leased from a dairy farm on Mt. Pleasant Avenue. The players shared their nine-hole layout with the grazing cattle who kept fairways at manageable heights.

The club continued to grow and flourish and by 1912, the members had a decision to make. Still a nine-hole course, the club had to look at options for property acquisition and whether to expand to eighteen holes. Tom Bendelow was called in from Chicago to look at the issues. At the same time, he was consulting in town with Elberon GC members about some property to build Western Hills CC and working with Richard Cass at Hamilton County CC as they built their course in Bond Hill.

Wyoming CC was still playing on their twenty-two-acre site and Bendelow's options were to build an amazing nine-hole layout or to squeeze the eighteen holes onto the fifty-three additional acres now available after a land purchase. This was nicely situated only a block from the street car line. Bendelow knew he could build a fine nine-hole course on the property with a length of 3400 yards and provide a challenge to the new Haskell ball (see "Equipment" chapter) being played. This was at a time when even the nation's best courses in the country, like Shinnecock CC and Chi-

An 1897 *Cincinnati Post* caricature of George Kinsey, founder of Wyoming Country Club.

cago Golf Club, were less than 6500 yards for eighteen holes. In addition, there would also be room for a nice clubhouse and tennis courts.

The membership wisely chose to build the quality nine-hole layout. The only decision left was whether to construct the clubhouse within the village limits (and no liquor) or at the far end of the property over the city line so a bar could be installed. Dave Mentiply was recommended by Bendelow to come in as Head Professional, Superintendent and to direct the building of the new course. Mentiply moved to Wyoming CC from his job in Omaha, Nebraska, and started in 1913. He would stay on the job until the 1940s.

The nine-hole layout has been rated as high as 14th Best in the United States and has been the home of some tremendous amateur golfers. Martha Kinsey was a dominant Women's player, winning her first Met in

Losantiville Country Club clubhouse was built in Pleasant Ridge.

1917 and following up with two more while at Cincinnati CC. She was also a great tennis player. Carol Clark and Nancy Porter were team mates on the Wyoming HS Boys Golf Team since there were no opportunities to play competitive golf as a girl. They completed locally for many years including a memorable 1944 Women's Met final when Porter beat Clark in the finals while both were sixteen years old. Martha Kinsey won the Women's Met in 1917 while playing at Wyoming CC. Men's players during this early period included two-time Met winner and former caddy Ralph Shelton (1929, 1932), John Busemeyer (1945) and Dr. Harry Duccilli (1963, 1964, 1966).

Golf Moves from the Race Track to Pleasant Ridge

Before the turn of the twentieth century a small group of Globe-Wernicke executives and friends built a small layout behind the company's Norwood plant. Many were members at Avondale Golf Club and were using the yard for practice but one player, Louis Rauh, visited the nearby Oakley Race Track and thought the infield would be a good spot for a full golf course.

Paired with local banker Simon Kuhn they obtained a lease of the infield for $10 per year per member with the proviso that the course must be closed during the two-week Summer racing season. The new club was incorporated under the name Losantiville Country Club under the leadership of men like Edgar Johnson, Alva Goldsmith Jr., Morris Freiberg and Leo Lowman.

Tom Bendelow laid out the new nine-hole course in 1902 and

three years later was brought back in as the members were losing interest in the race track property and its amenities. After considering many properties, including the present sites of Maketewah CC, Avon Fields GC and Hyde Park CC, the club moved to the present location in Pleasant Ridge. The first ball was hit from the tee in 1907.

That course as laid out by Bendelow was quite a bit different from the remodels that have brought it to its present routing. In those days the holes were given names. For example, the original #16 was called "Church Hill" and was an uphill climb with Pleasant Ridge Presbyterian Church as the backdrop for the green. A school building is now on the site of the green. Other hole names included "Beeches," old hole #9 located and protected by a strand of beech trees, "Toboggan"—old #2, and "Little Lake" old #13 a 137-yard Par 3 over water.

The club was the host of one of the most successful invitational tournaments in the city's golf history. For many years, the Losantiville Pro-Am included huge fields of golfers that counted almost all of the best local players—Pro and Amateur, a large contingent of Tour players like Sam Snead and Tommy Bolt as well as some new Amateur faces like a young Jack Nicklaus.

Throughout the years the club has been home to many great Professionals like Alex Taylor, Nipper Campbell, Arthur Boggs, Harry Boyer and Jim Flick and an outstanding caddy program that itself furnished more good Club Professionals like Clarence Dapper and Frank Gelhot. Ida Goldsmith (1918) won the third Women's Met and Olga Weil won eight of her twelve Met crowns (1945, 1946, 1947, 1948, 1949, 1952, 1953, 1954) while playing out of the Pleasant Ridge confines.

Ft. Mitchell CC A Foothold in Northern Kentucky

Even before the demise of Inverness CC in Newport (see chapter on "Ghost Courses"), a group led by Samuel K. Long began construction of a new country club

Officials of the Globe-Wernicke Company first started playing golf behind their plant in Norwood. Later they would build the first Losantiville Golf Club course on the infield of the Oakley Race Track on Robertson Road in Oakley.

CINCINNATI GOLF CLUB.
GRANDIN ROAD LINKS.

stward-bound . 199 yds.	7 Sunset Hill . . . . 212 yds.	13 The Alp . . . 167 yds.
he Paddock . . 209 "	8 Cypress Grove . . 273 "	14 The Hub . . . 230 "
he Orchard . . 301 "	9 Hyde Park Corner . 128 "	15 Cañon . . . . 193 "
lgecliff . . . . 195 "	10 Elmhurst . . . . 227 "	16 Rookwood . . 337 "
vernus . . . . 60 "	11 Esperanza . . . . 124 "	17 Highgate . . . 170 "
alnut Hollow . 333 "	12 Ridgeway . . . . 203 "	18 The Willows . . 207 "

Layout of the Cincinnati Golf Club for the 1905 Western Open. The course did not yet stretch to Observatory Avenue. The work was accomplished by the new head Professional, Phil Honeyman, and completed by 1907.

The City's First Major—1905

The Western Golf Association (WGA) and USGA were competitors until 1921. The WGA ran championships for states west of Buffalo NY. George Balch of the Cincinnati Golf Club (CGC) was one of the first Presidents of the WGA and his club was chosen for the Western Open in 1905. Fifty-four players teed it up for the seventy-two-hole medal play tournament played at about 4,000 yards on the Grandin Road course. In the tournament were ten amateurs plus a strong field of Professionals that included famous architect Tom Bendelow, Robert White (former Head Professional at CGC and Avondale GC), Laurie Auchterlonie (1902 US Open Winner),

Action over Bedford Avenue in the 1905 Western Open at Cincinnati Golf Club.

Laurie Aucterlonie on the #1 green at the 1905 Western Open.

George Low (runner-up in 1899 US Open and Head Professional at Baltusrol) and Horace Rawlins (1895 US Open Winner). The tournament was won by Englishman Arthur Smith, the Professional at Arlington GC in Columbus, OH. The WGA and the Western Women's Golf Association (WWGA) visited the city three more times. In 1941, The Women's Western Open was waged at Cincinnati CC and Professional Patty Berg defeated Olga Weil, the great local amateur from Losantiville CC in the finals. The Camargo Club hosted the Women's Western Amateur in 1953 won by Clevelander Claire Doran and the Men's Western Open was waged at Kenwood CC in 1954 as Lloyd Mangrum won a playoff over Ted Kroll.

about two miles south of Covington on the Lewisburg street car line. The street car could hold up to twelve people and there were 128 charter members committed to bringing golf to Kenton County. By 1904 Tom Bendelow laid out a nine-hole course and it was built by member Tom Creaghead. The club also built tennis facilities, a baseball diamond and a beautiful new club house. The course would be built on seventy-four acres of the Perkins Farm and property was leased for five years with an option to purchase.

Play began in earnest on the first design of 2,800 yards and it took only two years before Brad Eldridge, Beatty Warner and other very good players were to

make Ft. Mitchell CC a golf powerhouse in Kentucky and Greater Cincinnati. The club quickly grew to its limit of 275 members and one key to the success and stability of Fort Mitchell CC was the early decision to purchase the property for the club rather than engaging in a continuing lease relationship.

In 1920, the course was completely rebuilt under the direction of A.N. McPheeters as length was added to just under 3,000 yards. McPheeters' services were borrowed from the French Lick Resort and he would stay on as Superintendent for many years. Like Wyoming CC, the subject of becoming an eighteen-hole layout has been discussed on occasion but the nature

Ft. Mitchell Country Club stars Ben Hart, Tom Craighead and T.F. Walker. Craighead built the first Ft. Mitchell Course in 1904 using a Bendelow design. (Photo circa 1913)

Ft. Mitchell Country Club clubhouse. (Photo circa 1912)

of the property would diminish the quality of the golf. In 1927 William Jackson, the pro working with Seth Raynor on the building of the Camargo Club course, was consulted about a property about six miles farther south. The consideration was for a new eighteen-hole layout but the decision from members was to remain at the present site and nine-holes.

As early as 1910 the strength of Ft. Mitchell CC players was known. They dominated the first Audubon competition in Louisville by besting Lexington CC and Audubon CC. The club hosted three Kentucky Opens (1912, 1920 and 1931) and three Kentucky Amateurs (1917, 1920 and 1931). Besides Eldridge (two Met wins in 1911 and 1912) and Warner, Ft. Mitchell was also the home course of Bill Deupree. Captain of the Duke University golf team, Bill went on to win Kentucky Am in 1950, the Northern Kentucky AM in 1952 and the Men's Met (1954, 1959). His club mates include Spence Kerkow, also a Kentucky Am winner (1938) and Northern Kentucky Am winner (1942) and Joe Turner, Jr. who racked up the Kentucky Amateur, the Northern Kentucky Am and the Men's Met (1956). Dennis Hurley (1968) was also the Men's Met winner. 1968 was a good year at Ft. Mitchell as Margaret Jones won the Women's Met also.

Maketewah CC
Leaving Avondale for Bond Hill

One of the city's first Ghost Clubs—Avondale Golf Club (AGC)—would move its members from the present Xavier University campus to the sleepy village of Bond Hill. Members of Avondale GC had tried to expand to 18-holes by purchasing adjacent land on Clinton Springs Avenue and then in the Rose Hill Subdivision but were rebuffed in both cases. They then had tried to squeeze an eighteen-hole layout on their property but were not satisfied with the results. Only two miles north was the discovery of five small dairy farms on what would be the site of Maketewah CC. AGC member Barney Kroger had left his home for a drive up dusty Reading Road in 1910 and had found the site. He immediately contacted Tom Bendelow for his assessment and design of the city's first 6,000-yard course.

Within a year AGC had relocated to the new location bringing the trophies, Head Professional Richard Cass and their members. The club considered many names before deciding on Hamilton County Golf Club. The Avondale property left behind was purchased by Xavier University in 1911 and is the site of the present athletic fields on Dana Avenue and Victory parkway.

Early members included Kroger, William Cooper Procter, Otto Armledder and Frank Ballman among others. And in 1919 they hired Donald Ross to design a brand-new course on the site. Ross's layout would retain the routing of only one hole (present #12) and he completed his construction work by the 1921 season. At the same time the club changed their name to Maketewah CC. The club tried an unsuccessful bid for the 1928 US Open but were turned down. Members then bought more property and Ross returned in 1929 to add the present #2 and #3 holes while surveying a location for the new Kenwood CC.

Hamilton County Country Club (Maketewah) first clubhouse that burned down in 1913.

Hyde Park Country Club clubhouse. (Photo circa 1925)

It is the only known Ross design with a Par-3 hole on #9 and #18.

Ross's friend George Bowden from Boston was hired as Head Professional and this led to a stable of players who would win among them ten Met's, six Ohio Amateurs and one Ohio Open championship. The Met winners were Neil Ransick (1928), Maurice McCarthy (1939, 1941, 1943), Bob Sulzer (1940), Al Joslin Jr. (1950, 1952, 1953) and Tony Blom (1961, 1962). Women's Met winners included Dorothy Moeller (1918) and Janet McIntosh-Mueller (three wins in 1956, 1960 and 1964).

One of the greatest woman players to grace the local scene, Marion Miley, joined Maketewah when her father, Fred, replaced George Bowden as Head Professional in 1937. Between 1931 and her tragic murder in 1941, Miley would win six Kentucky Amateurs, two Trans-Mississippi cups, two Women's Southern championships, two Western Women's Open trophies and play on two Curtis Cup teams. (See chapter on "Women's Golf.")

Maketewah CC and the Camargo Club were the first two local clubs selected as USGA Quali-

fying sites in 1931. At this writing and since 1912, Maketewah CC has hosted forty-eight US Open Qualifiers (a USGA record), one US Senior Amateur Qualifier, one US Pro-Am, fifteen Met Championships, Four Ohio Amateur's (three men and one woman), two Ohio Open's, one Ohio Mid-Am, five Tri-State Invitationals (four men and one woman) and numerous collegiate tournaments. Winners of those tournaments and Qualifiers include Jack Nicklaus, Otto Hackbarth, Frank Stranahan, Toney Penna, Betty Rowland and Al Espinosa.

Golf in the Western Hills

Another of the original pioneer clubs needed to seek a larger site for their golf activities. Elberon GC made their move in 1901 from 8th Street to Rapid Run Pike on the back side of Price Hill but a tornado leveled the clubhouse and play did not begin until 1903. Membership had soared from seventy-five to over 250 in their first four years and it was apparent they were here to stay. They had increased their nine-hole layout at the thirty-five-acre location and provided space for other activities like baseball and archery. By 1908, they had squeezed their Rapid Run layout to a full eighteen-holes and joined the Ohio Golf Association but yet another move was on the horizon. L.C. Rose and Russell Jones were early great players from Elberon CC and Jones won the Ohio Amateur in 1911.

In August of 1912, Tom Bendelow was again summoned to the Queen City to look at three prospective sites for a new course. The Board selected property for a new eighteen-hole layout on Cleves-Warsaw on the site of a summer residence for former US President Benjamin Harrison. Barney Kroger led the membership drive and Will Howard was selected as first President. The move was completed for the 1914 season with Ed Brophy selected as its first Head Professional, a post he held until 1952. Brophy was assisted by his wife, Catherine Cassidy Brophy ("Aunt Kate") who also served as caddy master and teacher to many men and women players. Kate would also serve as Head Professional at Woodland GC down the road.

Bendelow was again called in in 1925 to meet with the Board and Brophy to look at the opportunities for expansion onto thirty more acres already owned at the north end of the property. By 1927, the new layout with three new holes and a redesign of almost all

PAIRING SHEET

5th ANNUAL

United States Invitational

Professional-Amateur Golf Championship

Sponsored by

THE GUARDSMEN

SAM SNEAD,
LAST YEAR'S WINNER

(Cincinnati Enquirer p
by Fred Strau

LOSANTIVILLE COUNTRY CLUB, CINCINNATI, OHIO
Saturday & Sunday, October 10-11, 1964
Conducted by

The Cincinnati Pro-Amateur Golf Committee
IN COOPERATION WITH
The Greater Cincinnati Golfers League and The Cincinnati Professional Golfers Association

Program from the 1964 Losantiville Pro-Am Tournament featuring Sam Snead as the previous year's winner.

Losantiville's National Pro-Am

In 1960, Losantiville CC hosted the first in a series of Pro-Am Tournaments that were a big hit with touring and local Professionals. Started by Mort Olman and others, it was held at the end of the regular tour season in September and it provided an opportunity for a paycheck before the winter tours began. The winning team that first year was Coach Bob Kepler of Ohio State University with one of his players, amateur Jack Nicklaus. By the next year's tournament there were 240 entrants and every local Professional and crack amateur was in the field. In 1961, the Tournament was scheduled the same week as the Portland Open in Oregon and some touring Professionals chose to play in Cincinnati instead. This was against PGA Tour policy and Sam Snead and Tommy Bolt were both fined and given 180-day suspensions. These were eventually reduced to forty-five days but it cost

Sam Snead, won eighty-two PGA Tour events and seven Majors. He once played in the Losantiville Pro-Am instead of a Tour event, and was fined by the PGA and lost the opportunity to play in the Ryder Cup.

Jack Nicklaus returns to the 1962 Losantiville Pro Am as a Professional and reprises his previous victory as an amateur. He was the only player to accomplish that.

Snead a spot on the Ryder Cup team that year. In 1962 and 1963 there were no Tour conflicts and more Professionals participated including Jack Nicklaus's win in 1962 (this time as a Professional). In 1963, Snead, Bolt, Bob Charles, Lionel Hebert and others were in town and competing but the tournament slowly died away because of the Tour conflicts. It was reprised in 1970 as the U.S. Pro-Am, a non-sanctioned Tour event at Maketewah CC but that too was short lived and the tournament ended after a total of eleven years.

Amateur Hale Irwin (l) and Professional Dale Douglass accept the Championship Trophy for the 1967 Pro-Am at Losantiville Country Club; between them they would win twenty-three Pro Tour and fifty-six Senior Tour events, three U.S. Opens, three U.S. Senior Opens and three U.S. Senior PGAs.

of the others provided a new challenging test for the locals. Bill Diddel would return in 1931 to complete the redesign.

In the late 1920s a local Western Hills CC caddy would begin a career that would take him to the very top of American amateur golf. By age fifteen in 1927, Johnny Fischer had already won the Junior Met and was low amateur playing against a top field of Professionals and Amateurs in the City Open. Fischer would graduate from Western Hills HS, win an NCAA title at the University of Michigan and start a local amateur career at Highland CC in Kentucky and eventually win the US Amateur in 1936.

One amazing feat was the 1930 Met where three former Western Hills CC caddies trained by Ed Brophy (Johnny Fischer, Eph Collins and Larry Hendrixson) all made it into Match Play. The tournament won by Fischer (now playing out of Highland CC) at the Western Hills links. Fischer would

have an amazing 1930 with a win in the Kentucky Amateur, the Cincinnati Open and Met Amateur, three Invitationals, and set course records at four different venues. He remains Western Hills' and the city's greatest player. Clarence B. Wood (1917) was the Met champion from Western Hills.

Golf in the Eastern Hills

Another small village, originally called Mornington and then Hyde Park, was annexed to the city in 1903. The original founding members of the village wanted to build a private club in the new Cincinnati neighborhood. The founders originally bought a house and ten acres of land on what is now Marburg Avenue in 1909 and James Watson laid out a nine-hole course for play that year. The club quickly outgrew this layout, additional property was purchased and Tom Bendelow arrived on the scene for another Cincinnati design. During the next two years the club endured a couple

Butler County Country Club would later become Hamilton Elks Country Club. The clubhouse was destroyed by fire in 1961.

of clubhouse fires, sold off the livestock that grazed the golf course and moved to Erie Avenue for better access to a new street car line.

Hyde Park CC soon outgrew the Bendelow layout and formed a blue-ribbon Committee in 1921 to investigate a new and more challenging layout. Chosen by club President Harry Lockwood it included Bill Harig (architect), Frank Fisher (engineer), Huber A. Lloyd (specialist in soil and seed), Al Joslin (fertilizer and chemicals) and J.R. Edwards (finances). Harig and Joslin would go on to future golf architecture projects at Terrace Park CC, Ridgewood CC, and Naples Golf Club in Florida. Harig and others made fact-finding trips to Oregon, British Columbia and California where Pebble Beach was being built. All of the information was provided to architect Donald Ross to complete the new course on Erie Avenue.

The course was completed in late 1922 and opened with great fanfare. New Head Professional George Smith led membership to a completely new 6,293-yard course where only one hole remained from the original Bendelow layout. The Greens Committee continued to add improvements under the direction of Harig. Following the lead of Camargo where Bill Jackson was both Head Professional and Greenskeeper, the club later chose Bill Fruectemeyer to fill both roles at Hyde Park. New greens were installed on #3 and #6 and, with the coordination of Harig's experimental turf farm behind #2 green, the quality of greens and fairways continued to excel on the Ross layout. This included a complete reseeding of all greens in 1928 with a new bent grass

especially suited for the Hyde Park layout. The course had all of the advantages of the science, research and course care by many key members.

In 1923 the course was visited by Bobby Jones and he was beaten by then Assistant Professional Art Smith in an exhibition match. Smith, later as Head Professional, would lead a further remodel effort of the Ross design in 1940. The changes were minor but improved the layout and playability reflecting the technology advancements in the clubs and balls.

But the biggest and most long-lasting event at Hyde Park CC is the Braemer Invitational. It is the city's oldest continuous invitational, started in 1920, and originally began as a two-day seventy-two-hole competition among the members and invited guests. Over the years all of the city's great players have vied for the championship and many guests from all over the country have participated. Other great exhibition matches have occurred over the years including one particular 1947 event attended by Ben Hogan, Byron Nelson, Jimmy Demaret and Bing Crosby that drew over 5,000 spectators and raised over $10,000 for the American Cancer Society.

Several players would win the Met under the Hyde Park colors including Al Baumgartner (1914, 1919, 1923), Fred Lush (1918), Spencer Kuhn (1924, 1925), Milt Cook (1933), Neil Ransick (1936, 1946) and Tom Strange Jr. (1949).

Golf and Butler County

In May of 1908, the Hamilton Country Club was opened and there was an attempt to lay out a small course on the Pollock Hill property but it was not suitable for the play of the day. After property was found in 1914, the Butler County Country Club was formed and Professional George Dow was brought in from the east coast to build a nine-hole course. Play began in 1915 and would continue until the early 1920s when a decision was made to expand to a full eighteen-hole layout. The club also featured baseball diamonds and tennis courts. The original nine-hole course measured 3,280 yards with a Par of 37. Jack Swim replaced George Dow as Professional in 1916 and he was replaced in 1920 by twenty-one-year-old S.I. Baxter. Baxter eventually grabbed the course record of thirty-two and arranged several exhibitions including two featuring US Open winner Walter Hagen and one with Gene Sarazen.

The Board met in 1923 to expand the course to eighteen holes and William (Bill) Jackson was brought in from Chicago to design the new nine and tune up the front. Jackson would stay on as Head Professional but eventually leave for The Camargo Club in 1926 to finish the course installation there and started by Seth Raynor. Jackson's Assistant, John Buchanan, replaced Jackson as Head Professional in 1927. Butler County CC disbanded in 1932 and the course and property purchased by the Elks organization and renamed Hamilton Elks Country Club.

In the same period (1922), Middletown also built a nine-hole course on property leased from Armco Steel. It was occupied by the Middletown Community Golf Club and they competed within the Golf Association centered in Dayton. The club then added a second nine holes and changed their name in 1928 to Wildwood Golf Club.

World War I and Post-War Growth

This was a decade of expansion and refinements of existing courses. The new Haskell golf ball was keeping the pressure on course design. The first eighteen-hole course in town—at the Clifton Golf Club—was now defunct and its members had moved on to other venues. Most other 18-hole courses in town were less than 5,000 yards and players were looking for more tests of their skills. Course lengths used in the big national tournaments were starting to be over 6,000 yards and only Hamilton County CC and Losantiville CC had the length locally before World War I.

When Tom Bendelow again came into town in 1912 it was to look at the expansion of two existing clubs (Wyoming CC and Western Hills CC). But he also visited the site of the planned Highland Country Club. It was officially founded in 1915 but its roots went back to one of the original ghost courses—Inverness CC. Even before the Inverness clubhouse fire in 1910 basically ended the Samuel Bigstaff's pioneering effort, many players had already left for Ft. Mitchell CC and other venues. The original Inverness property had crammed nine holes onto twenty-two acres and it was not conducive to good play.

Eventually in August, 1914—almost to the day that was the start of World War I—newspaper accounts were announcing that Ft. Thomas golfers, led by Harry and Frank Stegeman and Hugh Head, were

starting a club on seventy acres at the end of the street car line in Campbell County. Much of the land had been used for orchards and Bendelow laid out the new nine-hole course. Eventually In 1954, Bill Diddel would perform a major remodel of the original nine-hole layout. There had been an attempt to use Diddel in 1931, while he was completing Kenwood CC, to build a second nine but an unfortunate auto accident and the Depression combined to stop the project. The second nine eventually would be accomplished by Arthur Hills in 1985.

From the opening of play in 1916, Highland would be known for its great golfers. Alex Baxter, a Scotsman who had been Head Professional at Little Falls CC in New York was brought in to run the golf program. He had been assisting Phil Honeyman at Cincinnati GC for a short time and had worked on many of the improvements there. The new members were so excited about joining the competition that they started a Sunrise Club to begin practice for city contests. Players would rise at 4:30 AM every day and get in a quick nine-holes before work. The extra practice would pay dividends fairly quickly.

By 1921, one of the Sunshine Club members, Frank Marty, would win the Braemer Invitational at Hyde Park CC and the following year two Highland stars—Darwin Stapp and Marty—finished one-two in the Met Championship. This was followed up the following year when member Hugh Stewart would be runner-up to Al Baumgartner in the Met. Finally, Darwin Stapp would be the first amateur to win the Kentucky Open in 1926 showing that the early and extra practice paid dividends.

In 1930, eighteen-year-old John Fischer from Western Hills joined Highland CC and continued on with a career there that included a Kentucky Amateur, two runner-ups in the Kentucky Open, a win in the Queen City Open, a win in the Met (1930), four separate course records and four Invitationals. While at Highland he won three Big Ten championships and one NCCAA title and capped all of this with a win in the 1936 US Amateur.

The Roaring 20s, Prohibition and New Private Clubs

There was one complication affecting golf and country clubs and that occurred at the 19th Hole. The Volstead

Clovernook Country Club was the dream of Powell Crosley and designed by the famous golf architectural firm of Langford & Moreau in 1923.

Act and 18th Amendment basically shut down all alcohol production from 1919 to 1933. Consumption would continue off the books in speakeasies and some clubs. Bootleggers and gangsters took over the alcohol trade and demand barely diminished but the supply through legal outlets was cut off at the spigot.

The Roaring 20s had started with the opening of the new Donald Ross courses in Bond Hill and Hyde Park. In addition, five more big eighteen-hole private courses would be built in the Tristate and remain active into the twenty-first century. But the nature of the country club was going through changes. It was more being recognized as a home away from home and not just a locker room for athletic activities. More lavish clubhouses were being built by great architecture firms and included ballrooms and sitting areas with large fire places and decorating. The social scene of the club was taking on new importance.

But one of those early pioneers who was in it only for the golf was Covington attorney Harvey Meyers. He identified a beautiful property along the Licking River in Rosedale, Kentucky, for a new private golf course he called Twin Oaks Country Club. Almost single-handedly he set up the project, hired a course builder and an architect (Arthur Lockwood who had designed courses in Maine and Pennsylvania as well as Delaware CC in Muncie, Indiana, and French Lick, Indiana). Meyers' vision was to make this a premier golf-only venue with just a few social events.

Meyers handled financing and membership as well as planning the building of the 6,650-yard course (with one hole over 650 yards long). Things did move slowly through the decade in spite of the club's promotions and frequent exhibitions with visiting stars like Tommy Armour and Johnny Farrell. Milt Cook, one of the dominant players of the 1930s, won his first of four Met's (1931) as a Twin Oaks CC player. Twin Oaks would survive the Depression and eventually would become a fine local public course.

Like Meyers, Powell Crosley was a builder too. He built cars and he built radios. And he also built a golf course. By 1920 golf was moving farther into the Cincinnati suburbs and Crosley's vision would identify another opportunity. He was not an avid golfer but liked the game, playing at Wyoming CC, and saw a void in the northern part of Cincinnati. He had just started to build radios and by mid-decade was the world's largest radio manufacturer. He and his brother Lewis already had a business manufacturing auto accessories. Building a large manufacturing plant and broadcast empire and owning the Cincinnati Reds were still on the near horizon.

But in 1923 the Crosley brothers identified a 111-acre property on Van Zandt (now Galbraith) Road and organized a new golf club. It was not far from Powell's estate on Kipling Rd and they named it Clovernook Country Club after the nearby Cary homestead in North College Hill. Soon after, they began the process of hiring a course designer and building a clubhouse. They chose William Langford and Theodore Moreau as architects. By 1925 Archie Simpson Jr. had moved over from Twin Oaks CC as Head Professional, replacing Herb Sutkamp. Archie Simpson Sr. would replace his son after Archie Jr.'s untimely death in 1930.

One of the city's great players, Nelson Ruddy, broke on the scene in 1926 as a sixteen-year-old and won the club championship. The next year he won the 1927 Met beating the great amateur players of his day and went on to a great career in Ohio and Kentucky. Other Met winners in this time period include Alan Whaling (1948) and Geoff Hensley (1969).

Harry Mesloh, also an accomplished player, was long time Greenskeeper and, with help from both Simpsons, re-located many tees and re-built many greens to keep the course current and modern as technology changed the game.

Hamilton Avenue going north toward College Hill in the early 1920s when Clovernook Country Club was being built. Most macadam roads were in similar condition at that time when outside of the city center.

The Camargo Club
Seth Raynor's Crown Jewel

On the last day of 1925, Ralph Love the golf writer of the *Cincinnati Post* wrote in his article, "Whenever a new golf course is planned, the promoters proclaim that when completed their course will be the finest in the city, state or country ... " But eventually those promises are fulfilled and that may have occurred in that same year when it was announced that The Camargo Club would be constructed in Indian Hill on a 200-acre site. When planning for the club was originally organized in 1922 there was a suggestion to move Cincinnati CC completely from the Grandin Road location to Indian Hill but that was voted down by the membership in 1924. The new Camargo club site included 500 acres total and the remainder would be used for home sites and recreation. The region would now have its world class golf facility and construction started in August, 1924.

Seth Raynor, a disciple of the great C.B. McDonald, was selected as course architect. Clifford Wright,

Frederick Chatfield and several other members at Cincinnati Country Club (CCC) organized The Camargo Club in order to enjoy all forms of sport. This included hunts, polo and other equestrian events that were not possible at the East Walnut Hills site. DeWitt Balch, winner of two Mets and two Ohio Amateur titles at CCC, was an eager early proponent of this new course that would measure as much as 6800 yards from multiple tees, have irrigated fairways and greens, and some bunkers as deep as sixteen-feet. This was a course designed for US Opens and world class events.

Raynor's design included many of the features of previous McDonald courses including a Par-3 "Redan" hole (#15 at Camargo), a Par-4 "Cape" hole (#6), a Par-4 "Road" hole (#17) and a "Biarritz" hole (#8). There was some large machinery used on the site but much of the fairway shaping was my slip scrapers and mule teams—sometimes twenty different mule teams on the course at one time. After two years of meticulous construction, the front nine was almost completed and finishing touches were being put on the back nine when word came that Seth Raynor had died suddenly in January, 1926.

That fall the club hired William Jackson as Superintendent. He had been Head Professional at Butler County CC where he had designed and built their second nine. A Committee of Jackson, Balch, and Chatfield completed the design of the course using Raynor's drawings and instructions left behind. This included some major work by Jackson to complete holes #16 and #17. Jackson was a very important addition to the group. Before coming to Camargo, he had become a master of golf course design and construction and, in particular, the art of selecting and applying the proper seeding to a new course. These were skills he developed as Superintendent and Architect at Olympia Fields in Chicago and had many other designs on his resume.

Through 1927, Chatfield, Balch and Jackson continued the fine-tuning and careful completion of the course. Play was permitted on the two nines but with strict instructions to play with respect for the new grounds until it could mature. Jackson took on the double role of Superintendent and Head Professional. In 1947 Taylor Boyd moved in as Greenskeeper and Jackson remained as Head Professional until retiring and being replaced by Art Smith in 1953.

With the new course came a new competition for the city's elite golfers. The first Fleischman Cup was staged in July 1927 but was played only over the one nine. Invitations were limited only to members and guests who had won the Met or state tournaments in the past and it took three separate victories to claim the Cup. Ira Holden won the trophy quickly as he triumphed in 1927, 1928 and 1930. The Cup has been one of the city's great Invitational tournaments with many golf celebrity participants. Johnny Fischer won four Fleischman Cup tournaments between 1936 and 1941 and also claimed the Cup.

Finally, in the Spring of 1928, the full course was declared ready for play and the golf world found a layout that was prime and ready for any competition. By June, practice started for the club's first Men's Met. It was quickly determined that the course was too tough for the field. Ira Holden, also a past winner of the Ohio Amateur, lamented that on the back nine he needed a Brassie (2-wood) for a second shot on five of the Par-4's after hitting good drives. Neil Ransick of Maketewah CC was the eventual winner. It has hosted four Women's Mets (1930, 1938, 1947 and 1957) during that period.

The Camargo Club was selected to be the US Amateur Qualifying site in 1931 and now shares the local honors with Coldstream CC. Over the years the list of Camargo qualifiers includes Jack Nicklaus (five times), Pete Dye, Gay Brewer, and Tom Weiskopf.

The Women's Western Amateur Championship was waged at The Camargo Club in 1953 and Claire Doran of Cleveland won the first of her two championships by besting Jane Nelson of Indianapolis. The list of Women's Met winners playing from Camargo include Elizabeth Cassatt Reid (1934, 1935), Grace Leyman Lull (1938) and Eleanor Wright Warner (1957).

Play through the years confirms the difficulty of this last of Raynor's gems. Bill Jackson continued as a lead architect on his own by designing Potter's Park (Hamilton, OH), Summit Hills CC and also being consulted on numerous other projects like Ft. Mitchell CC. Unfortunately, his layout at Olympia Fields fourth course is no longer in use but his work and the contribution of Dewitt Balch have helped to boost Camargo Club to a perennial Top-50 classic course in the world.

Ryland Lakes GC was built in 1928 in Northern Kentucky on the Licking River between Alexandria and Independence. A residential retreat and fishing club started in 1892, access to the course was restricted to the surrounding property owners. The addition of golf was not necessarily favored by all of the members but under the leadership of Fred Fischer and new Head Professional Cliff Sturgil the game was quickly accepted and membership grew.

After leaving behind the sites of many ghost holes among the village residences as early as 1898 (see chapter on "Ghost Courses"), Terrace Park CC incorporated in 1915 and kept their eyes open for a larger venue. In 1930, they acquired the Woodward Farm in Milford with 128 acres at the confluence of the Little Miami River and its East Fork and golf was firmly established.

William Harig, an expert player and Ohio Amateur veteran from Hyde Park CC was selected to lay out the 1930 course. Mr. Harig was an architect and builder with several major buildings like the Hotel Sinton in his resume. But he was also best known for his extensive knowledge of turf grasses. He was

Slot machines were a significant source of income in many country clubs during the Depression, outpacing dues and restaurant revenue at some.

a pioneer of golf planting and fertilizing and was nationally recognized by the USGA for his work. He had laid out several holes on the Hyde Park CC course but was especially adept expert at the design and installation of greens.

Taylor Boyd, using slip scrapers and mules built the whole course and the inaugural round was played in 1931. Boyd would later move to the Camargo Club and Kenwood CC and attain national recognition in greens keeping. In the 1930s and 40s up to the present time, Terrace Park has hosted many local tournaments and exhibitions. In 1946, a fire almost completely destroyed the clubhouse and a new modern one was built and completed in 1947. Judy Diem (1959) and Sandra Jones (1966) won Women's Met's while playing at Terrace Park CC.

The Great Depression and Golf Struggles to Survive

The Stock Market Crash of October 1929 was a portend of tough economic times for the country. As the economic Depression deepened, country clubs in particular started to lose members and soon resorted to other revenue sources like slot machines and gambling to augment their loss of dues. Slot machine operations were common at Crest Hills CC, Maketewah CC, Kenwood CC and Terrace Park CC among others and those

revenues helped many clubs stay solvent. In some cases, slot machine revenues were higher than traditional sources like membership fees and restaurants.

In 1933, Prohibition ended and some courses and clubs were able to secure more stable financial footing but much damage had been done to the game and the Depression was still going on. The number of country clubs nationwide shrunk from 1,100 courses in 1930 to 763 courses by 1936 reflecting a decline of over one-million members. For those clubs that did remain open, many went from eighteen-hole layouts to nine-holes. At many sites, bunkers were removed and greens shrunk to lower maintenance costs. Bucking that trend nationally was the increase in municipal and daily fee operations with growth from 184 courses in 1925 to 576 courses in 1936. Many of these new public courses were the result of government construction programs like the WPA and many others were country clubs that changed from private to public status.

The Greater Cincinnati area followed that trend as many clubs like Homestead, Twin Oaks, and Three Rivers tried daily fee operation and only Twin Oaks survived. Hillcrest CC was reorganized as Crest Hills Country Club in 1940 then went from eighteen to nine holes at their Seymour Avenue site. Members then bought the Ridgewood GC site on Ridge Road and made it private under the name of Crest Hills CC in 1966. It, too, would become a ghost site and many members went to Losantiville CC.

In Oxford, Ohio, a group of businessmen built a nine-hole golf course on a sixty-acre plot near the town. Working with the local Kiwanis and also using the WPA for assistance and then disbanding for a few years during WWII, the Oxford Golf Club was able to reorganize and reincorporate in 1949 as Oxford CC. It is a prime example of the fortitude it took during the Depression and WWII to stay viable.

Kenwood Country Club

In 1924, some members at Cincinnati CC had considered options to move from Grandin Rd and expand their golf course as well as add other facilities for equine sports and hunts. Two properties were considered, one in Indian Hill and another 350-acre site near Madeira. The membership of Cincinnati CC decided to stay put but these other properties were both cov-

LOCATION OF NEWEST AND LARGEST GOLF CLUB

KENWOOD
COUNTRY
CLUB
334 ACRES

A 1929 map announcing the new Kenwood Country Club site.

eted for big country club projects. The Indian Hill site was selected for the new Camargo Club.

In 1927, after the Camargo project was underway, an offer was made for the Maketewah CC property in Bond Hill to build a subdivision. The Maketewah Board appointed two members to investigate the same Madeira property for a possible relocation site. Maketewah membership also voted to stay put but the two appointees (who were members of the Cincinnati Club also) took an option on the land and then went to the Board of Cincinnati Club with an opportunity.

Nationally, there had been many previous operations where downtown clubs had expanded to golf operations, the most successful example being the Olympic Club in San Francisco. The Cincinnati Club with its 2,000 members also was strongly considering such a move. Cincinnati Club President W. H. Merten formed a Golf Committee and put up $50,000 to help get the project started. The first step was to hire Donald Ross for his opinion and also survey the site for two eighteen-hole courses. Ross spent two weeks evaluating the Madeira property and a few other locations and wrote a report strongly recommending the future Kenwood CC site. While in town he also remodeled two holes at Maketewah CC to complete his design there.

Bill Diddel from Indianapolis was given the task of designing and building the new thirty-six-hole layout at the newly named Kenwood CC and eighteen holes were already in operation by 1930. At the same time, it lobbied the USGA and secured the site for the upcoming 1933 US Amateur Championship. Preparation of the championship layout was proceeding quickly and Diddel was invited back to get the course in shape through a summer-long drought.

Kenwood CC required membership at the Cincinnati Club also and this requirement plus the Depression put an immediate strain on the golf club's finances. Originally 625 Cincinnati Club members had expressed an interest in joining the golf club but the Stock Market crash changed the plans of many. For the first few years of operation the Board and some other key members (with the help of some gambling revenue) were able to keep operations going, host a major tournament and rebuild membership.

After the 1933 US Amateur, Kenwood was the site of many great golf events but possibly the most star-studded at the time was in 1938 when local clothes company Palm Beach conducted a special Invitational called the Goodall Palm Beach Round Robin. The field held only fifteen players by invitation and eleven of the top fifteen touring pro's including Gene Sarazen, Sam Snead, Billy Burke, Tommy Armour, and 1938 US Open winner Ralph Guldahl were engaged in a round robin tournament. Snead won that first tournament in a playoff over Sarazen and the format continued nationwide until 1957 at Kenwood and later at other venues.

In 1942, Burke and other top professionals like Byron Nelson returned and played in the Hale America Open Qualifier—golf's replacement for the US Open during WWII. In 1954, The Western Open was played at Kenwood CC with a field that included Bob Rosburg, Roberto DeVincenzo, Gene Littler and a host of other top PGA Tour Professionals. Lloyd Mangrum took the title in a playoff over Ted Kroll. The club was also selected to host the 1963 US Women's Open and it was won by twenty-three-year-old Mary Mills who bested a field that included Louise Suggs, Patty Berg, Betsy Rawls and Kathy Whitworth. The tournament also featured the appearance of Althea Gibson, the first African American to compete in the Women's Open.

Kenwood Country Club clubhouse. (Photo circa 1935)

Women's Met golf champions included Dolly Schildmiller, a five-time Met winner at Kenwood (1939–1943), Ruth Heutle (1950, 1958) and Joan Comisar (1967). Comisar would go on to win three more championships in the future.

1930–1960 Three More Country Clubs

After Kenwood, in the next thirty-year period ending in 1960, there would be only three local country clubs built. One would be built before WWII and located at the highest point in Kenton County. Summit Hills was designed by William Jackson, Head Professional at the Camargo Club and built by Avon Fields' Bill Smith. The eighteen-hole layout would soon be under the leadership of three pros in two years. Al Hubbard, former assistant at Twin Oaks started as Pro but was replaced by George Stark from Ft. Mitchell CC after a few months. Stark promptly won the 1930 Kentucky Open and also left after less than twelve months and Art Smith then took over the helm. Nelson Ruddy (1942) and Johnny Meyers (1951) both won Met's while playing at Summit Hills CC.

Municipal and daily fee courses would continue to multiply and courses like Sharon Woods, Winton Woods, California, Little Miami, Neumann and Reeves would be completed before the end of the 1950s. Private clubs were built at Bel-Wood (1958) and Brown's Run (1958). There are many local stories at clubs of people and ad hoc committees who stepped up to bridge finances and extend loans to keep operations going. Without this occurring behind the scenes many of today's clubs would not be operating today. As it was, there was no more significant development of private courses through the rest of the Depression and WWII.

Coldstream—Last of the Classics

Any course built before 1960 had many construction roadblocks. Present day earth moving equipment with GPS controls were still in the future and although mule teams and slip scrapers were replaced by power shovels and bulldozers after WWII, the work of architects was still very close to the dirt.

Coldstream Country Club would be the first course in the area designed for over 7,000 yards (actually 7,450 yards from the tips). It was also unique that it sought and received special permission from the Queen of England to use the name and badge design for the Coldstream Guards for their logo. Built on 1500 acres of the Chaswil Farms in Anderson Township, it was an idea originally explored in 1952 and then planned by Jim Williams, Larry Kyte, Doug Hill and George Conwell in meetings starting in 1955.

By 1959, the Committee had selected architect Dick Wilson, who was fresh off of his renovation of the Royal Montreal CC in Canada. He also had designed NCR South in Dayton, the Blue Monster Course at Doral in Florida and Dub's Dread (Cog Hill #4) in Chicago among others. Wilson was a designer who felt more comfortable in work boots and hard hat. Very early in the project he rejected a suggestion that the course be built with house lined fairways and instead carved out the best 174 acres from the property on both sides of Asbury Road to give the absolute best golf course setting.

Walking the property for weeks with his associate Joe Lee, he then took his notes to the drafting table and worked first on topographical maps. He took these drawings to the field and set stakes locating every tee, green and bunker considering the lay of the land and natural contours of the property. During this period, he could revisit nuances of the property to fine tune the design. Modern architecture drawings are usually made from CAD layouts and do not get this hands-on treatment. In that sense, this was the one of the last great course designs built in this classic method rather than requiring modern detailed drawings, environmental permits and earth moving plans for contractors.

There were some concessions made to the landscape. A dam was moved fifty yards to create the water hazard in front of Hole #2, dynamite was required to removed rock deposits under #6 and #9 fairways and there was a need to dispose of hundreds of 2' x 3'

A 1933 U.S. Amateur Match at Kenwood Country Club between Johnny Goodman and Stanford University star Charles Seaver. Goodman was foiled in his attempt to win the U.S. Open and U.S. Amateur in the same year. Seaver was the father of Cincinnati Reds pitcher, Tom Seaver.

WESTERN UNION TELEGRAM
W. P. MARSHALL PRESIDENT

8:42P EST JUN 18 63 CT8708

CT CT &A111 GOVT NL PD THE WHITE HOUSE WASHINGTON DC 18

GREGORY LALONDE JR, GENERAL CHAIRMAN

11TH U S G A WOMEN'S OPEN CHAMPIONSHIP KENWOOD COUNTRY CLUB

STATION M MADISONVILLE CIN

I WELCOME THIS OPPORTUNITY TO EXTEND GREETINGS TO THE PARTICIPANTS,
SPONSORS, AND GUESTS OF THE 1963 WOMEN'S OPEN GOLF CHAMPIONSHIP.
THIS EVENT, BRINGING TOGETHER THE WORLD'S FINEST WOMEN GOLFERS,
IS A SPLENDID SHOWCASE FOR THOSE QUALITIES OF PHYSICAL SKILL,
GOOD SPORTSMANSHIP, AND MENTAL RESOURCEFULNESS WHICH ARE SO
VITAL TO THE SUCCESS OF OUR SOCIETY. WITH BEST WISHES FOR A
SUCCESSFUL TOURNAMENT.

    JOHN F KENNEDY

Telegram from President John F. Kennedy to Gregory LaLonde of Kenwood Country Club sending his best wishes to the club and participants at the 1963 U.S. Women's Open.

stone slabs that served as flooring in the abandoned horse barn on the property. (They were mostly buried between the present #13 and #16 greens.)

Club President George Conwell led the festivities off the first tee in May, 1960 with Jouett Brown on board as the first Professional. For many years it was considered the toughest course in the Tri-State with its length, 107 bunkers and huge greens. To this day it still remains a great test for golfers of all levels. Judy Anderson Diem won the club's first two Women's Met Championships (1961, 1969) and later won two in the 1970s.

On the Horizon

Miami View GC was the first private club entry of the Modern era being organized in February, 1960. Bill Diddel also did the honors as architect but the course was literally built by its original owners and founders. Applying their own skills on a 188-acre property above Miamitown, Ohio, the club was able to enlist 116 members in a little over thirty days and eventually counted 350 members. The first nine holes were in operation by June, 1961 with President Charles Ratterman leading play off the first tee. Arnold Toole moved down from Oxford CC as the first Professional and the second nine was completed in 1962 on the 6,552-yard layout.

After Miami View it would be some time before other private clubs would be built here as more emphasis was placed on public access and municipal courses. Hillsboro Elks (1962) and Royal Oak/Stillmeadow (1963) were also built in the 1960s and Beckett Ridge (1975) built a few years later, but it would be decades before another major country club would be built in the area. Even with the slowing of growth, the country club was critical to the beginnings of golf in the area. When the game was still emerging in America, it took the coordination, vision and resources of six or seven different clubs to get the game on firm footing locally and allow golf to become part of the fabric of the city.

CHAPTER 9

The Public Courses

Golf is not a mere plaything of faddists as some suppose, nor is it a rich man's game. It is the game for all classes.

—William Howard Taft in the *New York Times* (1913)

Introduction
Local Governments Slow to Act

Public access to golf in the United States required a unique set of circumstances to progress. First there needed to be a site of thirty or more acres within city limits to build even the smallest nine-hole links and the land had to be suitable for a course. Second, the city must have municipal leadership to consider the use of the land for a recreation that would be used by only a small percentage of the population at the time. This would require tax dollars or bond issues to secure the land, build the course and then maintain it.

Today's access to public golf with courses provided by municipal and county park districts and recreation commissions as well as privately owned daily fee courses were not always available. As early as 1895, public golf had been accessible to New Yorkers at Van Cortland Park and several remodels were made, including one by architect Tom Bendelow in 1899 to get the course suitable for hosting the 1905 US Open. Public tournaments were held there as early as 1897. Public courses were reported being built throughout the United States as early as 1898. Much of that was due to Tom Bendelow who was considered the "Johnny Appleseed of Golf" as he travelled the country designing courses for anyone who would pay his $50 or $100 fee.

Cincinnati was behind the nation creating recreation for its residents as its nineteenth century Park Boards were reluctant to build city parks and the available land was getting more difficult to acquire. Country clubs were buying many available sites for cours-

A 1914 *Cincinnati Post* headline hailing the first Met winner who learned the game on a public course—Burnet Woods Golf Course.

es near to downtown and close to trolley lines. Because of the downtown's population density, its water and air problems and its location in a basin surrounded by hills, the city was in most need of green space. But in spite of its ranking as one of the country's largest cities by population, city fathers just did not prioritize recreation. Even in the boom town days of the 1840s and 1850s city leaders did not see the need for parks or green space. There had been many rebuffs of property offers from Nicholas Longworth including most of the land on the present Mt. Adams. Their refusal was because Longworth insisted that the land be used for parks. Except for the commitment to build Spring Grove Cemetery in 1845, the city allowed more factories and housing tracts to be built with the available real estate.

By 1904, the city owned only six parks and just two (Eden Park and Burnet Woods) were even large enough to consider for golf. Burnet Woods was 163 acres and went all the way from Ludlow Avenue to Calhoun Street. The south end contained buildings for the University of Cincinnati and north end had a lake and band stand. Clifton Golf Club, (an exclusive private organization that was included in the city's Social Register at the time) was able to lease about forty acres between the two for their nine-hole layout in 1898. This did not provide public access as Clifton GC operated as a private club requiring dues and invitation to membership.

Burnet Woods had been public property since 1872 but the city fathers believed they had paid too much to W.S. Groesbeck for the land and considered this a bad use of city money (thus they did not buy other potential park properties for decades afterwards). They were happy to have the income from the Clifton CC lease but by 1902 the complaints of flying golf balls were too much for the picnickers and other visitors so the club was asked to vacate. Frank Wiborg, a leading civic figure and member of Clifton GC, offered to expand their lease and pay for all maintenance but the Park Board refused and so the club moved their whole course across to the west side of Clifton Avenue (see chapter on "Ghost Courses"). They stayed on that property (now part of Hebrew Union College) until 1907 but Clifton GC eventually became another Ghost Course as the new layout was neither entertaining nor challenging. Mr. Wiborg moved on and became one of the founders of Cincinnati Country Club in 1902.

Fernbank Golf Course was relocated to the present site in 1913.

Meanwhile there was continued informal play in Burnet Woods under the tutelage of Scottish Professional Tom McCormick and a young Clifton GC caddy named Al Baumgartner continued to practice on the grounds. The course was still maintained like any other park asset and Baumgartner continued to practice until the play eventually stopped altogether. In 1914 and playing out of Hyde Park CC, Baumgartner would win the Met and then won again in 1919 and 1923. He was the first product of public golf to win the city championship and Avon Fields was still in the future. Eventually there was a realization that golf was not going to succeed locally unless it was made available to all and not just the members of private clubs.

The First Public Access in the Community—Fernbank, Harmon and Avon Fields

Besides the Burnet Woods course, another defunct golf club in Fernbank had been left at the city park by the Ohio River. The course was carried on the books by the Park Board and some maintenance continued but there is no record of how much it was used. Eventually the players moved, formed a non-profit organization and settled at its present location on Fernbank Avenue in 1913. It is still in operation today on the fifteen acres there. With its crisscrossed fairways, the mound in front of #3 green and a layout completed by member Quentin Sprong in the 1960s, it is an enjoyable throwback to the way golf was played in the earliest days of the game.

The first true local public access for golf was actually the Harmon Golf Club in Lebanon, Ohio. Started by Judge J.W. Wright, it was a five-hole course built in

The Cincinnati Post

CINCINNATI, SATURDAY, JULY 25, 1914.

GOLF NOT FOR RICH ALONE; CITY LINKS FOR ALL

FREE GOLF LINKS OPEN

A 1914 *Post* headline about the opening of Avon Fields.

GOLFERS TO SEEK HONORS

By 1924, Neil Ransick led six Avon Fields players into the National Public Links Championship.

the Harmon Park in 1912. Wright had fallen in love with the game while playing in French Lick, IN and with the eighty-eight-acre parkland donated by local benefactor William Elmer Harmon, the course was an immediate success. Mr. Harmon was an amazing philanthropist who built 118 other parks in thirty-four different states. The course went through two more remodels and expansions to its present layout. Professional Dick James held the reins for fifty-one years starting in 1954 and was instrumental in gaining access for African Americans to public and tournament golf in the 1960s.

The city of Cincinnati had inherited Burnet Woods and Fernbank courses but they had been built by private clubs on land leased in city parks. Both were allowed to go to seed after a few years. Most other major cities had true public golf courses at this time. Indianapolis actually had two city courses (Riverside Park and South Grove) in the early 1900s and public courses were already in faraway places like New Mexico and North Dakota. Cincinnati was slow to the post for public access and this could be attributed to lack of Park Board vision and perhaps a lack of local public interest in golf. Interest was certainly growing among the players and caddies at private clubs but there still was no spark to engage the general public, even with its growing middle class.

There had been a petition in 1901 for the city to build a true public access golf course in Burnet Woods

or some other parks for "persons who would like to play golf yet they cannot afford to pay the dues exacted by some of the swell clubs." But progress was slow. The Park Board had limited funds and priorities like inner-city playgrounds and baseball diamonds were still being tackled. But when John E. Bruce came to the Board in 1914, he finally brought an opinion that the parks should also bring opportunity for amateur sports. His real focus was baseball but also wanted swimming, tennis, golf and other sports available to city residents.

Another Board member, Irwin M. Krohn, led the drive finally to build a new public course in Burnet Woods but that effort was short lived and eventually tabled as the University of Cincinnati expanded north. Instead, the Board acquired the sixty-five-acre Blechly Farm on Paddock Rd. and a seven-hole course was laid out by Thomas McCormick for its first eleven players in 1914. He soon added two more holes and then became

Golf Widows No Longer, Women Take Up Sport

THE CINCINNATI POST

Low Rates on City Courses Enable All in Family to Play

Efforts Are Aimed to Check "Bleacheritis" Among Sports Lovers

CINCINNATI AUTHOR

In 1936, female golfers were joining the fun at Avon Fields. Three of Cincinnati's greatest female golfers were Rhea Geilfus, Kate Cassidy Brophy and Dolly Schildmiller. They either played or began at Avon Fields and won thirteen Women's Mets amongst them.

Professional had been employed to help oversee the operations.

Initially, this was a very crude course and, as 1941 Avon Fields Professional Red Strauss stated, "(it was originally) patterned after a course (that) young boys would build in a cow pasture." Later remodeling by Harry Asmann and a consulting visit by architect Bill Diddel helped get the course in better condition after the new Recreation Commission took the property over from the Park Board in 1929. Asmann single-handedly developed a plan and improved the Avon Fields course one hole at a time keeping the finances and construction managed.

Avon Fields was on public property but private clubs still operated and maintained the course. The course had many separate clubs, including ones for bankers, one for transit workers and even one for professional baseball players with each running their own competitions and managing their own affairs and membership. Each club paid dues and greens fees to cover the course expenses and the city provided some support in tree management, maintenance, concessions and other general services. In 1921 one of these clubs, the Metropolitan Golf Club with its 400 members, became the first municipal club to join the Cincinnati Golf League. This allowed Avon Fields players to play in local competitions like the Met. Women's Clubs were soon added and able to compete for the Women's Met.

Many players who could not afford the high dues at country clubs were introduced to the game at Avon Fields. Some, like Met Champions Rhea Geilfus Johnson, Neil Ransick, Kate

its first Professional and course Superintendent. The course was named Avon Fields Golf Club and there was finally an attempt for public access golf in the city.

City Council still did not believe in golf as a city enterprise and warned the Park Board that they had better keep the young Avon Fields golfers under control or they would be ejected "unless accompanied by a baby or small child." By 1915, Secretary Hodgkinson of the Cincinnati Park Department reported that municipal golf was enjoying a great season. The Board began planning a second nine on the property in Paddock Hills, a new clubhouse was in the near future, and a second

Jimmy Woods was the premier player at Avon Fields Golf Course as well as the Sharon Woods Golf Course in the 1950s and 1960s and won several Cincinnati Public Links Championships.

In 1902, Burnet Woods stretched from Ludlow to Calhoun Street. Clifton Golf Club occupied the middle third of the park and then a public course occupied some of the area from about 1905 to 1909.

Early City Parks and Recreation

City parks in nineteenth century America were still a new concept. City administrations were not sold on the concept of setting aside green spaces that would usually be used only by the wealthiest citizens. In addition, there were those who were against any spending of government funds for public services and wanted less taxes. But there were also advocates for health, safety and welfare of the citizens especially in urban areas. And progressive leaders were also citing the European gardens and parks that were signs of beauty and culture that America should emulate. The conflict between the pragmatic and the progressive was occurring nationally and would be the story of green space in Cincinnati and eventually would spill over to golf and access by the public.

Adolph Strauch was a park builder, landscape architect, and planner.

Cincinnati had set aside over 400 acres to build the Spring Grove Cemetery in 1845 in a major commitment to green space but the grounds were not very impressive, there was no planning and maintenance was spotty. Fortunately for the city, a world-class landscape gardener named Adolph Strauch happened to miss a train connection in Cincinnati in 1852 and contacted an old acquaintance here. He was soon hired by several citizens to build their estate grounds and Strauch would end up staying in Cincinnati until his death in 1883. He was immediately hired to redesign the Spring Grove Cemetery and during that thirty-one years here he would be a tireless advocate for parks and green spaces. The progress was not without setbacks. Though he engineered the grounds of the two first major acquisitions, Eden Park (opened 1870) and Burnet Woods (opened 1873), there were years when corrupt politics, financial panics and conservative governments, allowed the grounds to go to seed. Almost every American city was in the "Progress versus Parks" debate. Here it was even more intense as a plan was even proposed to replace Lincoln Park with a rail terminal.

By 1876, an Ohio law intended to reduce political corruption in city governments was passed and this replaced their Parks Commissions with a Board of Public Works. This reduced spending even more as public funds were funneled to projects supporting businesses. Through the 1880s and 1890s the emphasis on building accessible green space continued to wane. In fact, the Art Museum took over twenty acres of Eden Park in 1882 and The University of Cincinnati eventually took over half of Burnet Woods starting in 1889. This was the state of conditions as the first golf courses were being considered for public access. Note that by this time St. Louis had over 2,100 acres set aside for public use and San Francisco had reserved 1,100 acres. It would take a while for Cincinnati to catch up, but we now have over 5,000 acres and 10% of our total land area dedicated to green space and parks.

Cassidy Brophy, Dolly Schildmiller and Milt Cook, went on later to play at country clubs and compete city and state wide. Johnson won her third Women's Met (1923) while playing at Avon and Brophy won her first Women's Met (1927) while playing there. The organization of using private clubs on public property like Avon Fields helped expand the game but it could also be used to deny access to the general public. Public access to African-Americans was not achieved until 1938 when The Greater Cincinnati Golfers Club organized at Avon Fields during the Roosevelt Administration. Unfortunately, this did not also gain access to the Met or other local championships. That would have to wait until 1967.

Post WWI and More Public Access

As the Roaring Twenties arrived there were more attempts to create public access to local golfers. Some were semi-private like Ridgewood GC. Started by Hyde Park CC member Al Joslin Sr., it opened for play

Potter's Park Golf Course in Hamilton, Ohio, was designed by Bill Jackson of Butler County Country Club. Jackson would later become Head Professional at The Camargo Club. (Photo circa 1926)

William Diddel laid out an eighteen-hole course built around the Reservoir at California, Ohio. (Photo circa 1936)

in 1926. Joslin knew that only Avon Fields provided the city with public access and he saw an opportunity. But he also saw the potential to improve access to junior golfers and caddies. An investment group that included Joslin and Bill Harig, bought a 132-acre property on the corner of Ridge Rd and what is now Galbraith Rd. Langford and Moreau were hired as consultants but James Muirden was the main course Architect. Many holes were altered by Joslin and Harig during the first few years in operation. Harig would also later lay out the new Terrace Park CC course in Milford in 1930 and Joslin would design the Naples (FL) Golf and Racket Club. Joslin's interest in youth golf gave him the idea to start the Junior Met Tournament.

In addition, Joslin gave special access to caddies from all courses to play and develop their game at Ridgewood. In the late 1950s and 1960s, the course was a powerhouse in city golf competitions featuring Tony Blom who won his first Met (1958) playing from there as did Marion Scheibly (1965). Scheibly would win two more Met's while playing from Sharon Woods. Catherine Cassidy Brophy won her last two Women's Mets at Ridgewood GC (1928, 1929) and Dolly Schildmiller-McCarthy won her last two of her seven Women's Met's (1951, 1955) while playing from Ridgewood GC.

Shortly after building Ridgewood, Harig, Fred H. Perry and others planned to build twenty-seven more

holes of public access golf. The site was 180 acres along Reading Road and Section Road and down the hill from Ridgewood. The course was laid out by Ernest Brickwood from Scotland with Joslin and Harig again assisting. Eventually this would operate as Stonybrook GC (see chapter on Ghost Courses). Later the course was renamed Sycamore Golf Club when part of the property was purchased by Gibson Greeting Cards and other businesses. The second Men's Met Champion from a public access course was Bill Clensy of Sycamore Golf Club in 1938.

In 1926 the Covington Tennis Club, another private organization, announced plans to build a nine-hole course in DeVou Park. It would be designed by local Professional John Brophy though his brothers and Benny Weichman participated. This would be the third course in Kenton County but the first with public access. By 1928 the course was up and running with Larry Weichman as Head Professional. Pete Stuntebeck who played out of both DeVou GC and Sycamore GC in Cincinnati won the Met in 1944.

In 1926, Butler County also gained a public course as Potter Park began the planning stage with their course on 100 acres with enthusiastic support by all of Hamilton's civic organizations. Bill Jackson from Butler County CC was the architect at Potter Park and play began in 1929.

Hartwell Golf Club was founded in 1932 with Tom McCormick as Head Professional. McCormick

Play began immediately at California Golf Course in 1937 but then was shut down during WWII because of concerns that the enemy could possibly sabotage the city's water supply; it reopened in 1945.

had served at many locations including Clifton/Burnet Woods, Cincinnati Golf Club, and Avon Fields. Though not a private country club, the membership was limited to employees of the Union Gas & Electric Co. (forerunner of Cincinnati Gas & Electric Co.) Sixty players, including ten women, signed up for the initial season. Bob Lindenschmidt later served as Professional and Hartwell GC was active in the free lesson program offered to the general public during the Depression. The course was able to survive the Depression due to the company support and it developed some fine young players including caddy Curt Sears who won the 1940 Junior Met. The Golf Club also featured other sports such as baseball, softball and trap shooting. Bob Gutwein later took over for a short period until Lindenschmidt returned as Head Professional and the club stayed active through WWII, surviving a fire that destroyed the first clubhouse in 1943.

The Depression and the Growth of Public Golf

By the Stock Market Crash of 1929, the area now had several options for public play. Besides Avon Fields, these included semi-private courses like Ridgewood

GC and Stoneybrook GC as well as community courses like Potter Park, Harmon GC, Hartwell CC, Woodland GC, Fernbank GC and Devou Park GC. Even so, the economic conditions in the region were worsening.

As part of the solution, President Franklin Delano Roosevelt had installed new work programs to relieve the country's 25% unemployment. Agencies with acronyms like CCC (Civilian Conservation Corps) and WPA (Works Progress Administration) hired millions of workers to plant trees and build bridges, roads and public buildings. Included in these projects was the construction or upgrading of over 600 public golf courses nationwide. Golf star Bobby Jones was called in to consult on that effort.

Many golf architects were also suffering the pangs of unemployment and names like Allister Mackenzie, Donald Ross, Perry Maxwell and Robert Trent Jones Sr. were idle during this period and able to answer the call of the WPA projects. Architect A.W. Tillinghast was hired to build the Bethpage Black course among other projects during that time period. And two new WPA projects would be brought to Cincinnati in the 1930s and led by an architect already familiar to the area.

Strauss providing free instruction to beginning golfers. (Photo circa 1937)

Strauss, head Professional at Avon Fields, headed to the 1933 U.S. Open.

Strauss was barred from the 1923 Caddy Tournament at age thirteen because he chose to move into Pro Shop and learn club making. This designated him a Professional.

Robert (Red) Strauss—In Service to the Game

There were many Professionals and Administrators who could have been included here. People like Harry Asmann, Hank Wilms, Marty Kavanaugh and Dick James who worked inside the public golf arena to bring the game literally to tens of thousands of local players. Red Strauss served his whole Professional Career there, first as Head Professional at Avon Fields and then as Director of Golf at the Cincinnati Recreation Commission. In the latter role he supervised the building or acquisition of California GC, Reeves GC, Woodland GC, Neumann GC, and Glenview GC. He always considered himself a "Recreation Professional" as much as a Golf Professional as he worked on the installation of city driving ranges, miniature golf, playgrounds, day camps and the Airport Playfield.

Red started is golf career at age eight caddying at Losantiville CC for head Pro "Nipper" Campbell. In the caddy shack there at that time were fellow Pleasant Ridge youngsters and future Pro's Frank Gelhot and Clay Gaddie as well as future golf sports writers Wally Forste and Lou Smith. Losantiville dominated the city's caddies in all competitions. In 1923, at age thirteen, Red knew that he wanted golf as a career and decided to move from caddying into the Pro Shop to learn the art of club making. By doing so, he could no longer qualify for Caddy Championships. Between his Junior and Senior year at Withrow HS he took a Head Professional's job at Crooked Lake GC in Michigan and, when he lied about his age, beat out all candidates on the Civil Service exam and claimed the Head Professional's job at Avon Fields GC at age nineteen. He was the sole city employee involved with golf supervision. Except for a three-year stint in the US Navy during the WWII, Red retired from the city of Cincinnati in 1976 with forty-seven years' service.

But that does not take away from Red as Golf Professional and competitor, as he won the local PGA championship three times, the Cincinnati Open twice and the Southern Ohio Open as well as numerous other local competitions. He made it to the US Open in 1933 at North Shore CC in Chicago and, after some local Avon Fields players chipped in for travel expenses, he was four-under after seven holes but then admitted he succumbed to nervousness and failed to make the cut.

But what also sets Red's career aside, besides his administration and his competitive play, was his devotion to teaching the game of golf to beginners. The Depression brought a reduction in players for the game with the loss of jobs and time for recreation. For almost a decade the *Cincinnati Post* sponsored free golf instruction to the public and Strauss led a cadre of the city's best Professionals to provide the teaching. Driving his little Ford around town to teach and manage the operation it was such a success that there was national recognition. Indoor instruction was even provided during the winter for ten-cents an hour (to cover the cost of heat and electric). All the while this built the game and the dividends would be realized when golf had its great growth spurt after the war. Much of that additional play can be traced to the efforts of *The Cincinnati Post*, Strauss and his fellow teachers during the Depression. And many of us who play golf today have benefitted from those 1930s efforts to keep the game viable for the working class and later generations.

Cincinnati Red's Hall of Famer Lays Out First "True" Public Course—1890

It is accepted that the Van Cortland Park in the Bronx was the first public course in 1888. But in the purest sense of playing golf in a public park with no requirement for membership in a club, that honor might go to Franklin Park in Boston. George Wright of the 1869 Cincinnati Red Stockings and the star player on baseball's first professional team, was part owner of Ditson's Sporting Goods Store in Boston. He had seen some golf equipment listed in an English catalogue and had been introduced to it by some of his cricket players but when his order for clubs and balls arrived there were no instructions how to play.

The clubs went on display in the store window but, until a bypassing Scotsman saw them, they went unsold. That gentleman also instructed Wright on the fundamentals of the game and how to lay out a course. But Wright needed a place to play and so he met with Frederick Law Olmstead, the architect of nearby Franklin Park, and petitioned the local Parks Department. Over Olmstead's objections (he was worried about damage to his landscape), Wright was granted a permit and proceeded to the park. There, Wright and Scotsman Willy Campbell laid out a rudimentary nine-hole course, using a pickax to make holes in the frozen turf and mounting three-foot sticks with red flannel attached to mark their location. On that December day in 1890, golf was truly played on public property. It would take six more years after that initial round to get a permanent site in Franklin Park for public golf but the William J. Devine Golf Course is still in operation. Later, the city of Boston honored Wright's contribution by building the George Wright Golf Course in nearby Hyde Park. It was a WPA Project and designed by Donald Ross in 1938.

George Wright's plaque in the Baseball Hall of Fame. Wright was the star player of the 1869 Cincinnati Red Stockings. He went on to begin public golf in Boston and have a Donald Ross course named in his honor.

By the middle of the Depression demand for public golf was actually increasing. Public rounds played in Cincinnati climbed to over 10,000 *per summer month*. This compared to 23,000 rounds *per year* in 1923 and reflected the fact that country clubs were losing members because of costs but that interest in the game still remained. Avon Fields and other public access courses represented a place to keep playing golf. Things were improving but by now Toledo, Ohio, had three public courses (and 75,000 patrons) and Indianapolis, Indiana had four (and 180,000 rounds). As a region, we were still lagging behind.

The Cincinnati Recreation Commission had attempted to lease the grounds and golf course at Three Rivers CC (See chapter on "Ghost Courses") west of Cleves but that fell through and they then began a project on Kellogg Avenue near the water works

in California, Ohio. In 1935 renowned golf architect William Diddel, who had built Kenwood CC, laid out eighteen holes around the reservoirs of the Cincinnati Water Works. Opened in 1935 it became the city's second municipal course. The stone clubhouse and other features are a reminder of the WPA workers and the contribution they made to local golf.

One more public course opened in Montgomery, Ohio, where the Swaim family converted a farm on Cooper Road into a public course in 1934. It was not a WPA project and was built by private money like Ridgewood and Woodland. Bill Diddel also was architect on this project. Fred Miley came out of retirement to become one of their first Professionals and stayed through 1955. By 1941 they had purchased more property and expanded to eighteen-holes. It joined the ranks of the Ghost Courses when sold in 1976 for development as

Bill Lewis Sr., an architect and builder of Woodland Golf Course; technically an executive course, it was the main access to the public on the West Side for many years.

An excellent amateur player, Bill Diddel, designed many of Cincinnati's public and private courses including Kenwood Country Club and Sharon Woods Golf Course.

ball off the tee in 1938. The beauty and function of many of the access roads, bridges, clubhouse buildings and other features are still evident from the days of the WPA.

Sharon Woods was quite the construction project. Thousands of tons of topsoil were dredged from the East finger of the lake to build the greens. More than 31,000 feet of tile and 18,500 feet of pipe were laid for course drainage. As WWII began, Sharon Woods was claiming over 35,000 rounds of golf per year. In addition, the course provided free play to active duty servicemen during both WWII and Korean War. This was all done at the suggestion of Marty Kavanaugh Sr., the Head Professional.

Kavanaugh was key to the golf operation at the Hamilton County Parks projects. Like many others, he started as a caddy and worked his way up into the Professional ranks. The early years were spent at Avon Fields where he became Caddy Master and then Assistant Professional under Elmer Gerth. He then moved on to be Head Professional at Three Rivers CC in Cleves, Marion (OH) CC and then Ft. Mitchell CC before taking the helm at Sharon Woods in 1939. He would remain with the County system for forty-one years.

A second county course was planned right away and Diddel again was selected to design it but the onset of WWII delayed the construction in Winton Woods near Greenhills. The Hamilton County Park Board had tabled the project so they could put over 600 acres of the site under the till to raise corn and soybeans and support the war effort. In addition, the lake was stocked with bass and fifty head of cattle were purchased to increase the output of foodstuffs. Archery was the main sport at Winton Woods but the 6,420-yard golf course was finally ready for operation in 1951. This included a whole year's delay to get the greens in shape. Marty Kavanaugh, the Sharon Woods Pro was promoted to County Supervisor of Golf Operations and his assistant at Sharon Woods,

a subdivision and public park. By adding the country clubs that had gone public there were now twelve places for public play: Harmon, Avon Fields, Potter Park, California, DeVou, Fernbank, Homestead, Hartwell, Ridgewood, Sycamore, Swaim Fields and Twin Oaks. Unfortunately, California GC would close down in 1942 for the duration of WWII because of the possibility of sabotage to the city's water system but public golf was now firmly entrenched in the region.

In 1935, the Women's Golf Association also opened the Women's Met to seasonal members at these courses for the first time so a champion could now come from all public venues.

Hamilton County Gets into the Golf Business

Three years after Swaim Fields GC and California GC, Diddel also begin his design of the new WPA course at Sharon Woods. This was the first foray by Hamilton County Parks District into the golf business. Under the leadership of William Albers, the Board quickly acted on purchase of property and plans for public access to bigger and better parks. With the purchase of 730 acres on the north edge of Hamilton County, Sharon Woods GC was in business when Bobby Jones hit the first

Golf legend Bobby Jones hits the inaugural tee shot at the opening of Sharon Woods Golf Course on May 27, 1938. Jones was a consultant on the project and the one at California Golf Course, both designed by famed architect Bill Diddel for the WPA.

Jones was brought in as consultant for the WPA projects at California Golf Course and Sharon Woods Golf Course during the Depression.

Carl Rohmann, became the first Professional at the Greenhills site.

By 1948 William Albers and Hamilton County Park Board were also planning another facility on the west side to be called Miami Whitewater Golf Course. Marty Kavanaugh at Hamilton County was lamenting

the shortage of public access on the west side as the demand continued to increase. His Miami Whitewater project seemed on permanent hold waiting for the voters. The first nine at Miami Whitewater would not be in play until 1962, almost fourteen years after planning started. Bob Manly was named the first Professional as construction proceeded slowly. The second nine was made available in 1963 and 1964. Most of the construction of both nines was provided by the County workers and design was mostly accomplished by Kavanaugh and Alph Wright, Greens Superintendent.

The Trend Continues to Public Courses

When the Great Depression had begun in 1929, the *Cincinnati Post* reported that metropolitan Cincinnati boasted 324 holes of golf on twenty-two courses either in play or on the drawing board (including the new courses at Kenwood CC and Terrace Park CC). These courses were placed on 2616 acres. In a little over thirty years it had grown from soup cans and flower pots sunk in pastures in a few isolated neighborhoods across the area to a local sports phenomenon.

But of those 324 holes Avon Fields, Fernbank, Ridgewood, Devou Park and Stoneybrook provid-

Parks Help Feed Nation at War

A tractor, John Ruhl, Springdale, at the wheel, tears up Winton Woods park land for the planting of a corn crop.

Women Training As War Inspectors

An inspection training course is being offered in Cincinnati by the War Department.

Winton Woods to Produce Soybeans, Livestock, Fish

The War effort took precedence over golf as Winton Woods was plowed under for crops. (Photo circa 1943)

Semi-private courses like Ridgewood, Homestead, and Stoneybrook gave players the option of buying locker space and other amenities.

ed public access of only seventy-two holes (22%) in Greater Cincinnati. As the Depression deepened, the focus turned more to municipal and other public access course construction while country clubs either failed or were converted to public play. During the decade of the 1930s and the construction of

Woodland, Hartwell, California, Sharon Woods and Swaim Fields, seventy-two more holes of public golf were made available. Public access courses increased to over 35% of the total holes in the city. Even with the closing of Homestead CC and Three Rivers CC, public access courses would increase to over 50% of the golf holes in Cincinnati by the end of WWII. That trend would continue on into the post war period as more public courses were put on the drawing board.

This would soon be manifest in tournament results. In the 1951 Met, there were fifteen players from public access golf course in the Round of 64 for Match Play. Up to that time from 1910 there had been only four winners from

Marty Kavanaugh Sr. and Marty Kavanaugh II of Hamilton County Parks Golf.

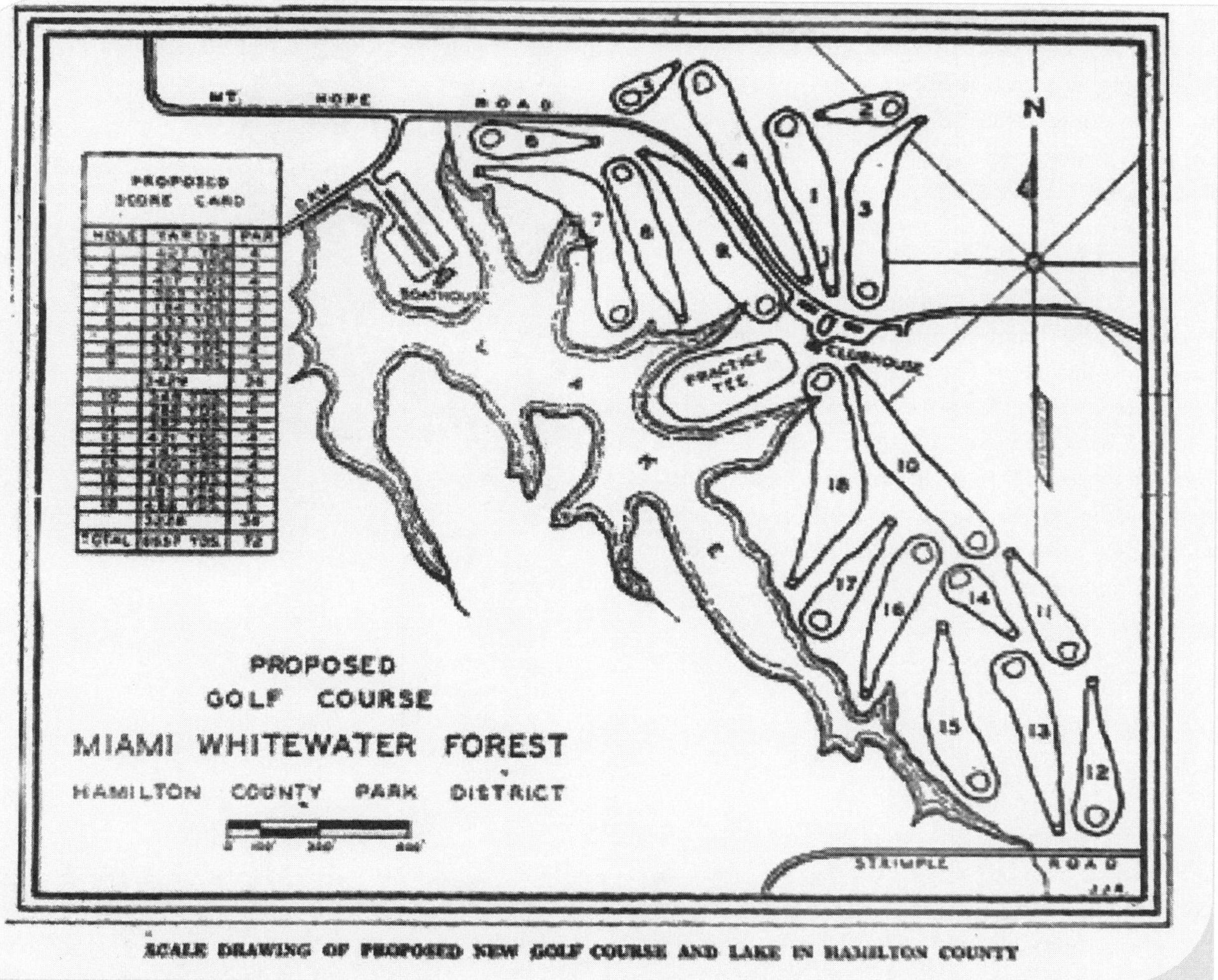

A 1957 *Post* article about a proposed Miami Whitewater course that was up for vote by the public; the opening had to wait several failed bond issues.

public access courses (1931, 1938, 1944 and 1947). In addition, the first Cincinnati Publinx Tournament was started in 1954 at Sharon Woods with an entry fee of $4. After the war, there was another new wave of public access courses but no local large country club was built in Cincinnati after 1930 until Coldstream was started in 1959.

The City of Cincinnati started planning the construction of a golf course on the Lunken Airport site right after WWII but operation of the first nine-holes of Reeves GC did not occur until 1955. It was another Diddel design on the flat grounds adjacent to the runways. Amazingly, the low water table due to the adjacent Little Miami River was dealt with by a series of three pumps that removed water from the course and sent it back into the river at a rate of over 1600 gallons per minute. Briefly the city considered lights for the whole course but that was nixed because of interference with air traffic.

Woodland GC and the Lewis family would have to hold the fort as the only public access game on the west side but that was a shorter Executive course. By that time Sycamore GC and Homestead GC had also disappeared under new commercial and suburban development. Ridgewood went up for sale by Al Joslin's widow and eventually would be bought by Crest Hills CC in 1966 and made into a private club.

In addition, a significant obstacle for public golf interest was finally eliminated in 1958 when a rule was implemented by the USGA to allow players from public courses access to the big tournaments like the US Open and US Amateur. In that decision, a group of players at a public course could band together and obtain a club status by submitting a fee to the USGA and registering as a club member. Using prescribed rules, the club could issue official handicaps. These could then be used to meet the requirements for entry into the major tournaments.

On the Horizon

Soon there would be more public access as A.J. Jolly, Glenview, Neumann, and Kenton County golf facilities were built but it would take years to satisfy the continued demand for public play in the area. Teaching and promotion expanded public golf and would also provide more champions in local tournaments. In time, most golfers in the region would be playing at public facilities. Quite a change from 1895 and the game's beginning in Cincinnati.

Woodland Golf Course names Kate Brophy one of the nation's first Female Club Professionals in 1931.

CHAPTER 10
The Ghost Courses

Gentlemen have leased links on Walnut Hills. Golf has reached Cincinnati.
—*Cincinnati Tribune* headline, November 3, 1895

Introduction

Under the parking lots, school yards, subdivisions and shopping centers of the Tri-State lay the remains of many of golf's earliest venues. They had names like Stonybrook, Ridgewood, Inverness and Avondale. Later they would be joined on the roster by other abandoned sites as the region expanded farther from the city center and Depression, Prohibition and wars took their toll on the game itself. Even today there

Inverness Golf Course clubhouse. (Photo circa 1902)

still are the telltale signs of abandoned bunkers, tees and greens and overgrown weeds on vacant lots waiting for their own new use for progress. These old names may not be familiar to us today but they occupy a special part in the beginning of the game in Cincinnati.

There were fledgling groups in at least seven or eight parts of the Tri-State who were trying to start the game on their own terms. A few succeeded, like Losantiville CC, Wyoming CC and Ft. Mitchell CC, and eventually developed into thriving organizations today. Even some of these successful clubs went through reorganizations and moves to better environs, leaving ghost sites in their path. Still others joined the list of Ghost Clubs and were never to be seen or heard from again. They only exist in record books and news articles now but they were still key to getting the game moving forward.

There were two main factors that caused this evolution and one was the golf ball. The Haskell ball, developed

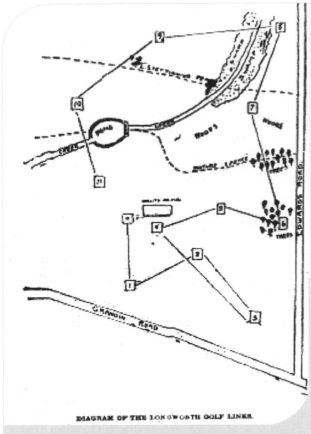

DIAGRAM OF THE LONGWORTH GOLF LINKS.

The first ghost course at the corner of Grandin Rd. and Edwards Rd. (Photo circa 1894)

The golf course in Glendale on the Procter Estate.

The infamous water hazard at Glendale Golf Course. It had to be traversed on several holes.

in Akron, Ohio, in 1899, flew farther and higher and the game now needed more real estate and over 6,000 yards of length to provide good competition. The golden age of golf architecture with Seth Raynor, Donald Ross and others now created new important courses that no longer were impeded by elevation changes on the property and embraced the challenges of the newer sites made available. This left old and land locked courses quickly out of date.

Transportation also had an effect. By 1899, there was only one automobile in Cincinnati and one in Northern Kentucky and courses were built near the street car lines. The Ohio automobile was owned by Cincinnati GC member Jacob Schmidlapp so he probably could drive to his golf game but all others were on horseback, in carriages, on bicycles or riding one of the city's electric street cars. Initially, the game started to expand out through the rail system that was centered in downtown Cincinnati. As the automobile entered more into the picture, roads were built and transportation

routes changed so courses could be built in locations farther from the city center and not limited by the street car rails.

The thirty- to one-hundred-acre sites of the original country clubs found themselves stuck near city centers where there was now competition for subdivisions and business sites. By 1910, the eventual requirements for even larger properties of 140 acres or more were now needed to build courses of over 6,000 yards. It was easier to pick up stakes and move farther out into the country and leave their original sites behind. So, the old fairways were paved over or plowed under.

Early Ghost Clubs
Golf Fighting for Survival

Play was continuing and membership grew from the earliest seed planted at Cincinnati Golf Club (CGC) in East Walnut Hills in 1895. But even CGC had left their first site behind farther down Grandin Road near Edwards Road as they moved to their present site nearer to Madison Road.

At the north end of Hamilton County there actually may have been golf even earlier than 1895. William Cooper Procter, grandson to the founder of Procter & Gamble, had learned the game as early as 1882 while a student at Princeton University. At that time there were still only a handful of formal golf courses in the country. Procter introduced the game to his father and both were known to play at their summer retreat in Watch Hill, Rhode Island, At The Oaks, their Glendale residence, some holes were installed and perhaps this became the first location for golf in the region.

By 1897, a large number of fledgling golfers met at the Lyceum in Glendale, Ohio, and founded the Glendale GC. The attendees included many from the Procter family, including William Cooper Procter, as well as sixty other representatives of the society in the village. Play began almost immediately on the nine-hole 2,302-

GOLF CLUB

Organized at Clifton With Sixty-four Members.

The Clifton Golf Club, organized at the Clifton Town Hall Tuesday evening with 64 members. The membership is limited to 100. The links will be located on the grounds of Mr. Sherlock, Mr. Rowson and at other places along Ludlow and Lafayette Avenues. A series of contests will be arranged with the East Walnut-Hills Club, beginning the first Friday in June.

An 1897 announcement for the Clifton Golf Club. The first grounds were near the intersection of Lafayette and Ludlow. The club quickly moved to Burnet Woods and remained until 1907 on Clifton Ave.

yard course on the Procter estate. It was famous for a particularly difficult water hazard that came into play on several holes and competition still continued into

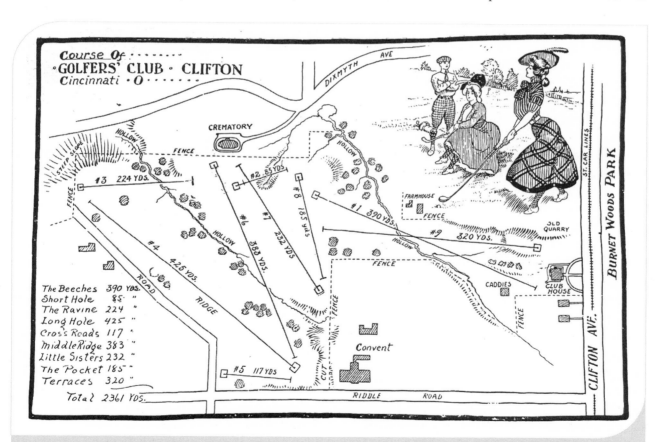

Layout of Golfers Club of Clifton on the west side of Clifton Avenue across from Burnet Woods. The course was most likely laid out by Robert White Jr. (Photo circa 1904)

1905. But it also joined the Ghost list with many of its members eventually moving down the pike to Wyoming CC. William Cooper Procter would be an active member at many clubs as he continued his love for the game. Eventually, The Oaks and the course were razed to build a subdivision.

The Ghosts of Burnet Woods

Tommy Morrison returned from Belfast Ireland early in the 1890s with news of this new golf game and carrying his hickory shafted clubs. He convinced his two brothers and others from the University Club to form the Clifton Golf Club. By 1897, they were setting up a course near the corner of Ludlow and Lafayette (near Cincinnati State University) and soon moved to Burnet Woods (on the #6 street car line). Two years later the group purchased more land and a building used for their clubhouse on the west side of Clifton Avenue. This allowed them to expand their layout to eighteen holes, the first in the city, with nine holes on either side of Clifton Avenue. Scotsman and Professional Robert White Jr., originally at Cincinnati GC and Avondale AC, most probably built the new course. Eventually flying golf balls and picnickers did not mix well and in 1902 Clifton Golf Club and their President Frank Wiborg were rebuffed by the Park Board for continued leasing of Burnet Woods as a private club for one of their nines.

Burnet Woods ran from Ludlow Avenue to Calhoun Street at this time and the Park Board did suggest the Clifton club might use some of the forty plus acres dedicated to University of Cincinnati activities (the University was located in Burnet Woods also). In 1902, Clifton GC and Cincinnati GC were the only locations with full eighteen-hole layouts and losing the Burnet Woods site was a blow to the Clifton golfers. The club tried to squeeze eighteen holes on the west side of Clifton Avenue but the course was not suitable and many members left.

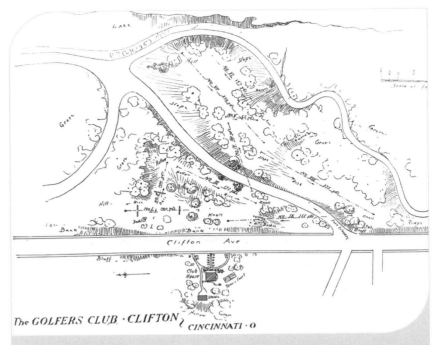

The original nine holes for the Clifton Golf Club were located near Ludlow and Lafayette Avenues in 1897, but soon moved to Burnet Woods on land leased from the city (as shown). Later, a second nine were added to the west side of Clifton Avenue. When the city did not renew the Burnet Woods lease in 1902, the club was left with only the nine holes. (Map circa 1899)

The clubhouse was sold eventually and the club disbanded officially in 1905. A few players remained and the course stayed in operation until 1907 before going defunct. It would become the first of a group of "Ghost Clubs," this one replaced by the campus of Hebrew Union College. The city continued to run a public golf facility in Burnet Woods for a while but the Park Board thought the game to be for the elite and never really bought into public golf. Eventually the Burnet Woods public access site also was added to the list of Ghosts.

An offshoot of Clifton GC was the Golf Club of College Hill. It was begun with members of that community and some players from Clifton's club, most likely when that organization moved from Ludlow up to Burnet Woods. They were only in existence for 1898 and 1899 but long enough to experience a caddy strike. It would take another twenty-five years until Powell Crosley came to the area and built Clovernook CC.

The Ghost of Avondale

Even before closing, some of Clifton Golf Club's pioneers had moved on to either Cincinnati GC (where Frank Wiborg helped to found Cincinnati Country

Clubhouse of Golf Club of Clifton, located north of Riddle Road on the west side of Clifton Avenue. (Photo circa 1904)

An 1896 map for city annexation of Avondale Golf Club parcels to Cincinnati; the map is overlaid to present the city map for reference. The C.C. Bragg lot is the site of the Avondale Athletic Club golf course; immediately north is the Blachly Farm where Avondale Golf Course was planning to expand further. After that sale fell through, Avondale Golf Club moved to Bond Hill in 1911, and eventually changed its name to Maketewah Country Club in 1921. The Blachly Farm would also become a golf course as Avon Fields was built there in 1914.

Club) or to Elberon GC up on Price Hill. But most of the exiting Clifton GC members moved on to help lease the grounds of the Avondale Golf Club (AGC) (on the present Xavier University campus) in 1903. Avondale Golf Club was itself an offshoot of Avondale Athletic Club that had been hosting golf at the site since 1897.

In 1897, Avondale Athletic Club (AAC) had come on the scene as the most expensive and exclusive country club in the area. With an unheard of $60 annual dues and an extra $10 annually to access the golf course, they built a beautiful clubhouse on Dana Avenue near Winding Way on the present Xavier University campus. One hundred golfers were in membership and Robert White was hired as Head Professional the same year. He built a new nine-hole layout that was located basically at the present Xavier soccer stadium and ran up the hill toward Woodburn Avenue.

AAC immediately had disputes with their landlord and were forced to add more members to cover the expenses of the extensive grounds, indoor pool, baseball fields and golf course. By 1903, AAC was in financial trouble and the facilities were padlocked except for the golf course. There the golfing members paid rent and were allowed to continue to play while renaming themselves the Avondale Golf Club (AGC). After being rebuffed in their attempts to build in the Rose Hill Subdivision or expand north to the Blachly Farm (site of today's Avon Fields), AGC would relocate to Bond Hill in 1911 and rename themselves the Hamilton County Country Club.

Eventually they were renamed again to Maketewah Country Club in 1921. But the ghost course that was Avondale Athletic Club and Avondale Golf Club remained behind on Dana Avenue. Eventually the site was purchased by Xavier University in 1911 so they could move their college campus from downtown. It was done with the proviso that the Park Board would build a wide tree lined Boulevard for automobile traffic through the property. Originally called Bloody Run Parkway it was later renamed Victory Parkway. The Avondale Golf Clubhouse was the first building on the new Xavier campus.

Ghosts Dotting the Region

Across the Ohio River, Scottish native Samuel Bigstaff started a project in an unincorporated area in the hills above Newport, Kentucky. He built a street car line out from Newport into this district of the Highlands and started the Inverness CC in the late 1890s. The nine-hole course was built on twenty-five acres. The club had 400 members by 1903 and the district was renamed Ft. Thomas. Eventually, Inverness would also close its doors after a severe fire at their clubhouse. It became a Ghost in the history books as the property was too small for a full-size course and there was pressure to develop their site for more new homes. Some of its members moved over to Ft. Mitchell CC while others eventually helped found Highlands CC in 1914.

In 1898, the Fernbank Country Club was formed by Mrs. Burnham Merrick and Miss Nancy Wilson. It boasted over fifty members and was located behind their clubhouse on the corner of Pecan Lane and County Road in Fernbank Village. The course site would eventually revert to a public access course and while the original club has achieved ghost status, golf is still being played in Fernbank near the original site.

A little farther east, an excellent female tennis player and athlete, Nona Closterman, gathered a group of twenty-five sportsmen at her father's house on Price Hill in 1899 to organize a golf club. The Price Hill GC soon occupied eight acres on 8th Street near Wells Road and built a six-hole course that stayed for a few years. The need for more real estate resulted in a short-lived move farther out 8th Street to end of the #12 Street Car line and Nebraska Avenue. There they built a more challenging nine-hole course and changed their name to Elberon CC. After another move to Rapid Run Pike and weathering a tornado that leveled their clubhouse, Elberon CC became a force in local golf competitions with some of the city's best players. Eventually the club moved to Cleves-Warsaw Pike in 1914 and renamed itself Western Hills Country Club leaving three ghost sites in their wake.

At about the same time, a group of executives from the Globe-Wernicke Co. started to knock golf balls around in the yards behind their Norwood plant. By 1902, under the leadership of Simon Kuhn, the group negotiated to build a golf course on the infield of the Oakley Race Track and hired Tom Bendelow for his first design effort in Cincinnati. The new club, now calling itself the Losantiville GC, used the locker

Golfers and other passengers disembark at the station for Inverness Golf Course in Campbell County.

The driveway into Elberon Country Club on Rapid Run Road with Kentucky hills in the distance. (Photo circa 1912)

Avondale Athletic Club grounds and clubhouse in 1903.

facilities in the grandstand as their clubhouse but the confusion and traffic of racing fans and track operations began to take the toll of the golfing enthusi-

Golf Manor

There were not too many towns or cities named for the new game of golf but if you are surrounded by golf courses, it might be inevitable. Golf Manor, Ohio, (one square mile in area) was started as a new community in the 1920s. It had been occupied since the 1800s, mostly by German immigrants farming the land but it was uniquely located among five golf courses operating or being planned. The Britton and Brown Realty company started buying the property and laying out lots as Cincinnati spread to the north. The pricing was relatively simple. One dollar down and as little as seventy-five cents per week would secure a lot and many faced Losantiville CC across Langdon Farm Road. Hillcrest CC was down the road and Ridgewood GC and Maketewah CC were within walking distance for caddies. Even a little farther west you would find Stoneybrook GC and then Sycamore Golf Club. All but Maketewah and Losantiville became Ghost Courses but a lot of golf surrounded Golf Manor at one time. Golf Manor was incorporated as a Village in 1947.

Where Would You Go if the Landlord Doubled the Rent?

Join hundreds of far-sighted people in building NOW for the future. Only those who own their homes know the true feeling of independence—living without fear of the landlord, appearing before the world as substantial property owners.

Start To-day by Buying a Lot for

$1 DOWN AND 75c A WEEK and up

With No Taxes or Interest for Two Years, in

GOLF MANOR

(Adjoining Losantiville Golf Club in Pleasant Ridge)

$250 UP

Liberal Discounts for Payments of $25 or More Within First 30 Days.

COME SUNDAY

Or Any Day During the Week

FREE ROUND TRIP FARE REFUNDED TO ALL

BRITTON & BROWN, Owners

An ad for Golf Manor Real Estate, a community surrounded by three golf courses.

Elberon Country Club clubhouse. The building was eventually remodeled as a church when the club moved to Cleves-Warsaw Pike and was renamed the Western Hills Country Club. (Photo circa 1912)

asts. Six holes were inside the infield and three other holes were outside with one hole touching the B&O Railroad right of way. When the race track began to have financial problems, the members picked up their gear in 1907 and built a new eighteen-hole Bendelow course in Pleasant Ridge, leaving a ghost site behind in Oakley.

Also, before the turn of the century, golf came to the Village of Terrace Park. Urban pressures were not yet as strong in the area but the town was still planning for the future and golf was using real estate perhaps better suited for residences. Will Irwin returned from a trip to Scotland in 1898 and began to play on a course he laid out among vacant lots and fields. He got his friends Sam and Huber Lloyd interested in the game, soup cans for holes were sunk in the turf

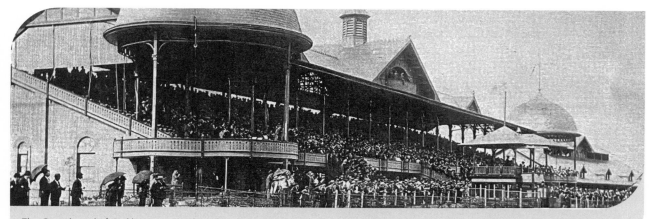

The Grandstand of Oakley Race Track and Locker Room for Losantiville Golf Course, the first course in the infield of a racetrack. (Photo circa 1901)

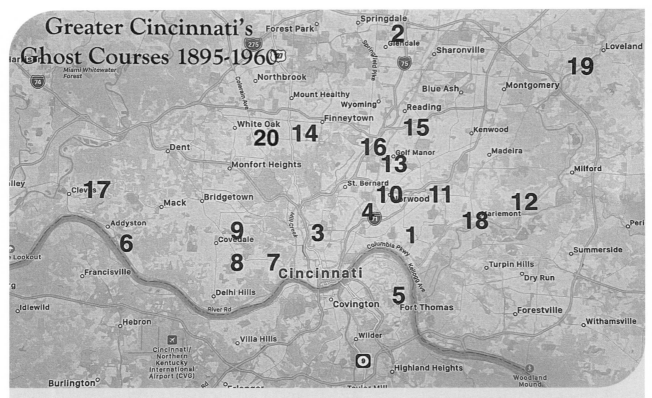

Greater Cincinnati's Ghost Courses 1895-1960

Ghost Courses between 1894 and 1960: (1) Cincinnati Golf Course (1894-1895); (2) Glendale Golf Course (1897-1905); (3) Clifton Golf Course (1897-1907) two sites; (4) Avondale Athletic Club/Avondale Golf Club (1897-1911); (5) Inverness Golf Course (1898-1904); (6) Fernbank Golf Course (1898-1908); (7) Price Hill Golf Course (1899-1900); (8 and 9) Elberon Golf Course (1900-1914); (10) Globe-Wernicke Co. (1900-1901); (11) Losantiville Country Club/Oakley Race Track (1902-1906); (12) Terrace Park Golf Course (1898-1930); (13) Phoenix Golf Course/Hillcrest Country Club/Crest Hills Country Club (1916-1966*). *Operated as city course for three more years; (14) Homestead Golf Course (1924-1953); (15) Ridgewood Golf Course/Crest Hills Country Club/Ridge Club (1926-2003); (16) Stoneybrook Golf Course/Sycamore Country Club (1928-1950s); (17) Three Rivers Country Club (1926-1935); (18) Mariemont Golf Course (1928-1937); (19) Elmstead Golf Course (1922-1960s); (20) Golf Club of College Hill (1898-1899).

and play began. Around 1900, Robert White, at that time Professional at Clifton GC, laid out a nine-hole course on the property of Judge Phillip Swing but it is unknown if this was ever open to public play.

The Terrace Park Country Club formally incorporated in 1910 but play was still among the homesites. This resulted in many broken windows and neighbor's complaints. Temporarily, they built a small course and tennis court on the property of Huber Lloyd and in 1914 a six-hole course was finally located on ten acres near the Little Miami River. A clubhouse was built in 1915 as well as five tennis courts and golf began in earnest with over seventy members. However, the broken windows were now replaced by errant shots into the river and so the club kept looking for more land to build a full eighteen-hole course. Eventually they would move to Milford and its present location in 1931

leaving numerous ghost holes among the gardens and homes of the village and along the Little Miami River.

The Second Wave of Ghost Courses

After WWI, the game continued its growth, stabilized and flourished during the Roaring Twenties. No longer would location be an impediment as the automobile allowed access to more sites. The early clubs had left ghost sites behind and, except for Clifton GC, Inverness CC and Glendale GC, all had established themselves in new locations albeit under different names. But as the Depression hit in 1929 there were new pressures on all golf clubs to stay viable and survive. Even the courses in the early wave that did make it to their better locations had to depend on outside revenue from slot machines, gambling and bootlegged drinks to stay afloat. Municipal courses and daily-fee

Terrace Park Golf Course clubhouse in the 1920s.

Hillcrest Country Club clubhouse, built in 1924.

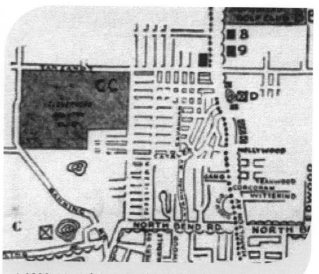

A 1930s Map of Homestead and Clovernook courses.

courses also felt the squeeze from the reduced number of players and the costs of maintaining their sites.

In 1916, the downtown Phoenix Club had exercised options on three tracts totaling 116 acres on the northeast corner of Seymour Avenue and Reading Road. The new Phoenix Country Club would include a beautiful new clubhouse, pool and tennis courts. This followed the lead of many other social clubs throughout the country that were getting into the golf business. The course was laid out on a flat piece of ground by architects Langford and Moreau and play began the same year. The golf club and downtown club members immediately saw the problems with operating two sites so far apart (and a requirement that everyone be a member of both clubs) so the two organizations split in 1919. Phoenix GC became Hillcrest GC. Later, to control costs, the club reduced to a nine-hole layout and changed their name to Crest Hills Country Club in 1940.

Hillcrest was the home course of Olga Strashun Weil for four of her Women's Met Championships before she moved to Losantiville CC in 1937. Milt Cook won two of his three Mets (1934, 1937) and Neil Ransick won one of his Mets (1935) and the 1935 Ohio Amateur while playing out of Hillcrest CC.

In 1924, a group led by William Holmes bought a tract of land on the east side of Hamilton Avenue just north of The Clovernook Home for the Blind in North College Hill. George Bowden of Maketewah CC laid out a nine-hole course that operated as a private club ($25 per year) but also provided some access to daily fee players ($1 greens fees on weekdays and $1.50 on weekends). Homestead GC became the home for many junior and caddy tournaments and was also the site for many years for the Cincinnati Post Hole-in One Tournament. This was especially popular during the Depression when any player (Amateur or Professional) could take five shots at the 135-yard Ninth Hole green with hopes of winning a set of Bobby Jones woods and irons. Homestead was the home course of the North College Hill HS golf team featuring future Professional Tom Nieporte and Lenny Wirtz, who would be Tournament Director for the LPGA. NCH would have three teams as State runner-up in the 1940s. Eventually the

F.H. Perry (center) and Ernest Brickwood, Head Professional (second from left), founders of Stonybrook Country Club. (Photo circa 1928)

A 1938 aerial photo of Mariemont looking west showing the location of the Mariemont Golf Club, now abandoned after the 1937 Great Flood.

lin was also the original founder of the Junior Met. Ridgewood GC was not just for junior players and it was once said that the ten best players there could beat a ten-man team from any club in the nation.

The Ridgewood project had been so successful that another group of investors led by F.H. Perry and Scottish Professional/Architect Ernest Brickwood took options on more property farther down Galbraith hill on the east side of Reading Road, north of Section Road. Begun in 1928, Stonybrook Country Club would start with bad timing as the Depression hit almost immediately and play did not actually start until June, 1930. They tried several pricing strategies to keep players at the course and eventually the club was sold and renamed Sycamore Country Club in 1934. There was an attempt to go private but soon operated as one of the new "semi-private" courses where members maintained special privileges like locker rooms but access could also be made by paying a daily fee. Eventually Sycamore CC sold off half their property in 1947 for development and reduced to nine-holes before going defunct and leaving that area of Roselawn to businesses, housing and restaurants.

In 1926, a group of businessmen from Cheviot, Cleves, Harrison, Price Hill and other neighboring towns banded together under the leadership of Judge George Eyrich to form the Three Rivers Corporation. Immediately they had over 250 members and plans for 150 more. Not waiting for a new clubhouse, the members converted an old farm house previously owned by President William Henry Harrison and hired Ed Brophy from Western Hills CC to build a quick nine-hole layout. The old stone building on the site was selected as a clubhouse and members quickly donated stoves, furniture, and utensils to get the operation ready. H.C.C. Tippet was hired and came in from Florida to complete the course design and Marty Kavanaugh Sr. was installed as Head Professional. At one time Three Rivers CC had almost 400 members before it also became a ghost course during the Depression. The city of Cincinnati considered buying the course for a few months in 1936 but eventually declined because of its remote location. That same year the property was purchased by Mrs. Flossie Brown, Manager of Jenny, Inc. a woman's apparel shop on West 4th Street.

Also, in 1928 the Mariemont Company decided to add a golf course to their planned community. Locating a site by the Little Miami River and under the leadership

course would close in the 1950s and the land used for a subdivision, stores and restaurants.

Ridgewood Golf Club, the original occupiers of the site on Ridge and Galbraith Roads, had been built in 1926 as a public daily-fee course. Avon Fields GC and Homestead GC had been the only significant sites north of the Ohio River to provide opportunity for public golf and Al Joslin Sr. and some fellow Hyde Park CC members like Bill Harig had a vision to provide golf for this new market of players. They were especially friendly to young golfers and Ridgewood became a location where caddies and other youngsters could play for a small fee and develop their game. Jos-

The Great Floods of 1936 and 1937 spelled the end for the Mariemont Golf Club.

Mariemont Golf Club clubhouse almost submerged from the 1933 flood. Floods in 1936 and 1937 totally submerged the clubhouse and forced the closure of the course and club.

of Gregory T. Des Jardins, Mariemont GC built a community course but allowed non-residents to play for an annual fee of $20. Jack Crook was the first Professional but several others served including Archie Simpson Sr. and Otis Bishopric. The Little Miami River floods of 1936 and especially 1937 washed away most of the course and clubhouse and the operation closed in 1937. For its brief time in operation, Mariemont GC had a great rivalry with Terrace Park CC.

Elmstead Country Club and The Arrowhead Inn

Farther up the Little Miami River was one of the more bizarre stories of the ghosts of Cincinnati golf's past. As early as 1909 and even before, the University of Cincinnati football team trained at a little camp near Branch Hill on the county line between Hamilton and Clermont Counties. Later, a nine-hole course was laid out and the Elmstead Golf Club was in business. About 1928, Ed Gaither purchased the golf course, its large barnlike dance hall and a small adjacent farm. Perhaps the city's wealthiest Black man, Mr. Gaither was an entrepreneur who had operated a pool hall, drug store, theater and other enterprises in the West End of downtown and was famous for having the only Rolls-Royce in Cincinnati.

The saga of the barn and its transformation into the Arrowhead Club was the story of the Roaring Twenties and organized crime. It was told most thoroughly by Gene Trimble in his blogs about the era as well as a series in *Poker Digest* and revolved around the entry of the Cleveland mob into the area as a pit stop

THREE RIVERS COUNTRY CLUB

For Reservations Phone Whitewater 7354   Cleves, Ohio

An Invitation is Extended to you to Visit this Beautiful Place. Open All Winter. Lunches, Dinners, Card Parties, Dances and Banquets.

T.R.C.C.
8720 Bridgetown Rd.
Near Cleves

C. W. CAINE, Cleves, Ohio
Phones Whitewater 7075 or Cleves 159

Invitation to Three Rivers Country Club at 8720 Bridgetown Road near Cleves.

to getting into illegal gambling in Northern Kentucky, St. Bernard and Elmwood. And it started with a machine gun attack on Gaither's house in 1929.

The barn was transformed into a supper club with local entertainment and gambling. The clientele were the residents of nearby Indian Hill and the payoffs to the politicians and law enforcement were made through a local minister. The organizers were a local gambler, Joe Bauer, and the Nason Brothers from Cleveland. The initial bankroll for the operation came from Detroit with mobsters like Sleepout Louie Levinson and Lefty Clark involved. After an initial failure in the rundown barn, new money from Cleveland remodeled the facilities and the Nasons called in Sammy Schrader from the Cleveland syndicate to help improve the grounds and the action. The Arrowhead Inn became the forerunner of the Beverly Hills operation in Northern Kentucky with

Arrowhead Supper Club at Elmstead Golf Course. (Photo circa 1930)

acts like Bing Crosby and big bands from Chicago and New York.

By 1935, the Arrowhead Club was on a roll and the little Elmstead GC course also became the site for some expensive betting games. However, Prohibition had ended in 1933 and speak-easies were no longer in vogue. Besides, there was increasing pressure from local authorities to close betting operations after the minister/bag man died suddenly and no one else knew who was being paid off. By 1937, the syndicate was gone. Gaither kept the Arrowhead Inn open until 1939 but eventually it closed its doors and many of the furnishings ended up in the offices of the new county court house in Batavia, Ohio. The Arrowhead got a reprieve later as it reopened for parties and weddings in the 1950s and the Elmstead course remained open for a few more years. It is now an apartment complex.

On the Horizon
Eventually Al Joslin's widow sold the Ridgewood course to the Crest Hills CC membership in 1966 as that club moved from Seymour Avenue. The nine-hole course on Reading Road became a public access site for a few years in the 1960s until replaced by a strip mall and office building. Years later, the Crest Hills CC membership would combine with Losantiville CC at their property in Pleasant Ridge and the Ridgewood/Crest Hills site in Amberly Village would also be abandoned as a golf course. Such was the fate of many courses during the early days of Cincinnati golf.

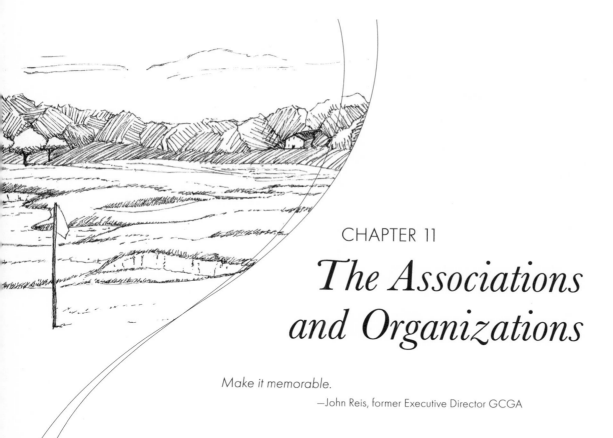

CHAPTER 11

The Associations and Organizations

Make it memorable.

—John Reis, former Executive Director GCGA

Introduction

The first attempts to organize golf and manage competitions were in Scotland. The Royal Burgess Golf Society, near Edinburgh, might have been the first but the Royal and Ancient Golf Club of St. Andrew's founded in 1754 had become the preeminent organization in Great Britain by the nineteenth century. In the United States, it was obvious the game needed similar organization at the national and local level and quickly the game's leaders made the move to standardize the game and formed what would be the United States Golf Association (USGA). Almost at the same time, some states, regions and cities were also organizing but eventually most would be under the umbrella of the USGA.

United States Golf Association (USGA)

In the United States the need for organization really became clear in 1894 when two separate golf clubs offered their own version of a national championship. With some organizational skill, four clubs along the east coast plus the Chicago Golf Club formed the Amateur Golf Association of the United States and

later changed their name to the American Golf Association. Eventually it was named the United States Golf Association (USGA) and within ten months the new organization conducted the first US Amateur, US Open and US Women's Amateur championships.

As the game grew in North America, the USGA grew with it and eventually provided the Rules and Regulations for the United States, Canada and Mexico. In addition, the USGA runs national competitions, establishes standards for playing equipment, manages the handicap system and provides services to local and state organizations in such fields as turf management and conservation. This is coordinated with the R&A who provides these services to the remainder of the golfing world.

The USGA also manages the unique handicapping system that provides equitable play among players. In America, we had originally adopted the R&A's method of averaging the player's three most recent scores to determine a handicap. But one of the key accomplishments of the USGA occurred in 1911 when a Committeeman named Leighton Calkins introduced a new handicapping method that included setting a par rating

George Bowden, a local Professional, worked with the USGA to design the handicap system.

Bill Jackson, Head Professional at Butler County Country Club and The Camargo Club, consulted with USGA on turf grasses nationwide.

for each course and requiring each club to have a Handicap Committee to manage the process. And Cincinnati had a hand in the further development of the system.

The new method would require that the individual courses had to be compared in some ways other than par. A player's score of 72 on one course might not be equivalent to a 72 on another and a local meeting helped create a new plan. In 1926, D.S. Horan of the USGA visited Cincinnati and met with George Bowden, Head Professional at Maketewah CC. Bowden had earlier floated the idea of having a handicap system in Cincinnati that would be similar to the one used back east in his hometown of Boston. During the Horan visit they developed the proposal and submitted the idea to James Clark, President of the Cincinnati Golf League.

Basically, a Committee of one hundred golfers around town played all of the local courses and assigned a par value for each layout so there would be equitable scoring reported. So, two courses might have the same scorecard Par of 72, but the Committee might vote that one course should have a real Par value of 69 and another 74, based on their own playing experiences. This data would then provide the handicaps of the players on the two different tracks. The same basic system exists today though it is done with more sophisticated course rating methods for a scratch and bogey player utilizing mathematical tables and computer calculations.

There have been many other connections between the USGA and Cincinnati golf. Not all involved the playing of the game but were just as important in the development of golf nationally. These include the work by Bill Harig in the 1930s on turf research at Hyde Park CC and later with Bill Jackson at The Camargo Club on grass seed application and turf management. Both local experts were called in to consult with the USGA as well as provide support to other clubs throughout the nation.

Cincinnati has also been the site for several USGA championships. The 1933 US Amateur was held at Kenwood CC and won by George Dunlap. The 1963 US Women's Open was also held at Kenwood CC and won by Mary Mills and the 1977 US Women's Amateur was held at Cincinnati CC and won by Beth Daniels. The US Amateur Public Links has been held here twice. In 1987, the tournament was won by Kevin Johnson at Glenview GC and the 2005 tournament was won by Clay Ogden at Shaker Run GC. Today, Cincinnati remains the site for numerous Local and Sectional USGA Qualifiers, a tradition started in 1931 and the ties are strong between USGA and local golf associations and players.

The Western Golf Association (WGA)

Many today think of the WGA only in terms of the Evans Scholarship program for caddies. But at one time the WGA and USGA were competitors for the organization of American golf itself. In the 1890s, the perception from 'Western' golf clubs (those west of Buffalo, New York) was that selection of competition sites and other rulings favored the clubs from the eastern USA.

The Western Golf Association (WGA) was founded in Chicago in 1899 to represent the courses out west, including Cincinnati. George Balch from Cincinnati GC was one of the first Presidents of the WGA. Other golf associations were started on a regional and state basis but the USGA and WGA guided golf through the early years in the United States.

Actually, the two organizations ran separate tournaments and sets of Rules in competition for almost

JUNE 9, 1931

CINCY GOLFERS AMONG 'ELECT'

Fischer and Bowden Qualify for National Open Tourney; Jordan Is Low Qualifier Here

By Chick Porter

Harold C. Jordan, professional at the Piqua Country Club, was low scorer in the trials for the National Open Golf Championship at the Maketewah Country Club Monday. His total for the 36 holes was 145.

Jordan started the morning round with a par and two birdies on the first three holes and finished the first nine holes in 35, two under par. He had a little difficulty with his putting on the 18th green, took three putts and finished with 38 for a total of 73.

Jordan's first nine holes in the afternoon were very good golf, but he was three strokes over his morning score. However, on the last nine he shot four birdies and finished with a 34 for a total of 72.

and he finished with a 34 for a gross of 73.

Neil Ransick, Red Strauss and Jimmy Brophy just missed being among the select six by one stroke.

Each had a total of 153. Strauss had 74 for his first 18-holes, Ransick had 75 and Brophy 77. Strauss easily should have been the low man in the morning, but he became careless with his putting on the last few holes and tossed off about six strokes. He turned in six birdies in the morning and had six three-putt greens.

Ransick has been ill during the early part of the season and has not regained his normal strength. His game was good, but he seemed to tire on the last round.

Brophy said he had no complaints and was pleased with his showing. He scored 77-76-153.

A 1931 Post article about the first U.S. Open Qualifier in Cincinnati, staged at Maketewah Country Club. John Fischer and George Bowden both qualified.

Qualifiers for US Open and US Amateur

As the major championships of the USGA became larger with more national and international participants, there had to be a way to qualify the field. Before 1913, anyone who filed an entry could enter the Championships. The number of golfers kept increasing and by the 1920s there were over 300 entries for the men's championships and the number kept growing. This required some qualifying strategies, first using the tournament site for several days before competition and eventually two remote locations handling the eastern and western halves of the country. The USGA further expanded the number of Sectional qualifying sites and also added some exemptions in 1926. In 1931, Cincinnati was favored to be a site for both the US Amateur Qualifier (The Camargo Club) and the US Open Qualifier (Maketewah CC). In 1959, the qualifying became a two-stage process with a Qualifier and the Sectional round. Clovernook CC, Western Hills CC and Hyde Park CC were also major local sites for those events through the years. The Camargo Club, Coldstream CC and Maketewah CC remain as Qualifier sites.

twenty more years before compromising and recognizing the USGA as the one source representing all American golf. On a local level, Cincinnati GC had hosted a prestigious Western Open Championship in 1905 won by Arthur Smith (first time by an American). Kenwood CC also hosted the 1954 Western Open with a victory by Lloyd Mangrum.

State and Local Organizations

By the turn of the century in 1900 organized golf was just a little over five years old in the eastern USA (USGA) and about a year old in the west (WGA). Like Great Britain, more natural evolution of the game provided competitions between clubs in addition to the normal internal club games and tournaments. At the beginning there was one organization in each state to run both men's and women's tournaments but eventually the two were split to meet the needs of the players. See the chapter on "Women's Golf" for women's organizations, both amateur and professional.

Ohio Golf Association (OGA)

The Ohio Golf Association was started in 1904 and hosted its first Amateur Championship that year at Cleveland CC. There were eleven founding member clubs including Cincinnati GC and the second tournament was held here and won by Charles Stanley. Elberon GC (Western Hills CC) joined the OGA in 1908 followed by Hyde Park CC, Losantiville CC and Hamilton County (Maketewah) CC. To win the State championship it was required to be a player at a member club at that time.

The state tournament returned to Cincinnati GC in 1911, 1913 and 1916 while Hamilton County CC held the tournament in 1917 as well as the first Ohio Open tournament the same year. Since then the state amateur and open championships have been held many times in the Cincinnati area. The Ohio Am has had a star-studded list of champions including Arnold Palmer (twice) and Denny Shute, as well as Cincinnatians Maurice McCarthy (Maketewah CC) (three times), Tony Blom (Maketewah CC) and Dewitt Balch (Cincinnati GC) (twice each) and Neil Ransick (Maketewah CC), Ira Holden (Cincinnati GC) and Russell Jones (Elberon/Western Hills CC) once each.

Kentucky Golf Association (KGA)

The Kentucky Golf Association was founded in 1911 and began conducting amateur competitions almost immediately. In addition, state-wide Professional championships were being held unofficially and by the first year Ft. Mitchell CC held the Open title (Peter Hendie) as well as the Amateur title (J.B. Warner). Darwin Stapp from Highlands CC won the Kentucky Open as an Amateur in 1926 and other local Professional win-

A 1933 photo of the Cincinnati area's Greenskeepers. First row: (l to r) T. Boyd, L. Lanfield, A. Brandhorst, Tex Harvey, C. Forste, A. Chamberlin, H. Mesloh, J. Muirden; Center row: A. Boyer, J. Allen, J. Thompson, O. Woodhouse, G. Benvie, W. Sheppard; Back row: (unidentified), A. Conrad, W. Bidwell, G. Donau, G. Waring.

The Superintendents Organize

The Professional Golfers organized the PGA in 1916 and unofficially there had been meetings as early as 1905 in Chicago with the Western Golf Association. Many of those early Pros also served as Course Superintendents at that time. But, as the game evolved, golf courses got longer and there were more demands on the operations outside the Pro Shop, larger clubs started the trend to hire specialists in maintaining and operating their investment in the grounds. At the same time, there were new grasses and fertilizing techniques being introduced to provide longer playing seasons and power equipment for cutting grass and greens and it was evident that professionals were also needed on the course itself.

As the number of Superintendents started to increase and the USGA and universities became more involved with turf issues, there was a natural evolution of communications among the Superintendents in a region. They shared weather, soil conditions and playability and budget demands from club members and Greens Committees. The state of Indiana, particularly Purdue University, was quick to build an educational network and our local Superintendents would attend workshops and lectures there. The Cincinnati Golfers League had started some early form of organization as early as 1925 and, with the foresight of a few here, the Greater Cincinnati Golf Course Superintendents Association (GCGCSA) was officially formed in 1931 to provide more support locally.

Cal Gruber, course builder and Superintendent at Coldstream Country Club developed a light weight fairway cutting technique that became a world standard.

Taylor Boyd, Superintendent, architect, course builder and founder of GCGCSA.

The founders and influential early members included Taylor Boyd (Terrace Park CC, The Camargo Club and Kenwood CC), Al Chamberlin (Hamilton Elks CC), George Benvie (Maketewah CC), Harry Mesloh (Clovernook CC), Art Conrad (Potter's Park and Miami University) and Warren Bidwell (Cincinnati CC). Eventually membership was extended to Superintendents of similar properties, like campuses and cemeteries so people like Cliff Runyon (Spring Grove Cemetery) could contribute. Also, seed and fertilizer company representatives were included and pioneers like George Richardson and Dwight Brown (McCullough Seed Company) could provide the latest research results and new product information.

During WWII most activities of the group were suspended but Taylor Boyd led a new wave of Superintendents like Marion Mendenhall (Kenwood CC), John McCoy (Cincinnati CC) and Don Likes (Hyde Park CC) to improve the education, communications and viabil-ity of the organization. Over the years, many course improvements and innovations have been developed by local membership including the removing of clippings and light weight fairway mowing by Cal Gruber at Coldstream CC. That method has been adopted nationwide and recognized by the USGA for "being the 'norm' among top quality golf courses." The GCGCSA remains a vital contributor to the evolution of golf locally with names too numerous to mention. The dedication and professionalism of the Golf Superintendent remains a key element in the growth and enjoyability of the game.

ners included John Brophy (Ft. Mitchell CC) and 'Bunny' Berning (DeVou GC). Local Kentucky Amateur winners included Johnny Fischer (Highland CC) and Nelson Ruddy (Summit Hills CC). Gordon Leishman also won the Kentucky Open after starting his amateur career in Cincinnati.

Greater Cincinnati Golf Association (GCGA)

Almost from the beginning of the formation of local clubs there had been informal competitions among club members and between clubs in town. Local clubs were also scheduling matches against their counterparts in other cities. Cincinnati GC had played matches against St. Louis and Pittsburgh clubs before 1900 and had a home and home arrangement with Midlothian Golf Club in Chicago in 1904 and 1905. Avondale GC was engaged in matches with Highland GC in Indianapolis and Ft. Mitchell CC was scheduling regular events with other clubs in Lexington and Louisville, Kentucky.

But there was more pressure to organize locally into a similar format being used by Saturday afternoon amateur baseball leagues. William Strobridge of the Clifton GC and others organized a meeting of seven golf clubs in Greater Cincinnati in April, 1905. This was only one year after the Ohio Golf Association was formed. The invited Cincinnati area golf clubs were Clifton GC, Cincinnati GC, Inverness GC, Ft. Mitchell CC, Elberon CC, Losantiville CC and Avondale GC. Two of the invitees—Fort Mitchell CC and Cincinnati GC—chose not to accept the first year's membership and the remaining five started play immediately in June, 1905 as the Cincinnati Golfer's League (CGL). Eventually the organization was renamed the Greater Cincinnati Golf Association (GCGA) in 1988.

The first two matches officially were underway on June 3, 1905, and featured Clifton GC versus Inverness GC and Elberon GC versus Avondale GC. The league agreed to schedule matches on alternate Saturdays through October. Clifton GC had officially disbanded in 1905 but some golfers still maintained the property and competed in the league until 1907. Losantiville GC competed in the first year but dropped out for the 1906 and 1907 seasons as they built their new course in Pleasant Ridge.

The first Board of delegates to the League included Edward H. Hargrave (Avondale GC), William W. Helm (Inverness GC), Louis C. Rauh (Losantiville GC), Lovell C. Rose (Elberon GC) and William M. Strobridge (Clifton GC). By 1906 Ft. Mitchell CC and Cincinnati GC had joined and Losantiville eventually filled Clifton's spot in 1908. In 1909 Inverness CC closed permanently and Hyde Park CC filled Inverness' slot in the lineup.

By 1908, the League was also discussing the formation of a city tournament (called a "field day," a term used for outdoor competitions of all types in those days). The first Cincinnati Metropolitan Championship—"The Met"—was played in 1910 at Losantiville CC's brand-new Bendelow course in Pleasant Ridge. The inaugural event was won by William Groesbeck of Cincinnati GC. The tournament continues to this date and has grown to a size that requires two qualifying sites before final match play. Met Championships were eventually added for Women, Senior and Junior players as well as various team and handicap events.

The organization's scope of services continued to expand as it formed a group to organize Superintendents and Greenskeepers in 1925 and added golf course rating in 1926. And very early in its existence, the organization also was involved with resolving conflicts such as the Caddy Strike of 1914 and also instrumental in bringing USGA Championships like the 1933 US Amateur and others to local clubs.

The GCGA is recognized by the USGA as the organization responsible for conducting tournaments, interpreting Rules, providing handicap services and course ratings and is one of the few such organizations that has multi state coverage (Southwestern Ohio, Northern Kentucky and Southeast Indiana).

Intercity and Regional Organizations

As mentioned previously, intercity play had started in the 1890s but was sporadic in nature and dependent on the business contacts at individual clubs. There was a Tri-State Cup started in 1909 among Indianapolis, Louisville and Cincinnati. But these early competitions began to wane and other attempts for city teams to compete regionally also sputtered.

In 1925 a last gasp meeting among Cincinnati, Indianapolis and Columbus golfers at Losantiville CC got it rolling for one year. However, a Cincinnati team loaded with good players like DeWitt Balch, Doug Hill, Al Baumgartner and Spencer Kuhn more than doubled the points of the other two teams and the effort was short lived. As the Depression hit all golf, it also curtailed any interest in competitions outside of state or region and it would be a while before that returned.

By 1940, an improving economy and renewed competitive interests brought about an opportunity for the old idea to resurface. That year, a new organization and competition was started among Ohio, Kentucky, and Indiana amateur players. The Tri-State Invitational was announced using an annual format of two-man teams from the three states with venues rotating among the region's great courses. This had been the idea of Colonel Lee S. Read (Louisville, Kentucky) and Clifford Wagoner (Indianapolis, Indiana) and after some preliminary meetings and correspondence the Tri-State Golf Association was organized.

In addition to the above two founders, Cincinnati was well represented in numbers and prestige as Roy G. Elliott, Robert Bohne, Thomas Earls, Don Gill, Frank Loewe, Art Theler and Doug Warner all had a hand in getting the association and first tournaments organized.

The inaugural contest was staged at Cincinnati CC in August, 1940 and the State championship was won by Ohio and led by the two-man team of Tom Earls and Bob Sulzer. The tournament has continued annually with participation by such players as Jack Nicklaus, Fuzzy Zoeller, Gay Brewer, Bob Lohr and Frank Beard playing as amateurs. Just about every top local amateur since 1940 has participated for the Ohio or Kentucky team and it has been played at many of the local clubs through the years.

Professional Golf Association (PGA)

A national organization for professional players was taking a little more time than the amateurs. Since early Pros also sometimes acted as course Superintendents and club makers as well as teachers and pro shop managers, there was not much time to organize. There had been some regional groups formed and unofficial communication among Pros at local clubs. At the same time, there was still a stigma about being a Professional player and at many clubs they were not invited to club facilities like the dining rooms and clubhouses. Most early Professionals were immigrants from Scotland, Ireland and England and besides performing their club duties would also be involved in betting games and other gambling activities. Some club members considered the early Professional almost as a servant.

Nationally there had been no movement to organizing but when the Western Golf Association (WGA) was founded in Chicago it started a separate Professional organization in 1905. Robert White was chosen to run this new endeavor. White had been Head Professional at Cincinnati GC and Avondale GC in the 1890s and had worked

George Balch,
Cincinnati Golf Club,
President of WGA.

at resort courses in Michigan and West Virginia as well as his club positions back in Chicago. He was an excellent player, having played in about every US Open to that point, was an expert club maker, agronomist and businessman and had made many contacts nationally. Still there was no national organization to represent the interests and issues of the growing number of golf Professionals and White and others were starting to see the need for one.

Things stayed the same for several years but some untimely rulings on amateur status by the USGA and more confidence of playing professionals like Walter Hagen and Gene Sarazen provided the impetus for the formation of the Professional Golfers Association of America (PGA) in 1916. Sparked by Tom McNamara and supported by Louis Wanamaker at his department store in New York City, the first meeting was attended by over sixty people including Francis Ouimet and many playing Professionals as well as those who derived their livelihood from running golf clubs. With the formation of the PGA, and high-profile athletes like Hagen and Sarazen, the perception of Golf Professionals was slowly changing.

This was the first attempt to unify all of the members nationally. Robert White, was also named first President of the PGA at the meeting. He was perfect for the job with his connections throughout the Midwest and the eastern seaboard and his experience running the WGA Professional organization. The Association was initially organized into seven sections (Metropolitan, Middle States, New England, Southeastern, Central, Northwestern and Pacific). From that meeting it has grown to be the world's largest working sports organization with over 28,000 men and women members.

With the formation of the PGA, records and statistics were compiled for professional victories by its members. By 1932, Bob Harlow was named the manager of the newly formed Tournament Bureau and money list records were started but it was still up to individual players to know where and when key Open events were

John Shippen finished sixth in the 1896 U.S. Open and played in five more Opens when entered as a "Native American" even though he was Black. He had a great career as a club Professional on the east coast.

staged and how to travel between these venues. Sometimes local club Pro's like Otto Hackbarth, George Bowden, Clarence Dapper, Clay Gaddie and others ventured out to national tournaments but local Professionals would mainly play in regional and state Opens and sometimes in Florida, California or Texas during the winter off-season.

As the PGA got larger, the divergent needs of the Touring Pros and Club Professionals became apparent. The number of tournaments and the purses were increasing after WWII and new stars like Ben Hogan, Byron Nelson and Sam Snead had different priorities than the club Professionals. Now there was more structure to the informal circuit of tournaments but it still did not meet all of the needs of the players on tour. In 1968, the Tournament Players Division of the PGA split off and formed their own organization. It eventually changed its name to the PGA Tour in 1975. Most players from the various tours still maintain membership in the PGA of America but now the main organization could concentrate on the needs of growing the game through organization and teaching at the club level.

Southern Ohio PGA (SOPGA)

The original organization of the PGA in 1916 included Cincinnati in the Middle States Section. As the game continued to grow in the region and America, there were further subdivisions and in 1921 Cincinnati clubs moved into the newly formed Ohio Section. To provide a more responsive organization, the Ohio Section was then divided further as Cincinnati, Columbus and Dayton started their own chapters. The Greater Cincinnati Professional Golfers Association (GCPGA) was formed in 1930 and Clarence Dapper was elected President, Jim Brophy, Vice-President and Elmer Gerth, Secretary-Treasurer. In this initial organization, the Professionals in Northern Kentucky were included.

Finally, in 1946, the state reorganized and Cincinnati was added as part of the Southern Ohio Section. That year, the Southern Ohio PGA (SOPGA) had its

Left to right: Woodrow Brown, Arnold B. Walker, and Joe Dowell, helped found the first Black Golf Club (Greater Cincinnati Golfers Club) at Avon Fields GC in 1938. (Other members Charley Mitchell, Chaukey Payne, and Oscar Gamby photos not available.)

first meeting at Crest Hills CC electing Tom Bryant (Moraine CC) as President and Gene Marchi (Miami Valley CC) as Secretary-Treasurer. Later the Sections became more restrictive on crossing state borders so Northern Kentucky Professionals returned to the Kentucky PGA.

Many Professionals came from the links of Cincinnati to have great careers as club Professionals and tour players. These would include Tom Nieporte, caddy from Homestead GC (and Assistant Professional at Clovernook CC), who went on to become the Head Professional at Winged Foot CC as well as winning several PGA Tour events like the Bob Hope Desert Classic.

Tom Strange (starting as a caddy at Hyde Park CC) was Host Professional at The Greenbrier in 1960–61 and Head Professional at Bow Creek CC in Norfolk VA. A great teacher and tournament competitor, Tom is the father of PGA players Allan and Curtis Strange. Other locals included Jim Flick, Head Professional at Losantiville CC and one of golf's premier instructors with students such as Jack Nicklaus, Jack Grout, Tom Weiskopf and Tom Lehman.

Golf Course Superintendents Association of America (GCSAA)

Started originally by John Morley of Youngstown, Ohio, in September, 1926 as the National Association of Greenkeepers of America, the organization quickly grew from 60 original founders to its present 18,000 members. Morley was a tireless leader who was recognized by Architect Donald Ross for his " … great success, not only from the standpoint of the members, but also from the clubs that employ them." He visited hundreds of golf courses continuing education and supporting a profession that is normally forgotten by the players that enjoy the benefit of their labors. There was a lot of Cincinnati area representation in that first group of members including James Muirden of Ridgewood GC who served on the Executive Committee. Clubs and Superintendents who also were early members included George Benvie (Maketewah CC), Alex Baxter (Kenwood CC), C.F. Forste (Hillcrest CC), William Fruectemeyer, (Hyde Park CC), Ollie Hudson (Avon Fields GC), Harry Mesloh (Clovernook CC), James Thomson (Cincinnati CC), and O. Woodhouse (Losantiville CC). Today's Organization also supports their Environmental Institute for Golf to provide scholarships, research, education and advocacy for the game we enjoy.

Minority Golf Organizations

One situation where there was no even playing field was the access to Black golfers in amateur or Professional organizations. Even though one African American (John Shippen) and one Native American (Oscar

Bunn) played at the first US Open at Shinnecock in 1895, the remainder of the time period of this book was spent keeping the races separated in competition and clubs. Shippen went on to a long and storied career as a Club Professional including 1899 at Aronimink CC in Philadelphia. He also was able to play in six US Opens because he was entered as a Native American though 100% African American.

Organizations and clubs can be used to exclude as well as include and many national, state and local championships were limited to member clubs and thus controlled participation. This continued a world-wide trend that diminished the game for decades. Like baseball and other sports, it is unknown what impact this had on the records and achievements of early players. Jackie Robinson broke baseball's color barrier in 1948 but it would take until 1961 for the PGA to act by removing a "Caucasians only" section in their by-laws for access by Black Professionals. And it would take even longer to make any impacts on club membership, course access and other barriers to equality.

African-American players did form their own organization in the 1920s, to provide a place to compete professionally. Players like Lee Elder, Charley Sifford and Pete Brown honed their skills with the United Golf Association (UGA) and eventually made it to the PGA Tour. But it took many more years to get invitations to the Masters and other venues on the tour.

The amateur attempts to admit blacks was not any quicker. After four Blacks were denied admission to a Chicago public tournament and a failed subsequent lawsuit, the United States Colored Golfers Association (USCGA) was formed in 1925. Soon they were running Open and Amateur events and eventually changed their name to the United Golfers Association (UGA). Like their white counterparts, purses were small and most of the players in these organizations depended on side bets and hustling to make a living in the game. Mixing with celebrities like Joe Louis,

Pete Brown, PGA Tour winner and SOPGA member.

Duke Ellington and Billy Eckstine, more could be made in outside bets than in the tournament purses.

In 1930, Chicagoan Robert (Pat) Ball was able to play in the prestigious Western Amateur—the first Black to play in a national tournament since Shippen. But it would be more than forty years before all of the remaining obstacles would be eliminated.

Locally, African-American players were originally restricted from playing in the Met and formed their own organization called the Greater Cincinnati Golfers Club. It began at Avon Fields in 1938 and was started by six players—Charley Mitchell, Woodrow Brown, Chaukey Payne, Joe Dowell, Oscar Gamby, Sr. and Arnold Walker. The organization launched the careers of many local Black players.

Eventually, the Met was open to all players in 1967 and a forty-year-old Jimmy Woods was runner-up the following year. Kevin Hall became the first African American to win the tournament in 2003. Locally, Professionals like Dick Plummer at The Camargo Club, René Garza at Wyoming CC and Dick James at Harmon GC were able to use their influence to provide improved playing conditions and access for African Americans to courses and outings.

Pete Brown became the first Black member of the SOPGA and was Head Professional at Madden GC in Dayton, Ohio, for twenty years. Brown is most known as one of the the first African Americans to win a PGA Tour event when he took the Waco Open crown in 1964. Brown won the prestigious Legacy Award from the SOPGA in 2002 for his contributions to golf.

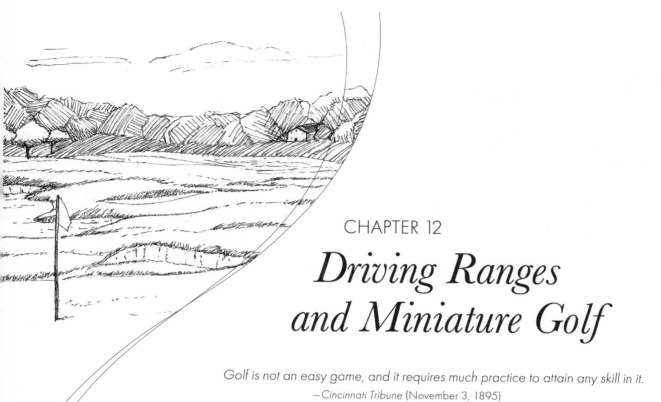

CHAPTER 12
Driving Ranges and Miniature Golf

Golf is not an easy game, and it requires much practice to attain any skill in it.
—*Cincinnati Tribune* (November 3, 1895)

Introduction

A driving range or a place to practice seems second nature to the game of golf today. But this

Early driving range ball retriever.

was not a consideration for the early golfers and architects who laid out the first courses. Golf, in its infancy in Scotland, had many layouts of only four to six holes on just a few acres. Even in the United States most early courses were located on very small pieces of property. Urban real estate was at a premium as parks and recreation competed against subdivisions, new manufacturing plants and even farms for available land. Golf courses had to fight for every available acre and there was little space for practice facilities.

Elberon GC started on fewer than eight acres on Price Hill before moving to larger lots on Rapid Run and finally Cleves-Warsaw to become Western Hills CC. The earliest course in Terrace Park actually was routed through vacant lots between village homesites before eventually becoming an eighteen-hole course in nearby Milford. Losantiville CC was built on the infield of a race track in Oakley before becoming a full-size course in Pleasant Ridge. Other local courses started on similar sized lots and available property was used for clubhouse, golf course and sometimes a swimming pool or tennis courts. There was nothing to spare for practice areas.

The Brendamour store downtown included an indoor practice facility for golf.

Johnny Fischer under the watchful eye of Professional Art Smith at his indoor practice facility inside the Brendamour Sporting Goods store on Main Street downtown.

Practice Facilities and the Professional as Instructor

Because of the lack of facilities at the course, the game first turned indoors for practice sites. They were already in operation in 1900 in New York and Chicago and Cincinnati was quick to follow. Many restaurants and hotels put in small indoor putting greens. Their courses were laid out on a woven carpet with a special heavy nap and fine sand was laid around the holes to duplicate outdoor conditions.

An indoor green and small putting course had been installed at Spalding Sporting Goods store on Government Square in 1909 and amateurs and Professionals would spend winter months practicing and even arranging competitions. Brendamour's also added a practice facility downtown. These early facilities were mainly for amusement and usually manned by a local Professional during the off season. But it was obvious that this was also an opportunity for teaching various aspects of the game.

In 1923, sixty-year-old Archie Simpson Sr., Head Professional at Ft. Mitchell CC, announced that he and his son would run an indoor golf school at the Central YMCA and be open to the public. They took over the instruction from the Brophy brothers who had started the program a few years earlier. By 1929, Simpson and Allan Brickwood, Head Professional at Stonybrook GC in Roselawn, began the Ruff Recreation Golf Club indoors at the old Central Turner Hall near 14th and Walnut Streets in Over the Rhine. Touted as the best facility of its kind in Cincinnati, it featured sand bunkers, water hazards, two driving nets and more opportunities for off-season instruction.

Almost at the same time, outdoor driving ranges were being built around town. Some, like the Dixie Fairway Golf Range (next to the Highland Cemetery in Ft. Mitchell, Kentucky) soon added lights but the technology limited visibility to about fifty—one-hundred yards from the tee. In 1931, a twenty-two-tee range was built on Beechmont Avenue near the present Levee. Two years later, Professional Jim Brophy opened his new Driving Range on Section Road in Roselawn and Art Fisher was there to assist. In 1934, Ernie Brickwood cut down seven acres of tough grass with a push mower to build his range on Reading Road just north of Maketewah CC but by then there were signs that golf on full-size courses was slowing in popularity. The economic woes of the 1930s was starting to take their toll on the game but that offered opportunity for the driving ranges.

During the Depression, many players gave up their private club membership and the few municipal courses left were also having trouble finding players. Many turned to driving ranges to keep involved with the game but the deepening Depression also started to have an effect at the off-course businesses too. By 1935, fourteen Cincinnati golf Professionals saw the trend and worked with the *Cincinnati Post* to introduce a new program of free lessons. They used the area's surviving driving ranges, private and public courses and Professionals like Bill Jackson (The Camargo

Club), Art Smith (Summit Hills CC), Clarence Dapper (Hillcrest CC), Ed Brophy (Western Hills CC) and Frank Gelhot (Ridgewood CC) actively participated. Babe Didrikson, at that time the nation's greatest woman golfer, was so impressed with the local program that she made a special stop in Cincinnati to congratulate the organizers on this effort to get new players into the game and keep interest high.

Toward the end of the 1930s, Cincinnati's economy started slowly to improve and a few new ranges started to appear again. Art Fisher eventually started his own facility in 1937 on Wooster Pike, and Clarence Dapper moved to the Eastwood Driving Range on Duck Creek Road in 1939. Other new ranges were in place on Reading Road near Summit and on Tennessee Avenue near Paddock Rd. With the coming of WWII, many ranges again closed as owners and instructors were joining the military service. Besides a shortage of golf teachers, there were fewer golf balls being made as country's manufacturing industry changed to support the war effort.

As the war ended, interest in golf again increased as men and women returned home from the military. Art Fisher returned from his three-year stint in the Navy to reopen his new range near Newtown. For a while, Fisher's wife had maintained the facility while he was gone. More facilities opened and a supply of new golf balls was now available. A new wave of owners came into the business and innovations like motorized retrievers and better lighting made the facilities more user-friendly. This also meant ranges could be open longer hours and service a bigger clientele.

New ranges opened at the Lunken Airport Playfield, Shady Shores Park in Covington, and out on Reading Road where the Drake Driving Range was built. On the west side there was Jon-Tom Driving Range at the corner of Queen City and Boudinot Avenues where John Mittlehauser provided golf instruction

Jim Brophy ran one of the city's first outdoor driving ranges on Section Road in Roselawn. He also ran a teaching operation from the downtown Brendamour's, replacing Losantiville's Harry Boyers.

out of a wooden shack. But he also later coupled the facility with his nearby Jon-Tom Sporting Goods Store on Glenway to supply clubs and other golf equipment. By 1960, golf practice facilities were transitioning to be more full-service suppliers and becoming family destinations.

Miniature Golf, Tom Thumb and Putt-Putt

In addition to the indoor putting facilities appearing at restaurants, hotels and stores before WWI, another special short-lived phenomenon hit the nation around 1929 that propelled the miniature game to where it is today. There had already been some putting courses built near resorts. At Pinehurst they built a miniature course called Thistle Dhu in 1916. The miniature game was used for the amusement of resort guests as well as a venue for the après-golf crowd.

But in 1929, a Tennessee promoter and salesman named Garnet Carter opened his first patented miniature golf course in Florida and, for the next couple of years, his concept swept the nation. Almost overnight "Tom Thumb" courses started to sprout. Named for the famous diminutive Barnum & Bailey Circus performer from the 1860s, the courses were normally outdoors and featured a special putting surface of cottonseed hulls, sand, green dye and oil. This was a big improvement over the carpeting in the indoor facilities and provided a close replica of regular golf greens. Locating courses was simple and at one time there were over 150 such layouts on the rooftops of New York City.

Ball retriever at Brophy's Driving Range. (Photo circa 1933)

John Mittlehauser at Jon Tom Range shack at corner of Queen City and Boudinot Roads. (Photo circa 1955)

Thistle Dew Putting Course in Pinehurst. (Photo circa 1916)

Cincinnati Reds pitcher Eppa Rixey proposed a similar course on the Cincinnati Club clubhouse on 8th and Race Streets. In Newport, the City Council built a course in Bellevue Park. The new Ken-Ridge miniature course on Montgomery Road featured competitions among some of the city's best golfers. D.J. Harding announced from his 13th Street offices that there were plans for ten new courses to be installed in the various Cincinnati suburbs in 1931.

By 1930, the city had formed a Tom Thumb Golf League and "Aunt Kate" Brophy, Western Hills CC Professional, announced that she would sponsor a Tom Thumb tournament for women. But regulations also followed quickly as Cincinnati City Council announced in their meeting that year that they appropriated $1,000,000 for the new Western Hills Viaduct and also an annual $100 tax on miniature golf courses. The USGA also soon announced that cash prizes won at the first Miniature Golf National Championship in Chattanooga would affect amateur standing of the participants and they would be considered Professional if they kept their winnings.

But as fast as Tom Thumb golf came on the scene, it was destroyed by the Economic Depression. Money for recreation took a back seat when so many people were out of work. By 1931, Cleveland had announced no more miniature course construction in the city parks. Most of the entrepreneurs who previously spread throughout the country carrying building plans and dreams and searching for vacant lots suddenly were going bankrupt. Prominent celebrities like sportswriter Grantland Rice and movie star Mary Pickford suddenly saw their investments turn to nothing. Pickford's Hollywood course had cost $100,000 and she did run it for a few more years until it too failed.

In November 1930, there were over 100,000 Tom Thumb courses in operation nationwide with an estimated investment of $175 million. At the same time there were 1,800 companies furnishing construction materials and supplies to keep the Tom Thumb courses running. By 1931, half of the courses had gone bankrupt and closed and most of those remaining were unprofitable. Companies that furnished raw materials like horse hair, cottonseed and cocoa fiber needed for putting surfaces suddenly found no buyers and went defunct. Prices were cut to entice players but the end was there. Tom Thumb golf was a two-year wonder.

Through the rest of the Depression and WWII, miniature golf continued to decline. Recreation locally switched to fishing lakes and twenty-five such facilities were built in the Cincinnati area during that time. Some miniature courses did last through WWII and into the 1950s. Locations like Airy Hills on North Bend Road (between Cheviot and White Oak) combined a swimming pool, miniature golf and two fishing lakes to cover all the bases for recreation. Fortunately, like driving ranges, the end of the war brought a resurgence of miniature golf facilities for recreation and competition. Miniature courses were soon added at some of the driving ranges and parks like Lunken Playfield.

In 1954, entrepreneur Don Clayton from North Carolina started the Putt-Putt franchises and the Cincinnati area was soon home to some of the nation's most popular locations. By keeping all of the gadgets off the course and making each hole thirty-feet long

New York City had 150 Tom Thumb golf courses on rooftops in 1931.

Miniature Golf in Mt. Auburn. (Photo circa 1930)

with a par of two, Clayton created a better venue for testing the skills needed on the full-size courses. He called Cincinnati the "country club of Putt-Putt" and matches would be televised here for over a decade. Some of the first installations here were located near other attractions like the Dairy Aisle in Silverton or the fifty-four-hole facility in Roselawn. Clayton also founded the Professional Putters Association (membership fee of $5) and held the second National Putting Championship at the Roselawn facility in 1961 with a Purse of $7,500.

Miniature golf remains a staple today in resort cities like Myrtle Beach or Atlantic City or near the beaches of Florida. But patrons still enjoy many sites in the Tri-State and it is a part of golf's lore and legend.

Executive Courses

Another recreational option was developed in the early days of golf. In fact, any player today when presented with the average course of the 1800s would think they are on what we now call today an Executive Course. Most of those early courses featured layouts with a length of 3500-4500 yards for eighteen holes. That would yield an average of 190-250 yards per hole. This was formidable in the days of hickory shafts and Featherie or Gutty golf balls but the same yardages today would yield a mix of Par-3 and short Par-4 holes, the perfect dimensions for an Executive Course.

By definition an Executive course is a layout designed for quick play, the need for less clubs in the bag and simple designs. It is made for the quick round or for beginners and players wanting to hone their short

game. But that definition meant nothing for an early entrepreneur on the west side who just wanted to build a golf course.

Bill Lewis quit his job with the Post Office in 1931 to pursue his dream of building a course on his farm property. Alongside his wife Dora, they laid out the 2555-yard course on Muddy Creek Road. Soon they were collecting greens fees, hired Kate Brophy as Head Professional and Woodland Golf Club was in business. Later the course was re-designed to 2161 yards as holes were shortened and some Par-4s converted to par 3s to make it more in the Executive design. Eventually the course was purchased by the Cincinnati Recreation Commission.

Fernbank GC was originally a private club using city property near the river for their course. Eventually it became a public course and moved to its present location on Fernbank Avenue.

Though the likes of Woodland and Fernbank GC could offer some challenging Par-4s, it wasn't until the 1950s and 1960s that specially designed Executive and Par-3 courses layout would become reality. In 1959, Len and Joe Macke built Delhi Par-3, the first true local Par-3 layout, on Ebenezer Road. It included nine holes ranging from 80 to 150 yards on rolling and hilly ground. Greenhills CC built their Par-3 course that year also with a design by Professional Marty Kavanaugh. Executive and Par-3 courses were now also filling a niche in the local golfing scene.

On the Horizon

The crown jewel facility of the period was the 1962 opening of the Golden Tee Amusement Center. Located at the Sharon Road exit off of I-75, it included a fully lit nine-hole Par-3 course, double-deck teeing area with fifty tees and "12,500 snow-white quality" golf balls. In the clubhouse were pool tables and other amusements. Practice facilities had arrived at the modern age and were now a family destination.

The following year the Bonair Golf Center was opened on Newtown Road with an Arnold Palmer putting course. A double deck driving range with thirty-four tees was added in 1964. Soon a nine-hole full-size course was built as well and the name changed to Ironwood Golf Club in 1971. In 1975 the property and facilities would be purchased by the Hamilton County Park Board and renamed Little Miami Golf Center. Later, a Par-3 course was added also.

Putt-Putt courses in Western Hills, Roselawn and Mt. Washington were still operating in the late 1960s though the Roselawn site had been moved to Even-

Lunken Playfield Miniature Golf Course in the 1960s.

dale. Eventually only two franchises remained, one in Hamilton and one in Northern Kentucky. But miniature golf, executive courses and driving ranges remain integral to the golf tradition in Cincinnati.

CHAPTER 13
The Media

It is the opinion of prominent physicians that (Red's Pitcher and Manager) Christy Mathewson hastened his own (end of baseball career) by taking up golf, which undermines the intellect ...

—Ring Lardner, *Cincinnati Post* sports page (July 26, 1916)

Introduction

In Cincinnati, the word "golf" appeared for the first time on September 1, 1890, in an article in the *Cincinnati Commercial Tribune* and it was unrelated to the game itself. It was only a comment about a cartoon in the British magazine *Punch*. It would be interesting to know if any readers even knew what "golf" meant. By 1960 there were over ninety golf establishments in the Tri-State and the media had a big part in that growth.

Local sports news in the 1890s and into the 1900s mainly focused on competitions in baseball, boxing and horse racing. Golf, bicycle racing and tennis were just coming on the scene but all of those stories appeared intermingled with the news of the day. Golf would be treated as much as a social phenomenon as it was a sport. But with the formation of the Cincinnati Golf League (CGL) in 1905 and new intra-city competitions, more and more articles and match results became newsworthy. It would be the 1920s before a separate sports section of papers began to be the norm for the daily publications and by then golf had begun to acquire its own local and national celebrities and the beginnings of the lore of championships and accomplishments. And these would be right alongside the stories of other athletes and sports teams.

Golf and Newspapers in Cincinnati

The first major newspapers in the area were started in the mid 1800s and were firmly established when golf arrived on the scene. The *Cincinnati Times-Star* started in 1840, The *Cincinnati Enquirer* was started in 1841, and the *Cincinnati Post* in 1881. Eventually the *Times-Star* and *Post* would combine in a merger in 1958 and the paper renamed the *Post-Times Star*. Previously the *Post* had also bought a radio station in 1935 and renamed the call sign WCPO for the voice of the *Cincinnati Post*. It would eventually also enter the TV business as WCPO-TV and went on the air in 1949. News organizations began to morph strictly from newspapers to radio, television and eventually to on-line availability. All would be a major player in the spread of golf news and the promotion of the game itself.

Many events sealed the relationship between golf and the media in the early years. Certainly, the Fran-

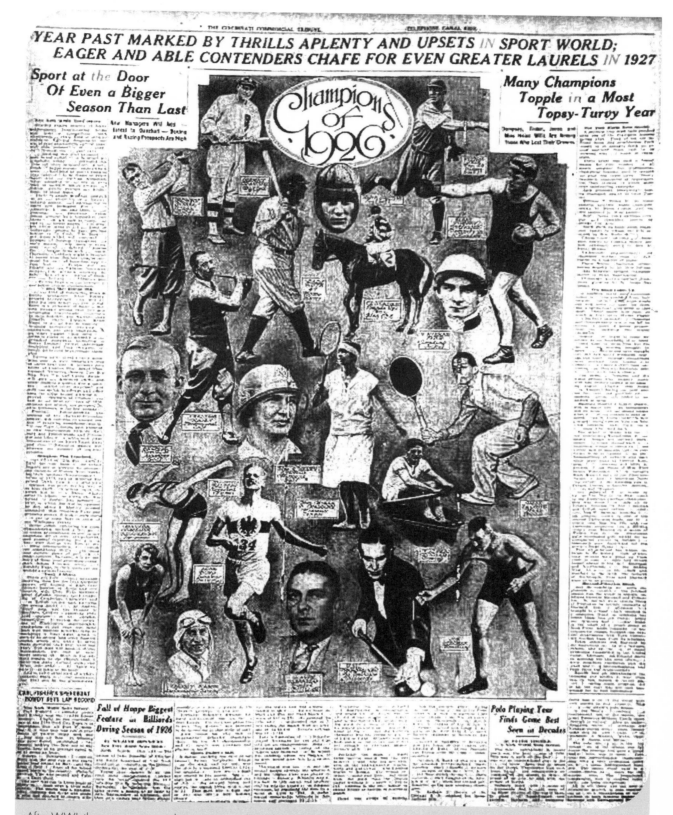

After WWI, there was a tremendous interest in all sports and sports heroes. Bobby Jones, Walter Hagen, Francis Ouimet and other stars were in the papers every day and local players and even caddies had scores posted regularly.

Sketch of Francis Ouimet in the *Cincinnati Post* after the 1914 U.S. Open.

Ralph Love, a *Cincinnati Post* golf writer and historian. He wrote about the history of golf for the newspaper's sports page in 1927.

Ralph Love was the golf writer for the *Cincinnati Post* and among his accomplishments was a twenty-plus series of articles written in 1927 and 1928 to document the history of golf in the city up to that time. Ralph was a member at Twin Oaks CC and Maketewah CC and an avid and competitive amateur golfer. During his tenure at the Post, golf became a constant item on the front page of the Sports section. Local players, Superintendents, Greenskeepers and even caddies became known by his articles and their fame spread throughout the city.

cis Ouimet win in the 1913 US Open whetted the American appetite for achievement in this new sport. Most did not know the rules or the history of the game but Ouimet's picture still appeared as an artist sketch in many papers. The sport needed its heroes and stars and Ouimet appeared in every American paper at the time.

It would be the early 1900s before many papers began to feature photographs routinely. And it was not until the 1930s that good quality wire photos could be transmitted over phone lines so pictures could be shared between cities and players could be seen in action. Before that, the game depended on the written word and the occasional sketch or cartoon to view the players of the day.

Cincinnati papers did pick up nationally syndicated sports columns and cartoons from the major sportswriters of the day including Grantland Rice, Ring Lardner, Murray Olderman, James J. Montague and Jim Murray. As the sport spread in town, certain writers became adept at the game and began to report it from a first-person basis. Through the years many notable news writers were on the local golf beat, including Pat Harmon, Bill Powers, Lou Smith, Wally Forste and Tom Swope, but one man in particular stood out as the its major local writer.

Caddie tournaments and major outings at clubs were publicized and you could follow the careers of golf stars like Johnny Fischer, Milt Cook, and the Brophy brothers from their days as caddies through their whole careers. Love eventually moved east and went into the insurance business but moved back to the Queen City during WWII and served with the US Army at UC. He was replaced at the *Post* by Chick Porter and Sue Goodwin who continued the tradition of great golf reporting. In addition to Love, Bob Newhall of the *Cincinnati Commercial-Tribune* also rates special mention for his contributions.

But one of the real signs of golf's acceptance by the general public was when its stories appeared daily in the funny papers. A popular comic strip was picked up by the *Times-Star* in 1928 and then moved to the *Enquirer* a few years later. "In the Rough" penned by Howard Freeman was nationally syndicated and followed the travails

Grantland Rice (1921)

IN THE ROUGH—*The Duke Considers All Emergencies.*   Registered U. S. Patent Office.   —By HOWARD FREEMAN.

Golf was even seen in the comic strips of the 1930s; the sport was becoming part of the everyday fabric of the city less than forty years from the time it was first played here.

"SO THAT'S HOW THEY USED TO DRESS FOR GOLF. WHAT A RIDICULOUS LOOKING COSTUME!"

A 1903 cartoon from *Golf Illustrated*.

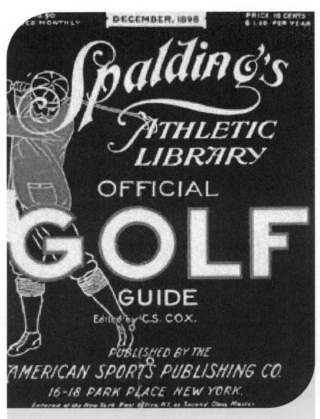

Spalding's Official Golf Guide in 1898 started arriving in mail boxes almost simultaneously with the first courses being built locally. Most were over 200 pages of facts, pictures and golf rules and included a catalogue of clubs, shoes, equipment, balls, even materials for building a course.

of "The Duke" and his buddies right alongside other strips like "The Katzenjammer Kids" and "Little Orphan Annie." Golf was now being seen daily by almost every reader and not just on the sports page.

Golf News in Sports Guides and Gazettes

Before 1900 in Cincinnati, there were few pictures taken at the golf course and little or no golf instruc-

tion available in books or magazines. Albert Spalding had formed a small sporting goods company in 1874 in Chicago and his marketing strategy included providing guides for all of the sports. This in turn would help sell his products and golf was a natural fit.

Bob Wilke (center), Western Hills Country Club Caddy, Elder High School student, stuntman and actor in over 400 movies and TV shows; shown with Lee Van Cleef and Sheb Wooley in the 1952 movie *High Noon*.

The Hollywood Connection

One interesting player of this era was Bob Wilke. Born in 1914 in Covington, Kentucky, and raised in Cincinnati, he attended Elder High School for a year. Wilke caddied at Western Hills CC but left home in the 1930s to become a life guard in Miami, Florida. There he gave high diving exhibitions, eventually performing them at the World's Fair. These skills led him to Hollywood as a stunt man and actor. He was most famous as a character actor in over 400 TV shows and movies but also had the reputation as the best golfer in Hollywood for most of his career, winning numerous celebrity tournaments and the Bing Crosby Clambake at Pebble Beach several times. Actor Claude Akins jokingly quipped that Wilke made more money on the golf course than he ever made acting. Note that this is different from another Robert Wilke, football star at Hamilton Catholic HS and Notre Dame University in the same time period, who was in Cincinnati playing and coaching for the first Cincinnati Bengals professional football team in 1937.

Bob Wilke shown with actress Barbara Eden at a golf tournament. Wilke was the top Hollywood golfer in the 1940s and 1950s.

American Golfer Magazine, edited by Grantland Rice from 1932.

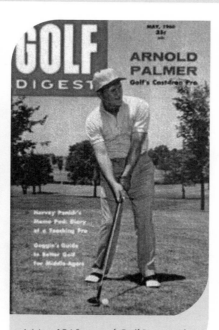

A May 1960 issue of Golf Digest with Arnold Palmer on the cover.

Spalding's 200 plus page golf guides started appearing by the late 1890s and included prices and availability for every product needed by the American golfer. The illustrated guides were advertised to be mailed free to any address. They also included the latest rules and interpretations by the USGA as well as tips on how to build a golf course and even suggestions for club committee management.

Almost as important, *Spalding's Golf Guide* was full of pictures of players and the champions of the day as well as landscapes of famous courses and clubhouses of the new clubs forming nationwide. It is no surprise that this became a key vehicle needed to get the game going nationwide and soon Spalding was opening branch offices in many cities, including on 5th Street in downtown Cincinnati.

In addition to the annual *Spalding's Guide* there were many other sources of information being published and some still operate today. *Golfers Magazine* was founded in 1902 and was edited by US Open winner "Chick" Evans. In 1908, golfing great Walter Travis founded *The American Golfer*, still considered by many the finest golf magazine of all time. So prestigious was this magazine that Grantland Rice

First Issue of *Golf World* in 1947.

Early radio broadcast on a golf course.

took over the editorship in 1932. *PGA Magazine* has been published since 1920 and *Golfdom Magazine* has been published since 1927 and still serves the game's Superintendents and Greenskeepers. *Golf World* was started in 1947 and *Golf Digest* was first published in 1950 as the post-war boom for golf began. *Golf Magazine* was started in 1959. All added to the promotion and expansion of the game locally.

Golf Makes it to the Radio and Movies

Some tournaments had been broadcast on the radio in the USA and Britain since the late 1920s. The Los Angeles Open was broadcast locally on radio in 1927 as was the 1930 PGA Championship. Unlike baseball, the game of golf did not lend itself well to radio with the technology available at that time.

There were experiments with recordings like those made by Chick Evans in the early 1920s. The proceeds from those recordings helped him start the caddie scholarship program in place today.

There were not many ways that golf could be visualized if not attending the events or seeing the instruction. After WWI, the movie theater became a place to see and experience the world. Almost at the same time, and maybe not coincidentally, America's attention turned to a new exciting generation of athletes. Competitors such as Babe Ruth, Jack Dempsey, Bill Tilden, Red Grange, the Four Horseman and even a racehorse like Man O' War achieved new celebrity status as they could be seen in news movies shown between the feature presentations.

News movies also provided action. Seeing a punch landed by Dempsey or a home run by Ruth had a different impact than a still photograph and one of the first golfing benefactors was Bobby Jones. Jones made eighteen instructional movies in the early 1930s for Warner Brothers where he coached famous movie stars like James Cagney, Edward G. Robinson, Frank Craven, W.C. Fields and Loretta Young. They were shown alongside

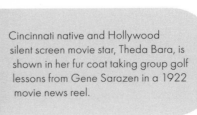

Cincinnati native and Hollywood silent screen movie star, Theda Bara, is shown in her fur coat taking group golf lessons from Gene Sarazen in a 1922 movie news reel.

Bobby Jones and a Warner Brothers camera at Belaire Country Club in 1930.

Bobby Jones instructs actor Frank Craven in Warner Brothers film shorts.

the feature films of the day in almost all movie houses nationwide. It is not surprising that golf took off nationally when these movies began showing in local theaters.

Fox Movietone News ran news reels in movie theaters starting in 1928. Stars like Byron Nelson, Sam Snead, Ben Hogan and even Arnold Palmer were first seen in action in the movie theaters on Movietone newsreels. RKO Pathe also ran Movie newsreel features on golf starting in 1938. They were extremely popular during WWII and featured stories about Professional golfers like Cary Middlecoff, Johnny Revolta and the Turnesa Brothers at venues like Pinehurst and Pebble Beach.

Hollywood also presented movies with golf themes and each made it to local theaters. Popular movie stars like Spencer Tracy and Katherine Hepburn (*Pat & Mike*—1952), W.C Fields (*The Golf Specialist*—1930), Dean Martin and Jerry Lewis (*The Caddy*—1953), Glen Ford (*Follow the Sun*—1951) played in films built around a golf theme. The genre also includes the oldest golf movie on film (*Spring Fever*—1927), a silent picture with William Haines and Joan Crawford. Of course, The Three Stooges got in the act with *The Three Beers* in 1935.

Golf and Television

There were some experimentations with early TV technology in the late 1930s in Great Britain but they

Crosley TV advertisement featuring sets made on Spring Grove Avenue.

were short lived as WWII began. As TV first came on the scene after the war (including the Crosley sets made in Cincinnati), it did not immediately catch on with the golfing public. Most golf fans were also players and TV was a distraction from the limited leisure time available to enjoy the sport on the course. But as the technology improved with multiple cameras, color transmission and better commentary, the unique ability of the TV to capture drama and develop stars began the love affair between the game and the medium.

The first time a golf tournament was televised was a telecast of the 1947 US Open in St. Louis. Broadcast was only to the local audience of KCD-TV and they witnessed a dramatic win by Lew Worsham over Sam Snead. Only one camera was perched atop a roof of a small truck behind the eighteenth green.

Of course, in 1948 there were only 102,000 TV sets in the whole United States and two-thirds of them were in New York City so there was a limited market. That represented 0.4% of the nation's households with sets. By 1953 that number increased to 55% and a shot from the eighteenth fairway in Chicago that year revealed the potential for golf and TV.

The World Championship of Golf was a national invitational event played from 1946 until 1957 at the Tam O'Shanter Golf Club in Chicago with purses that exceeded all of the other PGA tournaments combined. For example, in 1957 Dick Mayer won the US Open and a check for $7,200. The same year he won the Tam O'Shanter and pocketed $50,000. The ABC Network televised one hour per day from the 1953 tournament (with one camera and wide-angle lens positioned behind the eighteenth green) and Worsham won again in dramatic fashion, this time with an Eagle on the final hole to beat Chandler Harper. That shot was witnessed by the audience of about one-million viewers and the TV crowd went crazy. The next year promoter George May doubled the winner's purse from $25,000 to $50,000, in part based on the TV coverage.

It is difficult to measure exactly what effect that dramatic 104-yard wedge shot had on the future popularity of golf on TV but the next year USGA began to tele-

Worsham Outsmarts Snead
And Wins National Open

In 1947, Lew Worsham wins the U.S. Open on TV.

vise the US Open for a national audience. By 1958 the PGA Tour joined the party as CBS began broadcasting the PGA Championship. It coincided with the PGA Championship going from Match Play to a seventy-two-hole Stroke Play. Dow Finsterwald from Athens, Ohio, Ohio University and a frequent competitor in the Cincinnati area, won that televised tournament by two strokes over Billy Casper.

By 1956, over 75% of households now had a set and CBS televised the final three holes of the Masters in black and white. CBS was an early participant and innovator for TV golf especially under the direction of Frank Chirkinian. Truly a pioneer, he produced his first full Master's Tournament in 1959 at the age of thirty-three. Those early broadcasts also were in black and white and he had earned that position for CBS by directing the previous year's PGA championship in Philadelphia. He added so many features now thought of as normal in the watching of what many considered not a TV sport.

Among many innovations, he added more microphones to bring in the sounds of the game and the crowd, took cameras off of their stationary mounts to be more mobile, cut quickly from player to player to keep the action going and painted the inside of the cup white so it could be better seen on the screen. The union of The Masters, a new star in Arnold Palmer and the Chirkinian productions created golf on TV as we now know it. Early announcers for the Masters and CBS productions included Ken Venturi, Ben Wright, Jim McKay, Jack Whitaker and football star Pat Summerall.

All-Star Golf, filmed around Chicago in the 1950s was one of the first to produce a TV

WLWT remote camera bus used for early golf tournaments in the 1950s.

The first TV broadcast of the PGA Championship in 1958 with Winner Dow Finsterwald of Athens, Ohio.

Frank Chirkinian, father of TV golf.

Gene Sarazen hosts the *Wonderful World of Golf* in 1961.

Alan Shepard takes a golf shot on the moon.

Live local coverage of the Cincinnati Pro-Am in 1963.

series of matches. *Celebrity Golf* also started in the late 1950s with twenty-six episodes and featured Sam Snead playing nine-hole rounds against movie and TV stars like Dean Martin, Mickey Rooney, Harpo Marx with Harry Von Zell as the host. Eventually in 1960, the Shell Oil Company started the popular *Wonderful World of Golf* and the first match was played in 1961, filmed in Brazil and hosted by Gene Sarazen and Jimmy Demaret. The series was shown up until 2003 and was normally a one-hour broadcast on film that featured conversations between the match participants and information about the host country.

Cincinnati stations too provided coverage of local tournaments (and even miniature golf) with remote broadcasts starting in the 1950s. They also provided some features on local courses and golf instruction though most golf programming still originated from the networks.

On the Horizon

ABC would start its golf coverage in 1962 when it began covering the British Open as part of its *Wide World of Sports* programming. Later it would also provide the coverage of the US Open and PGA Championships with Chris Schenkel and Byron Nelson as announcers. After Jim McKay and Dave Marr took over in the booth, Bob Rosburg became the first on-course reporter bringing another innovation to the TV. NBC also did early broadcasts from local affiliates and some national circulation. This had started with the 1954 US Open.

Golf and Television, especially as presented at The Master's, started a relationship that made celebrities of the golfers of the day. The competition among the golf professionals of the 1960s and 1970s like Nicklaus, Palmer, Watson, Casper, Trevino and Miller was highlighted by color TV, improved camera technology and direction and the on-screen commentators. Golf needed the print media to get started but TV pulled the game into the mega-power it has become today even featuring its own network.

Today's golf fan takes a lot for granted. Immediately and live we can see a player make a shot from almost any major tournament in the world through television or video streaming on our computer or phone. A putt sunk in Australia hits our screen almost simultaneously via satellite, restricted only by the speed of light, and we have even witnessed a live golf shot taken on the moon. Obviously, it was not always that way, but the ability to communicate the game and its instruction and its drama ran almost parallel to the improved technology of the media itself.

Ultimately the game fell in love with television and vice versa. Arnold Palmer, Jack Nicklaus, Tiger Woods and their peers spread the game exponentially. But along the way, the likes of Albert Spalding, Grantland Rice, Ring Lardner, Jim Murray, Furman Bisher, Dan Jenkins and Ralph Love, among many others, carried the game forward from its very humble start in 1890.

Epilogue

Normally this is used for novels to tie up loose ends but we have reserved it to challenge other writers and historians. They can pick up the stories in the 1960s when the game comes to us in technicolor with Nicklaus, Whitworth, Palmer and Lopez. And locals like Volpenhein, Thompson, Metcalfe, Comisar and Elfers started to fill the pages with their accomplishments in the Mets. And add State tournament winners like Dorn, Green, Muething, Gerwin and Schultz. And Janie Dumler Klare winning the Ohio Women's State Junior Am, Amateur and Mid-Am titles during a great career.

Still others like Stahl and Williamson were taking their game to the National Amateur competitions. And Professionals like Hall, Kokrak, Wetterich and Herman were playing and winning on the Tour. And we can add stories of young players like Squires, Fitzpatrick, Grimmer, and Wetterich who started building resumes as teenagers. Media becomes electronic and equipment continues to evolve and the game continues to react. What great stories to continue.

And it may include sidebars that go full circle such as a young man from Chicago who made it to Cincinnati while still a teenager and who worked the first summer cutting greens, changing hole locations and edging bunkers for Cal Gruber, the Superintendent at Coldstream CC. He then moved on the next summer doing the same tasks at Royal Oak (Stillmeadow) CC, while attending Anderson High School and Miami University. After graduation, he joined Procter & Gamble as a Brand Manager and played his golf at Maketewah CC.

Career moves to the sports field landed positions at Wilson, Taylor Made and a stint in the hockey business and eventually he became only the eighth Commissioner of the LPGA in 2010. There, he increased the number of tournaments from twenty-four per year to thirty-four in 2020, building on the work done by Cincinnatian Lenny Wirtz in the 1960s. Finally, in 2021, Michael Whan was named to replace Mike Davis as only the eighth top executive in USGA history. And the ties between Greater Cincinnati and its golf history have been further cemented. The game conquered the hills and now has expanded to over a hundred sites in the surrounding counties.

Acknowledgments

The idea for this book began in June 2015, when I had the great fortune to be seated at a table with Mr. and Mrs. John Fischer III. We were attending a Cincinnati Country Club banquet celebrating the 100th Women's Met. They were so gracious and the conversation got around to history and John's position on the History Committee of the USGA. They had stories of the city's golf history and pointed out players in the room and their exploits. And I soon got on the list to receive John's blogs about golf history. Always written to coincide with an event like The Open or the Masters, it seemed to dig deeper into a little-known aspect and yet was presented with prose light enough to be a quick and enjoyable read. The stories had the feel of a Ken Burns documentary with the focus on presenting history as something to enjoy while it was absorbed. John has been with me through the whole project, always with insight and encouragement.

But it took until early 2017 when Dave Bahr, Head Professional and Alex Rodger (he would win the Met later that year) announced the formation of a History Committee at Maketewah Country Club.

The first meetings were full of promise and I was introduced to Newspaper.com and the possibilities of digital research. Like many, I remembered the days cranking the old microfiche machine and so sitting now at the home computer sounded a lot more efficient. Steve Moser, Mike Savage and James Devaney were there from the beginning and we started off with a blank sheet of paper. By mid-year we had a major discovery present itself when a 1910 Cincinnati Post article about Tom Bendelow revealed that Donald Ross was indeed the architect of our present course. This obliterated fifty years of urban legends and replaced them with a history. And it felt good.

Along the way I was accumulating research from other clubs and courses and events and players and was starting to expand the history to the region and I began to wonder why I did not know about these people and places. That summer I took a couple of the grandkids to hit balls on Kellogg Avenue and the young man behind the counter wore a Highlands Country Club hat. I asked him about John Fischer Jr. and the fact that he had won the 1936 US Amateur from his club but he did not recognize the name. Wrong answer.

Weekly trips to the Cincinnati Public Library and help from Stephen Headley in the Genealogy and Local History Department opened even more doors and discoveries. He was also a former caddy and a golfer and had an unbelievable fountain of golf knowledge and recall of facts. When news stories conflicted or hit a dead end, he had a knack to point me in the right direction. He showed me the resources available, especially the digitized newspapers and old insurance maps to locate Ghost Courses. And he also introduced another familiar name who had been looking into the same types of materials with him for a while.

Geoff Hensley was the Head Professional at Coldstream Country Club and I knew him only as a visiting Rules Official at tournaments. And I also knew his reputation as a young amateur golfer, a star player for UC, winner of the Met and Junior Met, and both a Club and competing Professional. We both had caddied at Clovernook and attended UC at the same time but our paths had never crossed.

Geoff had been on a similar path for longer than I and accumulating materials and ideas for a personal tribute to the game that he chose as his life's work. Todd Johnson, Executive Director at GCGA, knew we were both working on the same things and introduced us in December 2017. But after almost three years of collaboration it was getting clearer to both of us that our goals were different. We both had family health issues, work and other interruptions and it became inevitable that we agree to split our efforts and return to our own visions or else neither project would finish.

But you can't meet and discuss and share for that amount of time without spillover of concepts and ideas and material. There are parts of this book that are all Geoff. Ghost Courses, some chapter organization and pictures were there when I started my writing. We chose to share all of each other's research and hopefully my input to the collaboration will add to his book. This history could not have been written without Geoff's perspective and I am grateful.

And I am also grateful for the input and support of so many others along this journey. Some of these encounters have been face to face and some only electronic, some brief and some over the course of the whole book but all have been a factor.

Organizations: Cincinnati History Museum, Cincinnati Recreation Commission, Donald Ross Society, Golf Heritage Society, Great Parks of Hamilton County, Greater Cincinnati Golf Association, Greater Cincinnati Golf Course Superintendents Association, Greater Cincinnati Women's Golf Association, Glendale Historical Society, Hamilton High School, Hughes High School, Loveland Historical Society, Northern Kentucky Golf Hall of Fame, Reading High School, St. Xavier High School, Ohio Golf Association, Society of Golf Historians.

Individuals (alphabetically): Stuart Bendelow, Aimee Bollmer, Chris and Sara Carsten, Jim Cissel, Brian Critchell, Joni Copas, Sandra DeVise, Jennifer Nerone Donahue, Ron Dumas, John Earls, John Fanning, Pete Georgiady, Don Gleason, Coach Will Green, COL Dick "the skull" Johns, USA (Ret.), Carol Clark Johnson, Todd Johnson, Margaret Jones, Nick Kemper, Georgianne Koch, Gerry and Mary Lynn Lanham, Ken Lanham, Andi Lanz, Matt Lefferts, Tony and Jessica Minneci, Joe Nieporte, Patti and Ray Normile, John Reis, Joe Rouse, Bob Schultz, Teresa Silvers, Kevin Stanton, Allan Strange, Carlos Thompson, Peter Trenham, Skip Wallace, Ted White, Paul Wood, Joie Nieporte Woodstock, Jeff Zugelter. I hope I did not forget anyone.

That last name on the list is a reminder that historians do not always make friends. At this writing I still have not met Jeff but have a lot of correspondence and shared research yielding the same results. No one was more thorough trying to discover the truth. Some times that is not convenient, as he also discovered. But giving credit where credit is due is the most important thing we accomplish as historians. And the beneficiaries are those that really built the game with their talents and imagination and hard work.

Finally, the real dedication is to my wife, Susie, who stayed with me through this whole project. She put up with books and papers scattered through the first floor after it overflowed my office. She listened to the stories and even feigned interest after hearing them several times. She put up with me at the computer until two or three a.m. And she waited patiently as I completed a thought on the computer while a job waited (I tried not to do that too many times). Without her there would be no book.

Photo Credits

Images courtesy of USGA Photo Archives, Cover, 34, 35, 38, 52, 55, 72, 114–115

Images courtesy of Glendale Historical Society, 132

Images courtesy of Golfer's Club (Cincinnati, Ohio). Constitution and By-Laws of the Golfers' Club, Clifton, 1904. (Pamphlets 796.352 G624, 1904), 133, 135

Image courtesy of Golfer's Club (Cincinnati, Ohio). Constitution and By-Laws of the Golfers' Club, Clifton, 1899. (Pamphlets 796.352 G624), 134

Image courtesy of Cincinnati Museum Center from the original map: Plat Showing Territory to Be Annexed to the City of Cincinnati, n.d. (Map 977.14CP A961 n.d. D), 135

Index